COUNTRY
Women
IN MUSIC

QUARRY MUSIC BOOKS

Celtic Women: A Celebration of Beauty and Sovereignty
Mairéid Sullivan

The Real Patsy Cline
Doug Hall

George Jones: Same Ole Me
Jim Brown

Building a Mystery: Sarah McLachlin & Lilith Fair
Judith Fitzgerald

Falling Into You: Celine Dion
Barry Grills

Encyclopedia of Canadian Country Music
Rick Jackson

COUNTRY
Women
IN MUSIC

Man, I Feel Like A Woman

JIM BROWN

QUARRY
MUSIC
BOOKS

For Maggie and Fred,
Joanne and Larry,
Cathy and Bryan

☆ ☆ ☆

Country Women in Music is a serious critical and biographical study of country music and musicians. The quotation of lyrics from songs written or performed by the musicians under study illustrates the biographical and critical information presented by the author and thus constitutes fair use under existing copyright conventions. Every effort has been made to notify the publisher of these songs that the lyrics have been quoted in this context by the author.

The publisher gratefully acknowledges The Canada Council for the Arts and the Book Publishing Industry Development Program of the Department of Canadian Heritage for their support of writing and publishing in Canada.

ISBN 1-55082-247-0

Design by Susan Hannah.
Printed and bound in Canada by
AGMV Marquis, Cap-Saint-Ignace, Quebec.
Published by Quarry Press Inc.,
P.O. Box 1061, Kingston, Ontario K7L 4Y5 Canada
www.quarrypress.com

THE CANADA COUNCIL | LE CONSEIL DES ARTS
FOR THE ARTS | DU CANADA
SINCE 1957 | DEPUIS 1957

CONTENTS

☆ ☆ ☆

Foreword

☆ ☆ ☆

THE WOMAN IN ME

I'm not always strong
And sometimes I'm even wrong
But I win when I choose
And I can't stand to lose . . .

(Shania Twain)

One late winter afternoon in 1995, I was sitting at my desk in the Cyberstore offices on West Broadway in Vancouver and fielding follow-up phone calls from the media-launch of the web-zine *West Coast Music Review* or *wcmr.com*. There were plenty of calls. The media event had been well attended by reporters from the dailies, weeklies, and specialty magazines, a network television crew, and members of the music and business communities. They had all wanted to learn more about the investment opportunities and promotional advantages that lay in this mysterious region everyone was calling "cyberspace."

My webmaster, Al Medcalf, and I knew that our Cyberstore-sponsored internet music website was a pioneer effort in Canada, begun in 1991 as a syndicated electronic magazine for computer bulletin boards or BBS systems and first posted on the newly-created world wide web in December of 1994. Our *www.wcmr.com* site was not as huge as the International Underground Music Archive at *www.iuma.com*, and the artists who had their home pages at our site were not as prestigious as Madonna's personal message and video that you could download at *iuma*, but we had made a good start. We had posted dozens of CD reviews and sound bites. We had attracted interest from

Randy Bachman (The Guess Who, BTO) who would soon debut his "Guitarchives" record label at our web location. We were already tracking Michelle Wright's cross-Canada tour on the web and would soon host Ringo Starr's worldwide tour with personal audio file messages from both artists available to early cybersurfers. Other music related projects being hosted by Cyberstore included the Hudson Bay Company's Big Sky Festival website for a 100th birthday bash staged by Canada's original department store at High River, Alberta, starring the likes of Bryan Adams, Anne Murray, Michelle Wright, Colin James, and Blue Rodeo.

The phone on my desk rang and I picked it up. It was Ken Ashdown, the local Mercury Records rep. Ken wondered if I'd like to interview Shania Twain. She had a new CD and was doing media interviews the following day. I glanced at the clock on the wall. It was nearly 4 p.m. and I was bushed. I told Ken that I didn't have the CD. Without listening to it I couldn't very well tape an intelligent interview. "No problem," he said, "I'll express courier you the CD and promo pak. Would you like to have breakfast with my artist?" Boy, I thought, Ken was eager. Either the CD was gangbusters or it was a dud they were trying to prop up.

Before I left the office at six, the CD arrived and I just took the courier package along without opening it, drove home, and ate dinner. Shania Twain had put one album out, but nobody had sent me a copy. Though Larry Delaney, publisher of *Country Music News*, had raved about it in a cover story I read, I wasn't sure I'd even heard a single cut on the local country stations. Maybe a song called *Dance With The One That Brought You*. Had that been by this same artist?

I opened up the package, stuck the WOMAN IN ME CD on the stereo, and flipped through the promo pak. Hummm, I thought, Shania is a looker. They've got her pictured here in full-color Vogue fashions as well as the more usual cowgirl get-up. There was even a picture of the singer with a horse. By this time, the music had gotten to me. Hot damn, I thought, this is something new. It's like Garth, only exciting, like he was on his first records. As I familiarized myself with the Shania Twain story from the artist bio, I began to realize that Shania's producer and husband Mutt Lange had created a whole new kind of 'new country' music that was lush and glitzy pop but at the same time never really veered from its country roots. So, it was gangbusters, certainly not a dud, and I began to make notes for a CD review.

The music had been recorded in Nashville, but mixed at Morin Heights, in Quebec. Wasn't that the studio where Anne Murray had made some of her best records? I booted my Toshiba portable and wrote:

This splendid CD is infused with the deep love and affection felt between husband and wife team Lange and Twain who co-wrote all of the 12 tunes. From the opening strains of the tour-de-force ballad *Home Ain't Where His Heart Is (Anymore)* to the closing strains of the a cappella lullaby *God Bless This Child*, we are treated to songs which inspire rather than the usual cheatin', hurtin', drinkin', tragi-comic formula stuff.

There are plenty of twisted cliché Nashvillisms, waves of twangy guitars and spicy cajun fiddles, and even a number that has line dance mania served up with hand-claps and drum programs (*Any Man Of Mine*). But the bottom line here is country music through and through. Sometimes it is 'new country' as in the runaway chart hit *Whose Bed Have Your Boots Been Under*. Sometimes it is straight up traditional like the tear-jerker *Leaving Is The Only Way Out*. Always, you hear the expressive rich vocal from Shania. Continually, you get a changing, adapting production-mode from Lange that chooses to highlight the natural vocal, rather than force it into conceptual radio niches. An all-star cast of Nashville twangers: Brent Rowan, Dann Huff, Brent Mason and Larry Byrom (guitars), Matt Rollings (piano), Rob Hajacos (fiddle), Sam Bush (mandolin), Paul Franklin (pedal steel)....

I gave the CD the "most highly recommended" icon and prepared for bed. Breakfast with Shania — you want to put your brightest face forward for that, I told myself. Later, I added this final sentence to my review before posting it on the net: "As Shania Twain suggests (in the interview linked to this review), Robert Mutt Lange may have created a 'new standard for country' that is both acoustic and electric but neither rock nor pop pretending to be country."

The following morning, the tires of my vehicle humming over the paved surface of Lion's Gate Bridge, I reviewed the Shania Twain story in my head, recreating it from my memories of the bio. Shania (pronounced Shu-Nye-Uh) was Ojibway for "On My Way." Twain had been brought up poor in rural Ontario. An entertainer from age eight, her parents had wakened her up 'round about midnight to take her into the local water-ing-holes after last call and before closing time so that she could sing. It was a source of income for the family. So, she'd been in the music business just about all of her life. When her parents lives were tragically terminat-ed in a car accident, Shania was already touring with her own band, but came back home to raise her brothers and sisters before heading to Nashville to become a star.

She'd had over-the-phone songwriting sessions with Lange before meet-ing him, then worked with him, and finally married the lucky guy. It sound-ed like a page torn out of the Patsy Cline song book, only with a happy ending. Little did I know at that time that THE WOMAN IN ME would go on to sell more than 12 million copies in the United States alone. Little did I know that Shania Twain's navel would soon be as famous as the great pyramid at Giza. But I did wonder just what Shania Twain would be like in person.

The hotel was one of those elegant ones. I was told I was expected, then led through a quiet restaurant to a table set for two. The tablecloth and nap-kins were color-coordinated. The silverware had been polished till it gleamed. When Ken Ashdown arrived and introduced me to Shania Twain, she was just another person. No big hair. No gobs of makeup. Dressed sim-ply in soft hues. Her eyes *did* light up when I told her how good I thought her music was. They got real big. I realized then that Shania Twain was just another country girl who'd made it big in Music City, U.S.A. Right away, she wanted to know: What did I hear as the next single?

Ken Ashdown went off somewhere to make arrangements for the media party, which was to be held at the Press Club a few hours later in the day. Boy, I thought, I'm getting the royal treatment. Here I am alone with coun-try's next superstar. I don't know why I thought that, but there was something about Shania Twain, a quiet confidence that told me that the music was no fluke, and that if anybody could out-Garth Garth, it would be this woman sitting across from me nibbling at her toast. Nor did I know then that during Twain's first meeting with Mercury Nashville president, Luke Lewis, Shania had declared that "she wanted to be as big as Garth" or that record exec Lewis had "looked into her eyes and knew that she could do it." I didn't learn that until I read a cover story in the January 1999 issue of *Cosmopolitan* magazine written by Trish Deitch Rohrer that featured the Timmins, Ontario singer as the magazine's "Fun, Fearless Female of the Year."

When Shania and I finished our munching and had our coffees

topped up, I pulled out my trusty Sony Walkman and we began to talk on the record. "Your story," I began, "is kinda like the ultimate Cinderella story, the ultimate country music scenario, now that you've met the love of your life, your dream producer and co-writer, and gotten married to him. Especially, since your new CD seems to be one of the best releases to come out in a while."

Shania Twain's answer to my leading statement was confident and articulate. She even qualified my modifying phrases. "It *is* a Cinderella story," she said. "Not rags to riches, I'm not rich, yet. But certainly rags to something."

Instead of asking a question, I continued to just make conversation. "The unfortunate death of your parents is a visible focus to the story, a tragedy which you have survived and one which fans can see as an event that forced you to grow up quickly and assume responsibility at a very young age."

Shania thought about that for a second before speaking. "If you put it that way, it sort of makes sense, how I was able to cope with it at that time. The reason was, I think, because my parents — in developing a career for me when I was so young — *that* actually made me grow up very quickly as well. My childhood career matured me and, in a sense, prepared me in a way for what was coming."

I could tell that Shania was skilled at these interviews. She had thought everything through beforehand. I tried a question, the one used in the paperback biography that was published a few years later. "When you were only eight years old you were singing . . . did they have to stand you up on a chair so the audience could see you?"

That got a smile. "The guitar was bigger than me. I wish they would have made those half-width size guitars when I was 8, 9, 10, 11, and 12. I was so small that they couldn't lie flat on me. They were sticking out, like that . . . because I couldn't get my arm around them. I've been doing it for a very, very long time. I'm 29 years old, now, and it has been 21 years that I've been singing professionally. I remember Gary Buck and Dallas Harms. I used to be on shows as the opener for Anita Perras when I was just a kid and she was a teenager. I opened for people like Carroll Baker. Ronnie Prophet was one. Mary Bailey, my manager, was an entertainer when I was a child."

Good, I thought, the story just sort of rolls off her lips, all I have to do is guide this. I asked who were the stars on the radio who had inspired her.

"I listened to all kinds of music. We had a multi-format station happening in our home town. I heard *everything* through radio, but at home it was always country. And I only sang country music as a child. I had other influences. I was really enamored with the Carpenters. Their harmonies . . . were so beautiful . . . I learned so much, at a very young age from groups like that. Karen's voice is just like silk. It is so gorgeous! There were many influences along the way. I think Dolly Parton is the one from the beginning, right up until now, who has been the *one*. Dolly has done everything. She's an exceptional writer. She's an actor. She's a great personality. She's everything!"

If I had seen some of the videos that would soon be made, I would have made a reference to how Shania has become a music video star, acting in her own mini-movies. What I did say was more conversational. "I like Dolly, too. And one of the reasons I like her is her versatility. She's equally effective doing a simple acoustic bluegrass tune, like on the TRIO album, as she is in the larger country pop productions like *Islands In The Stream*. There's some splendid acoustic stuff on *your* new CD, as well."

Another smile. "I'm very comfortable with that. I'm not a great guitar player. I never spent very much time perfecting my skills on guitar. I'm a singer-songwriter. I use my guitar as an instrument to write. But I never performed without my guitar until I was at least 16, and when I first put it down, it was so awkward without it. I think any singer-songwriter is comfortable doing an acoustic-type thing. They are used to just sitting and singing with the guitar. It is one of my favorite things to do."

"Let's talk about the album itself," I said. "Your husband, co-writer, and producer has not come up with basically a pop album here. It is very country!"

"Yes! A lot of people are pleasantly surprised. Maybe they were even expecting it to be over-produced . . . or too rock. I think what he has done, through this CD, is created a new standard for country music. What people don't realize is, of course — yes, as far as Def Leppard is concerned, he is a major contributor to that success, of course, yes! But to go from Def Leppard to Billy Ocean to Michael Bolton . . . they are worlds apart."

I wanted a clarification, here, and said, "You are saying that he brings out the best in everyone he deals with?"

"He enhances the artist's music," she said. "A lot of the success of this album has to do with the writing and what he has done with the sound of it. Right from the beginning, he said, 'We need to go into your catalog. I want to know what you write, what you've been writing, then we'll go from there. You be the basis to the creativity of this album. Because it needs to be you not me.' And so that's what we did. Ten out of the 12 songs on this album are songs that I was writing before I even met Mutt. It feels very good. Like *Whose Bed Have Your Boots Been Under.*"

"The sounds on the album are pretty darn tasty," I commented. "I like the bursts of cajun fiddle." Shania's answer confirmed my suspicion that a lot of thought had gone into the instrumentation. It was not the usual paint by numbers approach.

"A lot of the album has a bit of cajun flavor, cajun fiddle. I think the whole idea behind the fiddle on this CD is we wanted fiddle that really *dug in* and was really aggressive, not just the fiddle as a background instrument."

"My favorite song is the second to last cut, *No One Needs To Know.*"

Shania surprised me by snapping her fingers to establish a rhythm. She sang:

Am I dreamin' or stupid
I think I've been hit by Cupid
But no one needs to know right now . . .

This pleasant outburst was a real bonus. But the thought that came into my head was, boy, Shania is a very healthy specimen and her mind is as clear as a bell. I applauded briefly, then said, "Many country albums only have 10 cuts, you've given us 12. Thanks for the extra music. The 12th is the show-stopper, an a cappella rendition of the song which came to you in the months when you were healing from the loss of your parents . . . *God Bless The Child.*"

"That was more of a . . . Mutt didn't want to do anything to that one. It is good the way it is. It is not really a complete song. What it is, is a musical thought, an expression. At the time, when my parents died, what that lullaby did for me was to comfort me. It soothed me. It was like a bellows of sorrow . . . I would go for long walks and just sing this."

"The healing process . . ."

"Yes. I think he really captured that on the CD without adding anything."

"Working with a producer who can get the right vocal out of you makes the difference between an average album and a killer one ..."

"Yes. Mutt's always been great at that with everyone he's worked with. I think that the advantage that we have together is that we love each other."

There it was in a nutshell. Shania Twain's THE WOMAN IN ME was music fostered by love and crafted by skilled hands. I put away my machine and we made small talk until Ken Ashdown returned. Later that day, I attended the Press Club meet-and-greet session and was knocked out by the extravagant spread of food and wine. There was sushi and quiche, for gosh sakes, exotic cheeses and fruit, everything gourmet and as tasty as Shania's entrance, this time looking like a million bucks and wearing a smile a mile and a half wide.

My next encounter with Shania Twain came a few months down the road at the Canadian Country Music Association convention in Hamilton, Ontario. For the press conference, 50 or so media types were ushered into a small convention room. By this time, Shania was an international star and she fielded questions from the floor that I found downright embarrassing. At one point, she flatly stated that she wasn't in the music business to win awards. If the awards came along, that would be just fine. But they were not the reason she was doing what she was doing.

Of course she did win. But the more she won, the more antagonistic some of the media got — or at least it seemed that way to me. Some journalists made a big thing out of the fact that she wasn't Ojibway by blood. Her father, Jerry Twain, had been a step-father. The First Nations people came back with a statement that she was raised native and they considered her to be an honorary member of their tribe.

Shania didn't seem to be winning many awards in Nashville, itself, however. Junos, yes, Grammies, yes, and an armload of *Billboard*, CMT, and American Music Awards, but no CMAs. I conjectured that a Nashville outsider — a Canuck, produced by a rock producer and a Brit to boot — just wasn't what the good ole boy system in Nashville really wanted, no matter that she was selling kazillions of records and that she'd crossed over from the country to pop charts just like Patsy Cline. Some writers seemed to feel that she had crossed over the other way, from pop into country, and that she was, basically, a pop artist. One onslaught of negativity seemed to center around the fact that Shania had not toured. When Shania did hit the road in the spring of 1998, she did so to rave reviews and sold out performances. By the end of the year she had sold more than one million tickets for a whopping total of $35 million, a figure that put her ahead of the pop divas for the time period.

Not only had Shania Twain and Mutt Lange set new standards for country, they seemed to be doing it in all of the relevant arenas. By that time, December of 1998, Shania's third album COME ON OVER had been released and been in the Top 10 on the *Billboard* Hot 200 albums chart for most of the past year, at number one on the *Billboard* Country chart for several stretches during 1997 and 1998. The new album was a little more pop-country than THE WOMAN IN ME, but the fans were buying it at break-neck speed. Sales figures were said to be more than nine million for COME ON OVER, putting her at a total of nearly 21 million overall. It was a Cinderella story, alright, and although Shania had told me in 1995 that she wasn't rich "yet," she surely was now. The January 1999 cover story of *People* magazine pictured Shania Twain collaged together with those pop divas that she had out-drawn during the past 12 months — Mariah, Whitney, Jewel, Celine, and Madonna. Here for all the world to see, Shania Twain was accepted as one of the top singers on the planet.

Not everyone was willing to accept her and her husband Robert Mutt Lange with such open arms, even outside of the Nashville influenced media. Why, I wondered, had her neighbors in upstate New York objected to Twain and her husband building a recording studio on their land, a spread that was said to be large enough so that no one could see or hear what the couple were doing while riding their horses and writing those number one songs? Why couldn't people let the singer alone? She'd already logged enough tragedy for one lifetime. Shania and Mutt, of course, merely bought houses in Florida and Switzerland. For that matter, why did some journalists still make a big deal out of the fact that she'd changed her name from Eileen Twain to Shania Twain? Had they done that when Leonard Slye changed his name to Roy Rogers? They hadn't kicked up much of a fuss when they learned that Randy Travis was born Randy Traywick or that Diana and Christina Judd had become inspired to reinvent themselves as Naomi and Wynonna before launching their recording career together.

In September 1998, Shania's performance at the CCMA Awards Show in Calgary had not been ruffled by any of this distracting behavior. For a while, though, it *had* been rumored that Twain couldn't make it to Calgary to appear on the show. She was busily engaged in making that tour some people had predicted she couldn't make. However, when Canada's brightest country star has become an international superstar, yet can't take the time to acknowledge the industry that spawned her...that industry might be in trouble, especially if Twain won all the awards and wasn't there to accept them. By the time I arrived at the convention, the dilemma had been solved. Shania was to fly in, rehearse, do the show, and get back to her tour.

During the rehearsals, I was in the Jubilee Theatre to meet in the green room with Randall Prescott and Tracey Brown. Tracey wanted to slip into the theater to catch Shania's rehearsal segment. I tagged along. The first go-round of *Honey, I'm Home* was in progress. I was intrigued by the choreography of the guitarists and fiddlers and would later ask Cory Churko, one of the fiddlers, how that was created. Churko said that there were some initial directions, but most of it just evolved. By this time, each segment of Shania's performance was tightly choreographed. The CTV production team had done their homework, too. For example, on the guitar solo, a camera person with a hand-held unit began the instrumental section tight-in on one guitarist who stepped away from a crouched position. Then the bass player peeled away to reveal the lead guitarist wailing away on his solo. On the monitors, we could see that Shania was in the background of the camera lens playing air guitar.

When the rehearsal segment ended with Twain walking back to her drummer and turning to face the non-existent audience, the singer began to make suggestions to the off-stage crew of producers and directors. It took one more go-through before it was right for Shania, who has admitted in interviews that she is a perfectionist. Later that night she would tell the television audience, "I'm a work-a-holic, you just have to be to be a success." I was impressed with Shania's take-charge attitude, something she did with a maximum of efficiency and without any evidence of a prima donna attitude. Each time her band and the television people went through the segment, things got better, with the superstar working as hard as anyone on improving the performance. I was also impressed by her physical stamina, her absolute physical perfection.

The choice of Terri Clark to host the 1998 CCMA-CTV Awards show had some eyebrows raised. The ex-Medicine Hat, Alberta singer was already an established Nashville star, but people knew her through her videos. They were not familiar with her as a personality. Clark had jumped to star status in Nashville when videos from her debut Mercury Records album, TERRI CLARK, featured her wearing a stetson and strumming an electric guitar. Here was a manifestation of K.D. Lang's "big-boned gal from southern Alberta." And Terri's big brown eyes seemed to be looking right out into your living room. The effect was highly personal.

At first, this fresh approach had created a mystique. Then country fans heard that Terri was accident prone. She might ride a Harley Davidson, but a Harley can be as ornery as a mechanical bull or a bucking bronco. She broke one of her hands in a bike accident. During a celebrity softball match in Nashville, she sustained a fractured cheekbone. Then, after a concert at a State Fair in New Mexico, she suffered a dislocated shoulder when a fan grabbed and held on to her arm as the car she was riding in accelerated away from the concert venue. As confident as she looked in those videos, Terri had a vulnerable side, too.

It was a curious mix of information to add to the success of her Top 10 debut single *Better Things To Do*. There was a strategy going on here, but just what was it? "We shot the video near Santa Fe, New Mexico," Terri told Larry Delaney for a November 1995 cover story printed in *Country Music News*, "and it was just the perfect rugged scenery to suit the story line of the song. As soon as the video struck, there was huge interest in the song and it really helped to launch my career at that level." Another strategy being used was to have Terri appear as a guest or backup singer on other albums being released at the same time. She was bubbling up in all sorts of places. When her second single, *When Boy Meets Girl*, was released, it rocketed up the chart.

> First it's baseball, arcades in the mall
> Skipping out of study hall to hang with the guys
> Then it's fast cars, rock and roll guitars
> Lighting up behind the barn and not knowing why
>
> But his life is about to change
> He's never gonna to be the same
> And he'll be living in a different world
> When boy meets girl ...

(written by Tom Shapiro, Terri Clark & Chris Waters)

Although she had been in Nashville for nearly ten years before putting out her first CD, Terri Clark was just getting to know Canadian country stars Michelle Wright and Shania Twain. "It was kind of neat at the CMA show last month," she told Delaney. "Michelle Wright was a presenter, Shania Twain opened the show, and I had a brief singing spot on the show. We were all together in a dressing room which we dubbed 'the Canadian Room', and both Shania and I were really nervous about our roles in the show...but Michelle was a real pro, having made several appearances and co-hosting the CMA Show, and she told us what to expect and how to handle the jitters...gawd she was just great. I admire her a lot!"

Shania Twain had swept the 1995 CCMA awards, but in 1996 Terri Clark had taken both CCMA Album of the Year and the Vista Rising Star awards. 1997 was the year that Shania first out-sold Garth in Canada, winning the CCMA's best-selling album foreign or domestic award. That year Terri Clark hauled in her second CCMA Album of the Year Award for JUST THE SAME and repeated as CCMA Female Vocalist. The two seemed to be running neck and neck, but they were a different as night and day. Where Twain was slim, petite, vivacious, and downright sexy in her videos, Clark still wore a hat and jeans, sometimes a longrider coat. Terri looked like she could wrestle a steer to the ground, no trouble at all. But few had been exposed to her sense of humor or her bubbly personality. These traits came out on the 1998 show, along with Terri's ability to ad-lib and improve on the cue-card mentality of the show writers. For example, when called upon to list some of Shania Twain's credits before Twain's performance on the show, Clark delivered the hard info, smiled, and then quipped, "...and she needs to eat a big steak dinner!"

During the rehearsal that afternoon in 1998, Clark — garbed in an all-leather outfit — had come dancing out of the wings during one of the go-rounds of *Honey, I'm Home*, hammed it up in a far-from-nimble imitation of Twain's lithe moves, and without really upstaging Shania, danced off again. It was a real yin and yang thing between the two on the show itself, as Shania came up six times to receive her awards. It went over the top a few times, like the moment when Terri Clark pushed a pun to its limits as she stepped on the train of Twain's costume and said, "I stepped on your *twain*." But it was fun and it was young women doing it with spontaneity, not stock-in-trade shtick from comedians or film actors.

Twain and Clark had rapidly bypassed the bevy of Canadian hopefuls who had been making their bid for success in Nashville during the early 1990s — Michelle Wright, Lori Yates, Lisa Brokop, and Patricia Conroy.

Shania had achieved the challenging goal of placing number one hits on the *Billboard* country chart. Anne Murray was the only Canadian female vocalist before Shania Twain to ever accomplish that. Twain was also right up there with Canadian pop vocalists Celine Dion, Alanis Morissette, and Sarah McLachlan, with sales large enough to put her albums in the Top 10 on the pop charts. Shania was a superstar, but she wasn't too snooty to take part in the Canadian country awards.

☆ ☆ ☆

The most serious downside of eras — when one or two superstars eat up a huge portion of the total album sales and airplay — is that there isn't much left for other people. Album sales in 1998 fell off considerably from the high numbers achieved in the early years of the decade for country. Today the competition is tough, indeed, among the newcomers for a share of the crumbs that remain. As the gap widens between the sales-obsessed mega-stars and the rest of the pack, a curious limbo is forming where the media, still hyped on how huge country is, continue to hammer the success of the few top-achievers home to a public that grows ever more cynical and reluctant to endorse country by purchasing CDs. The real tragedy, as always when country takes a downturn, comes further down the food chain. Local bars close and the work for journeyman musicians and bands dries up. Duos and singles with midi-tracks or beat-boxes replace bands. Karaoke and disco country replace live entertainment. Working musicians starve or get day-jobs. And as we approach the millennium, those good old days of the honky-tonk women and rhinestone cowboys who first made country music popular on country radio are gone forever. CMT and country videos have redesigned country music.

Despite downsides, and there are always some downsides to any situation, Shania Twain and many of the female vocalists featured on CMT in the 1990s have emerged as distinctive personalities while some of the male 'hat acts' seem to lack individual focus. And, where women once seemed in competition with each other, in the 1990s a feeling of solidarity often referred to as "sisterhood" has resulted in concerts where female performers gather their forces and present a unified stand. Backstage at the 1998 CMA awards in the press room for some photo ops and a brief barrage of questions from the media after six award wins, Shania Twain was genuinely complimentary when asked about the show's host, Terri Clark, saying,

"She's wonderful! A complete natural." There was no animosity between the two, as there might have been in previous decades.

A few weeks later, Shania performed on the 1998 CMA Awards show in Nashville, but the top female artist that night was Trisha Yearwood, who accepted her CMA award via satellite and sang her duet *Where Your Road Leads* with Garth Brooks from the stage of their concert in Buffalo, New York. Saying that she was surprised and thrilled by her win, Trisha added, "Tonight is amazing because *I* was not *my* prediction! Martina was my pre-prediction, because I'm a big fan of hers . . . she's had an incredible year."

That same night, Dixie Chicks won the CMA Horizon award and the vocal group award. The three young women were visibly excited when they stepped to the microphone. Natalie Maines stated the obvious, saying, "We are *so* excited!" Martie Seidel blurted, "The first thought that went through my head was *don't* blubber!"

When hundreds of local students joined Shania Twain on *Honey I'm Home* and her rowdy performance came to an end, Awards show host Vince Gill got in a shot of his own when he said, "That was Shania Twain with 'Honey, I'm deaf.'"

A great night for country women was made even better when the video for Faith Hill's *This Kiss* was named CMA Video of the Year. Along with her husband, Tim McGraw, winning album of the year, Faith Hill seemed overwhelmed as she ended her acceptance speech: "This year has been unbelievable. The biggest thing that we'll remember about this year is that we have a beautiful 16-month-old at home, and we were blessed with another beautiful little girl. There's nothing that tops that."

The only sobering moment of the evening came when Tammy Wynette's untimely death earlier in the year was addressed by her induction into the Country Music Hall of Fame. When Pam Tillis and Lorrie Morgan honored the 'First Lady of Country', singing their tributes before massive rear-projection images of Tammy, the audience showed their appreciation for all three singers.

A few months later, when the 1999 Grammy nominations were announced, Shania Twain was up for six awards. The list of nominees emphasized what had become apparent to many observers of the music business scene: women had really come into their own in the 1990s and Canadian women had surged to the forefront. Celine Dion walked away from the annual event with three Grammies. Shania Twain had two.

Alanis Morissette, one. Dixie Chicks picked up Grammies for Best Album with their WIDE OPEN SPACES and for Best Country Performance by a duo or a group with a vocal. Madonna won some Grammies, too, as did Sheryl Crow. And newcomer, Lauryn Hill, cleaned up. Women had never done better at the Grammies.

Shania Twain's performance on the 1999 Grammy show was to be her most controversial to date. Wearing the provocative black bustiere, ultra-short skirt, and thigh-high boots she had first revealed during a mock strip-show sequence in her video for *Man! I Feel Like A Woman!*, she seemed to have abandoned country music altogether, its inhibitions and conditions, perhaps even it traditions, as some Nashville critics would claim:

I'm going out tonight — I'm feelin' alright
Gonna let it all hang out
Wanna make some noise — really raise my voice
Yeah, I wanna scream and shout

No inhibitions — make no conditions
Get a little outta line
I ain't gonna act politically correct
I only wanna have a good time . . .

(written by Shania Twain and Robert John 'Mutt' Lange)

Perhaps all those comparisons to the pop divas had gone to her head. After all, that 'new standard' for country, which she and Mutt Lange had created on their first album, dictated that the recording artist walk that great divide between country and pop. However, with their second collaboration, COME ON OVER, they seemed to have thrown caution to the wind. Of course, by 1999 country radio had entered a phase that was often described simply as 'contemporary', not contemporary country, new country, or any kind of country at all.

It had been nearly 80 years since the first hillbilly string bands had trekked to New York to be recorded on the new RCA talking machine, and by 1999 country music had along with much of the rural population made the move to the city. During those 80 years, the music had made several approaches to the pop market. When it had faltered, singers and producers had gone back to the roots of the music to revitalize the genre. The current flirtation with pop began with Garth Brooks' early recordings and concerts. When Garth emerged as the top-selling solo artist in any genre of music in the 1990s, country music became more popular than it had ever been. However, beneath the smoke-screen of Garthmania women stepped up to claim ground they had been denied for far too long. Of course, the implementation of SoundScan in 1992 had revealed a fact that had sometimes been obscured by number fudging and reporting of the number of records shipped rather than the number actually sold. SoundScan had revealed that the women were selling a whole heck of a lot of records.

The long journey from hillbilly to contemporary has been spiced with an ongoing debate between traditionalists and modernizers. It is an discussion that will continue on into the 21st century. For example, Nashville columnist Charles Earle, writing in the February 23, 1999 issue of Nashville's City Weekly In Review, offered the following argument in favor of a return to traditional country radio: "The unsinkable WSIX here in Nashville has dropped a few spots in the recent ratings book, while KHYI, a full-time Americana radio station in Dallas, has jumped — in less than two years — from 59th to 29th in one of the largest markets in the country. WSIX is playing the current boring Music Row garbage we've all heard too much of, while KHYI is playing a hybrid of non-mainstream country music and classic hits from the genre's past. You do the math."

It was food for thought. However, the same Charles Earle writing about the 1999 Grammy show in the March 2nd issue of In Review seemed to hold something against the more talented young women who, I believe, have revitalized country: "Shania Twain — Her performance made me want to puke. She embarrassed the entire country music industry, and that's pretty hard to do in a business that is so shameless . . . The Dixie Chicks — I've finally figured out why I hate these girls so much. It's because they are working with Shania Twain in a secret conspiracy to make country music into a big, awful fashion show. The Chicks looked like morons in their silly little outfits that some designer charged somebody an obscene amount of money for. These catty little clotheshorses must certainly have had the folks in L.A. scratching their heads and asking, 'Who the hell dresses those people in Nashville?'"

Charles Earle may have been attempting humor in the above quote from his column, but woman-bashing has been a favorite pastime for male journalists ever since country music was invented. Perhaps Earle's venom comes from a deep-seated guilt felt instinctively from the seven decades of country where males dominated the charts, the tours, the awards, *and* the record sales. The 1990s have become the decade of the woman in country music, but to get to this point women have had to labor long and hard. They have endured many insults more damaging than the mere vitriol of chauvinist columnists. Unfortunately, country's flirtation with the pop market *has* diluted much of the music and, although Charles Earle's assertion that the Dixie Chicks are "just cutesy girls playing pop music with fiddles thrown in" may be an extreme position, Earle is merely personifying a growing critical concern that contemporary country is not country at all. The bottom line is, after all, the bottom line, as Charles Earle also says in his March 2nd diatribe against Shania Twain: "If country music disowns her, the yearly sales figures for the industry would look absolutely disastrous."

Meanwhile, across town at the historic Station Inn, the Nashville club that has been home to bluegrass performers in Nashville for many years, Steve Earle along with Jerry Douglas, Iris Dement, and the Del McCoury Band was tearing up the joint with fresh acoustic bluegrass music. The pickers and singers leaned in to a single microphone with increased enthusiasm as they performed Steve Earle's new songs from MOUNTAIN. That CD would sell 11,000 units in its first week of release on Earle's own E-Squared label and be listed on the *Billboard* Hot 200 albums chart at number 133 but not show up on the country albums chart at all. While sitting in the by-invitation-only audience and being dazzled by the flying fingers of dobro wiz Jerry Douglas and mandolinist Ronnie McCoury, I wondered if the message coming from *Billboard* magazine was that bluegrass was also "not country" in 1999. It most certainly was not 'contemporary'.

There was only one bluegrass artist who was consistently charted in the 1990s. Alison Krauss first hit the country charts as a guest artist on Shenandoah's *Somewhere In The Vicinity Of The Heart*. She became the first contemporary bluegrasser to break the Top 40 when she released *When You Say Nothing At All* to radio in 1995. This single hit the number 3 spot on the *Billboard* chart and won the CMA Single of the Year award. Krauss won both the CMA Horizon award and the Best Female Vocalist award that year. She has not compromised her music when encouraged to contemporize her style.

The movement from hillbilly to country & western, to country, then new country, and finally to contemporary has had a momentum all its own. Once the music was launched to the world by the early RCA Victor and Okeh Records recordings and by the barndance-style radio shows, it began to evolve. And it is far more likely that several strains of country music will survive to the 21st century than that traditionalists will reign in the frequent forays into the larger popular music markets.

At first, hillbilly singers tuned in to the *Grand Ole Opry* for inspiration and worked diligently to fulfil their dreams of becoming a star on the Opry, and, ultimately, the next Hank Williams, Patsy Cline, or Loretta Lynn. As the years went by, it became easier and easier to put out a 45 rpm single, and literally thousands of hopefuls entered the fray. When it came to 'making it' in country music, most were willing to sacrifice principles to make a buck. A dollar went a long way in those days and every country singer could remember a time that there had been no food on the table.

There were times, however, that singers resisted the temptation to popularize their sound. If Hank Williams had agreed to work with pop music impresario and roots music diluter Mitch Miller, who made a bid to become Williams' next producer, country music might have developed in a very different way. Mitch Miller was hugely popular in his day and, despite his betrayal of all genres to a subservience of 'Singalong with Mitch' mediocrity, is still listed as one of the top record sellers of all time. But Hank didn't do it that way.

The development of the 'Nashville Sound' represented ongoing attempts to appeal to a wider audience, but for several decades after Hank's tragic death whenever country music went pop, that sound seemed to retain only the worst of both worlds. In the 1990s, Garth Brooks and Shania Twain have led the way into the biggest country crossover of all time and both singers have found ways to popularize a sound that successfully captures the *best* of both country and pop.

HILLBILLIES COWGIRLS & HONKY-TONK ANGELS

☆ ☆ ☆

The increasing role played by women in writing, recording, and performing country music has changed the music in more ways than merely the obvious slide into pop. Women songwriters have begun to address female fans directly and the time-worn clichés of cheatin', hurtin', lovin', leavin', and drinkin' have been replaced with lyrics that speak to issues relevant in the 1990s. Of course, the history of country music has been built record piled upon record with songs that have provided both comfort and identity to a less privileged rural population. As the country music fan-base gained increasing levels of education and a measure of economic stability, the lyrics were bound to change, too.

For the early string bands, the quick money they received for their recordings was ample incentive to come out of the hills where a need to feed their large families drove the inventive to distil corn whiskey and the daring to over-plant their tobacco crops, despite strict enforcement of quotas by federal agents. Some hillbilly musicians went to New York. Others, like Jimmie Rodgers and The Carter Family were recorded by RCA Victor's Ralph Peer on his many excursions to the countryside. The prospect of earning a hundred dollars for a few songs was attractive. For women who sang country music in the early years, gaining recognition would be an uphill struggle all the way, and the lyrics and titles of early songs like Esmereldy & Her Novelty Band's *Slap Her Down Paw* reinforce the reality that the American South was a patriarchal stronghold.

Today, there are more hit records on the airwaves sung by women than ever before in the history of country music. It has been a long time coming, but in the 1990s according to facts and figures amassed by James Dickerson in his book *Women On Top*, female singers have come to dominate *all* Top 20 sales charts. Shania Twain's CD sales rival those of Garth Brooks, a phenomenon that never happened when Kitty Wells and Patsy Cline vied with Eddy Arnold, Ernest Tubb, Johnny Cash, Elvis Presley, and Marty Robbins for sales and airplay. An endless stream of new female performers in the 1990s suggests that the role model for young, determined and talented women has swerved somewhat from the long established goal of becoming a star of the silver screen to that of being a rock star, a pop diva, or a country sensation.

Before 1960, the role model for women in North America was fashioned in Hollywood, although basic education was taught in places as different from each other as Vassar College and Butcher Holler. The lure of the silver screen — and the mythic heights achieved by larger-than-life film stars like Lauren Bacall, Katherine Hepburn, and Marilyn Monroe who cavorted in and out of satin sheets, descended spiral staircases in silken gowns and were romanced by the likes of Clark Gable, Jimmy Stewart, Spencer Tracy, and Humphrey Bogart — was irresistible to young women who wanted to elevate their lives above that of the common lot. Young girls who attended the movie theaters in the 1940s and 1950s often studied and imitated stars like Grace Kelly, noting how she moved, spoke, and smiled. Mothers who were determined that their daughters had "star potential" moved to the Los Angeles area where they camped out on the doorsteps of Hollywood studios and groomed their offspring for the big opportunity, which, all too often, turned out to be no more than a sordid casting couch scenario never filmed for posterity.

After a few years, the practice of young women going to the film capital of the world all on their own to "make it" in show business, without being chaperoned by either of their parents, became an unprecedented feature of the liberation of women from centuries-old roles as wives, mothers, and housekeepers. However, in the South, the daughters of poor sharecroppers and displaced farmers were drawn by a different beacon. The *Grand Ole Opry* radio broadcast, which began as a barndance-format show in 1925 from the WSM radio station in Nashville, grew in a few short years to become a showcase where hillbillies had a chance to really shine. Hillbilly musicians and singers aspired to being an Opry star, and their fan base tuned in to the Opry and other barndance radio shows like the *National Barndance* and the *Louisiana Hayride*.

At first, hillbilly musicians and recording artists were mainly men, and with very few exceptions women merely performed as members of family acts. Beginning with a handful of singers like Patsy Montana and Molly O'Day, the situation began to shift. Born in Arkansas in 1912, Rubye Blevins surfaced in California in 1928 singing on the radio as the "yodelling cowgirl from San Antone." Three years later, when she joined Stuart Hamblen's traveling rodeo show as one of the Montana Sisters, Blevin, like her Hollywood counterparts, changed her name to Patsy Montana to fit the "cowgirl" image.

The cowgirl mystique derived from genuine female cowhands during the late years of the 19th century and began to evolve in the early years of the 20th century with the appearance of Annie Oakley, who toured with Buffalo Bill's Wild West Show and regularly bested her male competitors in shooting matches. The feats of champion rodeo cowgirls like Lucille Marshall and Fanny Sperry Steele were also real evidence that women could compete with men.

When Thomas Edison developed the first practical movie camera, he was eager to shoot a variety of subjects for his minute and a half clips. Among the subjects for his first action sequences were Bill Cody and Annie Oakley. A few years later, feature films began to replace the traveling shows as the primary entertainment medium in America and an early Hollywood actress by the name of "Texas" Guinan — a cowgirl aspirant who had logged 10 years as a dancer on Broadway — was signed to make a two-reel western in 1917. "Texas" Guinan portrayed a two-gun-toting shoot-em-up character, but this center-stage role was not to become the norm. Soon after this, film companies began producing a steady stream of dusters, often featuring Lucille Mulhall, and the rodeo cowgirl champions of the day would routinely spend their winters working in Hollywood. The downside of this was that all of the lead roles and action scenes featured men. Women, aka 'cowgirls', were relegated to supporting roles.

Through this evolution, the cowgirl image changed over the years, becoming blurred and romanticized. As Candace Savage in her book

Cowgirls notes, "As the cowgirl style was shifted away from its roots, it became available to anyone who wished to appropriate it. A housewife or a secretary could buy it off the rack, and an advertiser could pick it up as a ready-made image." It was a natural for women who sang hillbilly music.

Moving on from the Montana Sisters, Rubye Blevin kept the stage-name she had acquired while working for Hamblen, and it was "Patsy Montana" who joined the hot country band who called themselves the Prairie Ramblers. By 1933, Montana was the star of the *National Barndance* radio broadcast and in 1935 she recorded and released her original song *I Want To Be A Cowboy's Sweetheart*, the first million-seller by a female hillbilly singer. Breaking out on her own as she did, Patsy Montana first did so in California and Chicago. In the West, the example of Hollywood had to some extent freed women from the strict moral constraints placed upon them by religion and by their parents' strong sense of family values.

The patriarchal world was first rocked by the suffragist movement who succeeded in their aim in 1924. For the first time since the concept of democracy had been introduced to the Western world, women could vote. Of course, there were a few more hurdles to be surmounted before any measure of gender equality would be achieved. For example, even in California's film-making mecca, the roles women played in those feature film dusters were still written and directed by men. And the assault on patriarchal value systems were not made by a united front. Suffragists were urban-based political activists who advocated prohibition. They felt little in common with the wild west ways of the less-educated and far more worldly cowgirl. Cowgirls explored the wild side of life, often drank whisky, caroused, married more than once, and pitted themselves against the tough male cowhands and rodeo riders.

During the 1930s and 1940s, Patsy Montana was an inspiration to yodeling cowgirl singers like Louise Massey, Rosalie Allen, Texas Ruby, The Girls of the Golden West, The Melody Ranch Girls, and Bonnie Lou. By the time Dale Evans arrived on the Hollywood scene in the mid-1940s, the cowgirl image had been severely modified, and Evans reconciled herself to "the girl" role, saying little more than, "He went that-a-way." Other actresses like Barbara Stanwyk, who played the lead role in the 1935 feature film *Annie Oakley*, were outspoken when it came to disagreeing with the male writers, producers, and directors who saw frontier women as being limited to secondary support roles. However, through the medium of early television it was Dale Evans who became the quintessential air-brushed cowgirl.

In the 1940s, cowboy singers like Roy Rogers, Gene Autry, and Tex Ritter were the inspiration for the re-naming of hillbilly music to 'country & western'. A recent issue of *Country Weekly* magazine also points out that these silver-screen cowpokes were the first 'hat acts'. Performers on the Opry and the other barndance shows readily adopted the cowboy and cowgirl garb and were often clothed by Hollywood fashion designer, Nudie, who was first employed by Audrey Williams to make stage costumes for her husband, Hank Williams. Hillbilly was fused with the wild west and the change of name from hillbilly music to country & western music reflected the changing times.

As Roy Rogers' wife and partner, Dale Evans continued in the public eye, and the two were chosen to host the very first televised CMA awards show in 1968. Dale Evans was still in vogue in 1990 when she was remembered as an inspiration in the title of an early Dixie Chicks' album THANK HEAVENS FOR DALE EVANS. In 1999, at Canada's Cowboy Festival in Calgary, Dale Evans was the guest of honor and recipient of a Bully Award. The 87-year old Queen of the West told an editorial writer for Calgary's *Country & Western* magazine, "I think it's high time to celebrate the women — they kind of got short shrift. So, I'm glad to see it happen. Particularly for the women of the West — those women that came across mountain ranges, in wagons, had babies. They were unsung."

In the country music world, the rise of Patsy Cline during the 1950s began a move from cowgirl to a more urban image for the female country & western singer. During the early years of her career, Patsy wore cowgirl fashions made for her by her mother, Hilda. Later, she took to wearing designer gowns that she bought in New York.

During the 1950s the mainstream role model in North America slowly began to shift from the film business to the music industry. The emergence of Memphis-based rockabilly singer Elvis Presley created quite a stir, to say the least. When Presley was signed by Colonel Tom Parker and his recording contract was sold by Sun Records' Sam Phillips to RCA, he began to record in Nashville and the rockabilly took on a new fervor. Presley's RCA releases *Heartbreak Hotel*, *Don't Be Cruel*, and *Hound Dog* were played on both country and pop radio stations, but soon the rockabilly would give way to urban rock & roll.

When Elvis appeared in his first feature film, *Love Me Tender*, theater audiences were packed with young women, and whenever Elvis spoke or sang or got into a fist-fight, the movie houses were filled with spontaneous shrieks of adulation. It was no different when Bill Haley & The Comets appeared in *Blackboard Jungle* and launched their song *Rock Around The Clock* into the stratosphere. The spontaneous emergence of a whole generation of rock & rollers such as Chuck Berry, Buddy Holly, Little Richard, and Jerry Lee Lewis literally set the entertainment world on fire. When Elvis returned to performing after his two-year-stint in the U.S. Army, he was the world's first superstar.

Bing Crosby and Frank Sinatra had become major box office attractions through singing on film, and their records had begun to sell in the millions. It is interesting to note that all three of the major male vocalists of this era combined recording and making feature films. It was a double-whammy, which gave them infinitely more exposure than singers who just sang and toured. Presley made 33 feature films, but he wasn't primarily looked upon as a film star. Elvis was the King! A few years later, in 1963 when the Beatles invaded North America, they maximized their exposure by appearing on the *Ed Sullivan Show*. A year after that their first film, *A Hard Day's Night*, was released. The formula of combining film, television, and record releases had become established as the ticket to really big careers. It was a phenomenon that did not go unnoticed by the children of the 1960s who began to view becoming a rock star as the route to fame and fortune.

For the Nashville-based country & western industry, however, the rockabilly fever that infected Memphis in 1955 spelt disaster, and it has taken until the 1990s for sales of country records to catch up to the rock stars. The appearance of Elvis and the popularity of rock & roll posed the first real threat that the country music industry had faced, but — when Elvis began to live in Hollywood and Las Vegas as often as he did in Graceland, and his music moved further from its Memphis roots with every recording — his records no longer charted in the Top 40 on *Billboard* magazine's C&W chart.

Presley would return to favor with country radio DJs in 1970 with *Don't Cry Daddy* and Eddie Rabbitt's *Kentucky Rain*. He continued to chart even after his death in 1977 until the early 1980s when *Guitar Man* was his final number one country hit. The King had become bigger than life and done much to change the perception of children across North America that becoming a "rock star" could bring at least as much glitz and glory as Hollywood stardom. The collapse of the Hollywood studio system around this same time nudged the perception along.

From the invention of radio and records onward, women were looked upon with suspicion when they became entertainers. When they wanted to make it in the music business, women were often faced with compromising situations. And when they wanted to become "stars" more than they cared what people said about them, they suffered. Patsy Cline was publicly referred to as a slut and a whore by some of the townspeople in her home town. Molly O'Day's recordings like *Black Sheep Returned To The Fold* and her version of Hank Williams' *Tramp On The Street* provide further insight into the situation. Each assertion of a woman's point of view by a female singer, from Kitty Wells' *It Wasn't God Who Made Honky-tonk Angels* to Loretta Lynn's *Don't Come Home A-Drinkin' With Lovin' On Your Mind* to Tammy Wynette's *Woman To Woman,* opened the door to equal rights and opportunities a little wider, but it was really Dolly Parton who yanked it wide open, taking the whole issue to Hollywood when she starred in the feature film *9 To 5* with known women's rights activists Lily Tomlin and Jane Fonda.

When TNN *The Nashville Network* started up in 1983, country music had its own TV network outlet. The mixture of programming included opportunities like *The Ralph Emery Show* where artists could appear, chat with Ralph and his puppet, and sing their latest release. This show was viewed as being a country version of Johnny Carson's *Tonight Show.* TNN also devoted part of its programming to stuff like NASCAR racing, but they did play the new music videos that were being produced as country music promoters struggled to keep up with what was happening on MTV for the pop acts.

With the advent of CMT, a 24-hour-a-day video channel, a new land of opportunity was opened for exploration and the women of country began to shine in the new format like they never had before. Within the video medium they were to get to star in their very own mini-movies, and sexually provocative performers like Tanya Tucker, who had at one time been kicked off the Opry stage for rocking too hard, really came into their own.

At first, the country music video was regarded as a curiosity. However, early on, it became apparent that there were some special uses to which the medium could be put. Larry Delaney in a September 1987 story printed in *Country Music News* quotes Warner Nashville's Jim Ed Norman on the subject: "We are repeatedly seeing the effects of CMT, especially for our newer artists. It's one of the few media outlets where our newcomers can get the exposure they need." Joe Galante, Vice President, RCA Nashville, concurred: "CMT is one of the major tools in the focusing of new country acts." And Chairman of CMT parent company Caribou Communications, Jim Guercio, agreed with both record execs: "We feel CMT is already established as a 'starmaker' in the industry." CMT head of programming, Stan Hitchcock, put it in more vivid terms: "This is people music. It's like a radio station with pictures." Delaney also noted that, "with the recent marketing move into Canada, CMT has added several videos by Canadian artists. During August programming CMT aired Anne Murray's *Are You Still In Love With Me* and K.D. Lang's *Turn Me Round* in heavy rotation."

Michelle Wright and Patricia Conroy used the opportunity to gain exposure on CMT to great advantage. As the wave of new traditionalists gave way to a louder electric guitar-driven country-rock and sparse country-pop that would become known as 'new country', the "radio station with pictures" also demonstrated that the small screen medium was a forum where female country artists could sell their sexuality as never before. The marketing of Shania Twain's 1995 release THE WOMAN IN ME would see a record-setting seven music videos from the CD play-listed as Twain's provocative posing and bared mid-riff propeled successive singles toward the top of the *Billboard* chart. Before this demonstration in marketing was through, Shania's album had become the top-selling female country album of all time. It was the nth-degree extrapolation of what could be done when you used sex and country music via CMT to sell a newcomer.

Of course, long before Twain's success, music videos had been working very well for women with veterans like Dolly, Tanya, and Reba looking better than ever on their early videos, and newcomers like Pam Tillis, Martina McBride, and Trisha Yearwood using the medium as a springboard to success. Mary Chapin Carpenter rallied many of the top female vocalists who sang with her on the *He Thinks He'll Keep Her* video that was filmed during the production of the 1993 CBS documentary *The Women of Country*.

When CMT Canada announced their Top 100 Videos of All Time in

June 1998, a simple head-count revealed that there were 26 women in the Top 50 and 44 women in the Top 100. If you added in the three duets by Tim McGraw & Faith Hill, K.D. Lang & Roy Orbison, and Michelle Wright & Jim Brickman, the total was 47 videos by women out of the Top 100 videos. To get on CMT, however, your video product had to be contemporary, action packed, shot on 35 millimeter film, and much, much more than merely standing in front of a microphone, singing through your nose and strumming your guitar.

In 1999, four RCA/BNA recording artists — Mindy McCready, Martina McBride, Lorrie Morgan, and Sara Evans — would take the Judds' 1985 hit song *Girls Night Out* literally and celebrate the coming of age of women in country with renewed energy on a CMT *All Access* Special. The fact that this celebration was taking place on the country music video channel was not coincidental. CMT and TNN had been very good for women right from the beginning.

As Anya Wilson, TNN's Canadian rep, says, "the advent of music videos helped to contemporize country music. When country artists started to see themselves on video, they evolved and got more and more contemporary. A lot of them had pretty traditional haircuts, and they saw that, and they changed. All women have had to evolve. Not too long ago, all women in music were considered whores. Nobody wanted their daughters to be in the performance industry." Before coming to Canada in 1978, Anya Wilson had worked in rock promotion in England for 14 years. "I was the first female independent in the U.K. and men tended to treat you as a joke," she remembers. "You were existing in a man's world. Being viewed as 'one of the boys' meant that you were privy to what some of the boys perceptions were, and thoughts. And you could join in some of their conversations, but you could never be: one of the boys."

Anya's first assignment in Canada was to promote an Ernest Tubb record. It was a challenge, especially so, since working conditions in the Canadian music industry were no better than in the U.K. "I found North America pretty chauvinistic, too," she recalls. "No one would ask you for your opinion. I had some hard knocks. There were some *women* who didn't see me as anything else than how they viewed women. Women were raised to be wives and anything other than that was considered indecent. When I came over here, I got a job in country and I applied some of my rock principles to promoting country, and most of my clients, most of the music directors I dealt with, found it very, very refreshing."

When Anya made her connection with TNN, she began contributing a monthly "Nashville Scene" column to *Country Music News*. Through the years, Wilson widened her base of operations, working as publicist for the CCMA and as a record plugger to radio. And she witnessed first-hand the changing situation for women. "At one stage, when I came to Canada," she remembers, "it was very, very rare for a radio station to play two females back-to-back. It's changed totally. For years, women bought more male artist's records. Women evolved into record buyers, but it was a male audience, initially. A lot of that started with Elvis. Today, women will not only buy the men, they'll buy the female records. The women like the women. They identify with a female artist."

Anya Wilson's answer to the blunt question, "Are there any downsides to women working in the country music industry today?" surprised me. "Sure. There are! Going to Nashville with my husband, Larry, now . . . we have our own business . . . and I'm fine with my work with *The Nashville Network*. I've been their PR consultant for many years. But going to Nashville for my own business . . . it's still a very male town. The upside is that there is a women's network there, too."

From what she has to say about these issues, you might think that Anya Wilson is probably a radical feminist, but the opposite is true. She is merely a straight-shooter. And Anya hits a key word when she mentions the concept of a woman's network. It has taken time, but women who were formerly relegated to supporting roles have proven that they can cut the mustard, so to speak, especially when it comes to promoting country music. Where, a few years ago, booking a country music festival meant posturing and backslapping with a few cowboys in the back rooms at conventions and then filling in the blanks, today, with the critical margins that budgets for such events dictate, it takes a special understanding of all of the ingredients that go into such an endeavor to make it work. From the booking of headliners to the filling in of the set list with affordable acts and beyond to the minute details of assuring sanitary conditions on a festival site with adequate portable toilets, the containment of rowdy enthusiastic drinkers to beer gardens and the creation of family-friendly festival grounds, organizers must be on their toes or they will lose money. Women have proven to be very good at these considerations. They have proven to be adept at running publicity campaigns, signing contracts, and making things hum at all levels of the country music business.

Heather Ostertag, head of the Canadian funding agency for record-ing artists known as FACTOR, agrees with Anya Wilson that it was diffi-cult during in the 1970s and early 1980s for women in the industry. "I can still remember the times," Heather says, "when they were saying, 'Don't sign a Canadian female artist. They don't sell.' I think that when country women began to get rid of the old hooped-skirts and the old look and start-ed using sex like it is used in other genres of music to sell product, all of a sudden people discovered that women could sell records, too. I think they were being packaged in a very old-fashioned way, as opposed to the 'Helen Reddy, I am Woman! Hear me roar!'"

Ostertag remembers the not too distant past when things were very different than they are today: "I grew up on country music. Patsy and Loretta. The women were ladies, and as ladies you wouldn't say 'shit' if you had a mouth full of it. And you wouldn't swear. You wouldn't do any of those things that have been accepted in the norm of being a human being. There was so much that was being hidden . . ."

Ostertag, a true believer in women's rights, could barely restrain her-self from standing and beginning to lecture on the subject. Because we were in a public place, the lounge of the Palliser Hotel in Calgary, she settled for readjusting her lapel-clipped microphone. But she wasn't fin-ished her resolute description of how tough it had been only a few short years ago. "You could be a backup vocalist, but a lady didn't step up and be the entertainer. It was all around being a lady. It's totally been a man's world and we're re-writing history! We're creating a new history. We're becoming so empowered in so many ways outside of music. There's been a lot of change for women in the last 20 years. With that change we're taking more of our own power and we're owning ourselves and coming to recognize that, as women . . . it's okay to be people. We do not have to package ourselves as anything other than what we are. Because, you know what, the guys have never done it. They've been themselves and they've been accepted or not and judged or not judged by society and its standards at any given time. But the ones that we remember the most, like Elvis, are the ones who have pushed the envelope. And women are doing it. We want to be recognized as the artists. We can sell the prod-uct. We want to be recognized as part of the infrastructure. And we're not having to be the secretaries and answering the phones and typing the memos. It's a really exciting time."

When I veered in a sideways direction, alluding to the success of women in the video era, Heather knew she had more to say: "Look at how K.D. Lang pushed the envelope a few years ago ... when she wore the wedding dress at the Junos. It put a new identity in a face to Canadian country female artists. I mean what the heck was 'cowpunk'? She set a standard that it's okay to be different and to make fun of the old while still embracing it. Because, if you look at what she did musically, it was certainly respecting and honoring the history of Canadian country singers, but she was able to put her own identity on it."

At the time that I taped this interview with Heather Ostertag, I had just seen Wynonna's tribute to Tammy Wynette, a live performance of *Woman To Woman* on *Late Night With David Letterman*, which had elicited eerie electrical shudders up and down my spine. When I mentioned how powerful Wynonna's performance had been and how she had drawn energy from her female backup vocalists, turning to them and giving them a high-five during her performance, Heather Ostertag knew what I was talking about. It was sisterhood. "I was just about to use the word 'sisterhood'. If people can wrap their minds around it and use the word. I grew up in a family with five girls in Orillia, Ontario and we learned to work together on certain things. We were within a year, a year and a half of each other, and we would be competing with each other for husbands, boyfriends, for jobs . . . but what has happened is that women have realized is that we don't need to compete with each other. We have realized that we can work together and support each other and make a difference. And that is what sisterhood is really all about. I've been fortunate. I've been in the music business a long time. And I've had an opportunity to work very closely with a lot of men. For one reason or another, and I suspect my size and my directness has something to do with it, I get treated like one of the guys. And I see that they have their own bonding and support mechanisms. I see that they are there to help one another and take care of each other. And women are finding theirs and they're calling it the sisterhood. But men have been instinctively doing it and not calling each other on things. . . . There was a time when women would have chastised each other and gone after each other but we're realizing that we don't need to do that any more. I feel really good that I'm part of this thing, this movement that is seeing women go forward.

"In June 1998 at the *RPM* Big Country Awards, I was inducted into their Country Music Hall Of Fame. It was a very flattering thing to have happen. But, most important, I found that I was the first woman from the industry side of things to be inducted. And, I thought: What about all of the other women? There have been a lot of other incredible women in the industry. Today you have Lisa Zbitnew who is running BMG Canada, which is probably the strongest country label we've got in this country. And that's exciting. And you've got Jill Snell, who is head of country artists on BMG, and so you can see that the sisterhood is doing it, but it is not doing it at the expense of any men. Women are giving women the opportunity and that's all we ask for."

As Heather Ostertag had suggested at the beginning of her impassioned statement, the arrival of the video era encouraged country females to strut their stuff. Patricia Conroy — winner of the 1993 CCMA award for Best Album and the 1994 CCMA award as Best Female Vocalist — sees the breakthrough as being a natural. "Women like to dress up. They like to play house. And they like to play-act. I believe that's why female videos are so popular. It's a good medium for female artists and I've learned a lot about myself as a performer doing videos."

Conroy's supporting video for the title song *Bad Day For Trains* from her award-winning album was directed by Steven Goldmann. In Conroy's video, the juxtaposed image of a muscular, bare-to-the-waist man driving a glowing railway spike into place, each blow of his sledge hammer sending a new shower of sparks into the air, and Patricia's own provocative performance, was spectacular when viewed on CMT. Conroy's album sales soared as never before. A Conroy video in support of *Keep Me Rockin'*, from her 1994 Warner Canada album CAN'T RESIST IT, focuses on Conroy's sexuality and was listed as the Number 86 video on CMT Canada's 1998 list of the Top 100 Videos of All-Time.

However, Conroy, who was in Calgary for a taping of a CMT special during the 1998 CCMA convention, was not sure she wanted to see every single release supported by a video. "In some ways," she said, "it's changed the face of music, because I can remember the days when I'd rush to get a new album by an artist that I liked . . . just to read the liner notes and learn something about them. These days, you know everything about them before you even buy the album. You've seen the video, you know the background, you've watched the interviews on TV. It's great. But I wonder what kind of impetus there is to go out and buy the album when you've got it right there on TV. Videos are a good thing, and the television exposure, but I think we need to find a way to, you know, not go over the top and do a video for every single song. I think it's nice to hold back a bit. Believe me, I'm a hundred per cent behind videos. When I saw people's first videos, I was saying, 'Oh, I want to do one!' I had to wait until my second album, and when I did, I worked with a wonderful director, Steven Goldmann. I was very fortunate right out of the gate to work with someone like that.

"The CMT Special that we have just filmed is a lot more satisfying. It takes me right back to when I was just a bean-sprout in Montreal. It traces my first steps in music. It shows an overall view of who I am, musically, how it all fits together for me as a person and how it translates for as many people as it can. There's an interview segment, a rehearsal segment, and a performance segment. When you see a music video it's edited and all very nicely put together. *This* is the real thing!"

But what is the 'real thing', when, on the one hand, country women recording artists need to create an image that sells music, and on the other, they feel a deep need to be true to themselves and try to do so. Often these two aims are at odds. We need to roll back the years again and look more closely at the life and careers of the early country women artists to see how they managed to survive and sometimes thrive in this paradox, from cowgirl and hillbilly singers to honky-tonk angels like Kitty Wells and Patsy Cline. Then, perhaps, we can begin to glimpse the real thing.

PATSY MONTANA

During the summer of 1990, I heard Patsy Montana sing at Ivan Daines' "Country Music Picnic and Rodeo" near Innisfail, Alberta. Dressed in a fringed buckskin jacket, skirt and western boots, she was hail and hearty at the age of 78. Backed by the Alberta trio, the Great Western Orchestra, she delivered a short, charming set of real cowgirl songs on a narrow stage overlooking the rodeo oval where the women's barrel race competition was being run off. Despite appearing in her cowgirl stereotype, Patsy still exuded the confidence that led her to write one of the first country & western songs penned by a woman about women's lives, *I Want To Be A Cowboy's Sweetheart*. Recording a song that had a definite female point-of-view opened a new door and suggested new opportunities, but it was something Patsy Montana had to do herself. Candace Savage quotes Patsy as saying that I *Want To Be A Cowboy's Sweetheart* "is a *girl's* number, and that ain't supposed to happen. I had to write my own material. Nobody else was going to do it for me." It was by far her most noteworthy success as a recording artist.

> I want to learn to be a cowboy's sweetheart
> I want to learn to rope and ride
> I want to ride o'er the plains and deserts
> Out West of the Great Divide
> I want to hear the coyotes howlin'
> As the sun sets in the West
> I want to be a cowboy's sweetheart
> The life I love the best
>
> (written by Patsy Montana)

Patsy appeared in one Hollywood film with Gene Autry, although her role was minor and typically stereotyped as were all Autry's female co-stars, and sang and recorded with the Sons of the Pioneers. Her career was extended when she began touring with her daughter, Judy Rose, in the 1960s.

Likewise, the hillbilly singers of this era were 'liberated' by women songwriters like Cindy Walker, Sharon Sheeley, Mae Axton, and Rose Marie McCoy, though most of their songs were performed by men. The earliest female hillbilly singers in the South may have had the same feisty spirit of independence displayed by Patsy Montana in California and Chicago during the 1930s, but they were not encouraged to outshine men. It was not deemed acceptable for a woman to travel alone with a band in the South and women kept to family groups. The Singing Stoneman Family and the Original Carter Family were the groups who had the most success recording their music.

THE CARTER FAMILY

June Carter Cash, in her 1979 autobiography, *Among My Klediments*, paints very real pictures of the primitive living conditions facing mountain families. She also describes the role that religion played in keeping families together and how strict her upbringing was.

"I grew up afraid to wear make-up, afraid to dance, afraid to wear a basketball suit because it wasn't modest. I learned that I shouldn't use peroxide in my hair or go to beer joints. That's why I was so surprised about Daddy, I guess. It just never dawned on me that my daddy would take a drink of liquor." June Carter's revelation came when at an innocent young age she was out by the out-house and discovered a bottle of booze hidden nearby. Naturally, young June reported the find to her father. "Grandma Carter fixed Daddy good," June remembers in her book. "She went into the mountains one day and came out pulling a big copper kettle hooked over the end of a stick, dragging it downhill all the way, calling, 'Ezra, Ezra, come here Ezra. I've found the dandiest copper kettle for making apple butter.'"

This theme of men being into the booze and women either taking a stand, as in the Carter family's case, or taking a beating as was much more common, or suffering the humiliation of infidelity and divorce became woven into the lyrical fabric of country music songs. And, while the boozers often died out on the road or at the very least got divorced when they arrived back home, the singers who were rehabilitated, as was June Carter's husband, Johnny Cash, were usually 'saved' and brought back into the fold when they found the strength to deal with their addiction. It was the only treatment available before the creation of substance abuse clinics.

Doc Carter traveled a lot through the hills, collecting songs as he went, and the family act's music was a combination of originals and traditional songs that Doc had harvested. Their first recordings were made when Ralph Peer came to Bristol, Virginia in 1927. Over the years, they recorded more than 300 songs and were the first family act elected to the Country Music Hall of Fame. Mother Maybelle's career saw a second-coming during the 1960s folk revival when she was recognized for longstanding status as one of America's pioneer folksingers. Maybelle's 'scratch' guitar style gained notoriety, and songs like *Wildwood Flower* and *Will The Circle Be Unbroken* survive in the repertoires of country performers to this day.

The Carter Family's record sales were strong, but Doc Carter hankered after the bigger markets being opened up by singers like Jimmie Rodgers who toured extensively. During the early years of the Great Depression, Rodgers was said to be earning in excess of $100,000 a year. The singer who later became known as the 'Father of Country Music' was a womanizer and a heavy drinker and at the opposite end of the morality spectrum from the clean-living Carters. James Hefley in his book *Country Music Comin' Home* offers this description of the day that Rodgers first recorded for Ralph Peer: "When the 'Blue Yodeler' came to Bristol, he already knew he had tuberculosis and probably just a few years to live. He coughed and wheezed and had difficulty recording. Peer got only two songs from him, *The Soldier's Sweetheart* and *Sleep, Baby, Sleep* . . . Five weeks later, Jimmie took the train to New York . . . within six months the sickly, blues-singing yodeler was earning $2,000 per month."

Recordings by the Carters and Jimmie Rodgers were hugely popular from coast to coast, but the touring life took its toll on the Blue Yodeler. Hefley chronicles Rodgers' declining health with these brutal observations: "In 1931 Ralph Peer brought Jimmie and the Carters together for recording sessions in Louisville. Now in intense pain, Jimmie left a trail of blood from coughing spasms and could not stay on stage for more than 20 minutes at a time. He was making more money than President Hoover, yet he refused to slow down. Doctors warned him that he was shortening his life with cigarets and alcohol, but he refused to give up either. In Louisville, Jimmie cut a hymn, *The Wonderful City*, written by Elsie McWilliams. He was so weak that Maybelle Carter had to play his guitar while he sang. The Singing Brakeman was headed for the final downgrade. Hat still cocked jauntily on his head, he looked like a walking dead man when he sauntered on stage. Between recordings he had to rest on a cot."

Rodgers succumbed to his tuberculosis and his excesses in May 1933. In the face of this tragedy and other examples of the downsides to the touring life, Doc Carter couldn't convince his wife to hit the road. Sara was bent on staying at home and bringing up her children in a stable environment. The two divorced. For a time, Sara and the children joined Doc Carter and Maybelle singing on the radio in Mexico where they broadcast over the powerful 250,000 Watt radio station XER that was located right across the border from Del Rio, Texas, and the Carter Family was heard by audiences said to number in the millions. Record sales boomed, but Sara and Doc were not reconciled. By 1943 the original Carter Family had disbanded. The group was reorganized as The Carter Sisters & Mother Maybelle and went on to perform at the Opry and to record and tour with Johnny Cash.

Meanwhile, female vocalists like Patsy Montana, Rosalie Allen, and Molly O'Day were enjoying success with their solo records, and the focus slowly shifted from women singing in family groups to embarking on careers of their own.

ROSALIE ALLEN

Rosalie Allen was born Julie Marlene Bedra on June 27th, 1924, in Old Forge, Pennsylvania and moved to New York in the late 1930s to work on Denver Darling's *Swing Billies* radio show. Known as the 'Queen of the Yodelers', Allen had her first two Top 10 hits in 1946 with *Guitar Polka (Old Monterey)* and a cover of Patsy Montana's *I Want To Be A Cowboy's Sweetheart*. Rosalie went on to host a TV show, work as a disc jockey, and open her own record store. She was a true pioneer in many ways and one of the first female country stars.

The final missing ingredient necessary before female hillbilly vocalists would begin their assault on the charts in the 1950s was input from female songwriters. In the 1950s, Felice Bryant co-wrote many of the Everly Brothers hits with her husband Boudleaux Bryant. Sharon Sheeley became the first woman to solo write a number one, Ricky Nelson's *Poor Little Fool*. Sharon went on to write many hit songs, but her career was nearly ended when she was injured in the same London taxicab accident that killed her friend Eddie Cochran. Mae Axton co-wrote *Heartbreak Hotel* with Tommy Durden, but she wasn't the only woman to write a hit for Elvis during the 1950s. Presley's 1958 hit *I Beg Of You* was penned by Rose Marie McCoy.

CINDY WALKER

When Texas-born Cindy Walker pushed past a secretary into Bing Crosby's offices in Los Angeles and pitched her songs to Bing's brother, Larry, country music got its first significant female writer. Larry Crosby pitched Walker's *Lonestar Trail* to brother Bing who recorded it, and Cindy had her first hit. Cindy Walker remained on the West Coast where she wrote hundreds of songs for films and specific singers, but her success with her songs pointed the way for other women to follow in her footsteps.

When Cindy Walker was inducted into the Country Music Hall of Fame in 1997, a recital of her accomplishments could have taken up the entire CMA Awards show. Among her many successes were Eddy Arnold's *You Don't Know Me* and *Take Me In Your Arms And Hold Me*, Roy Orbison's *Dream Baby*, and Gene Autry's *Blue Canadian Rockies*. She also penned many of Bob Wills' classics, like *Bubbles In My Beer*. Cindy Walker had less success when she recorded her own records, but her 1944 Decca release of *When My Blue Moon Turns To Gold Again* was a number 5 country hit for her and a number 19 pop hit when recorded by Elvis in 1956. Walker and

**ORIGINAL
CARTER
FAMILY**

**PATSY
MONTANA**

**CINDY
WALKER**

**KITTY
WELLS**

BRENDA LEE

**SKEETER
DAVIS**

MYRNA LORRIE

DOTTIE WEST

**LORETTA
LYNN**

other singers like Rosalie Allen also filmed movie shorts, singing jukebox hits that were known as 'Soundies' during the 1940s. These film clips were early examples of the music video format and attracted a high proportion of women performers, but by the 1950s 'Soundies' died out in popularity. It was also during the 1940s that country radio stations began a switch from live shows and singers to disc jockeys who spoke to the audience and played records.

In 1944, *Billboard* magazine began to publish both juke box charts and hit parade charts and the modern era of country music was ushered in. Inadvertently, the charts also created several other terms and issues. For example, now that there were country and pop charts, the phrase 'that's not country' would soon enter the North American vocabulary. Before that happened, another new word, 'crossover', would take on significance.

In addition to creating the term 'crossover', the *Billboard* charts gave rise to the statistics game by which today's country music measures much of its success. *Billboard* began listing a Juke Box Folk Records chart on May 25, 1944. In 1947 this chart was changed to Most Played Juke Box Hillbilly Records. In 1948, the magazine began a Best Selling Retail Folk Records chart. In 1949, the name was changed to Best Selling Country & Western Records. That same year *Billboard* began to list its first airplay chart: Country & Western Records Most Played by Folk Disk Jockeys. That name was modified several times until the C&W was dropped in 1962 and the chart named Hot Country Singles.

A study of the early charts confirms the fact that most of the hits were by men. Joel Whitburn's Top 25 listing for the 1940s in *The Billboard Book of Top 40 Country Hits* shows only one woman, Margaret Whiting. The 1950s was not much more hopeful with only Kitty Wells (at number 9) listed in the Top 25. In the 1960s, Kitty Wells was joined by Loretta Lynn and Connie Smith in the Top 25 list. By the 1970s, we find Loretta Lynn, Dolly Parton, Tammy Wynette, Lynn Anderson, and Donna Fargo listed in the Top 25. Today's country music scene may not be dominated by women, but women have never before had such a high percentage of airplay and record sales.

The early charts were dominated by male singers and bands, but when female pop singers began crossing over into the country market, things began to change. Margaret Whiting was a pop singer who had success with c&w duets, which she sang with cowboy singer Jimmy Wakely. In 1949,

Whiting and Wakely hit with *Slipping Around* and were at number one for 17 weeks on the Best Seller chart. They charted two more number ones and half-a-dozen more Top 10 entries through 1951.

The Andrews Sisters (Patty, Maxene and LaVerne) struck pay dirt when they teamed with Bing Crosby on *Pistol Packin' Mama*, a gold-selling record in 1944. Two duets pairing the Andrews Sisters and Ernest Tubb also went Top 10 in 1949 but did not sell as many copies. In 1946, the King Sisters had a number 5 hit with *Divorce Me C.O.D.* And in 1951, Patti Page's recording of *Tennessee Waltz* achieved gold status. Patti was born Clara Ann Fowler and got her stage name when she was a regular performer on the Page Milk Company Show on KTUL. She became host of her own national TV show in 1955. During this era, the top male singers like Hank Williams and Slim Whitman had three gold records each, Eddy Arnold, Red Foley, and Tennessee Ernie Ford only one each. Selling a million copies was difficult in the 1940s and early 1950s, even for the male country singers.

When Owen Bradley began to produce records by Patsy Cline and Brenda Lee in the late 1950s, Brenda would crossover so completely that she wouldn't be heard on the country Top 40 until the 1970s. Patsy Cline, who already had a fan base throughout the South by the time she hit big on the radio, did see some of her releases cross over, but — unlike Brenda Lee who was a child phenom and more readily accepted by pop and rock audiences — Cline appealed so compelling to c&w fans that crossing over never posed a threat to her identity as a country star. But before he recorded these crossover stars, Bradley had produced Kitty Wells, the first "Queen of Country."

KITTY WELLS

Country fans got their first female star in 1952 when Kitty Wells' *It Wasn't God Who Made Honky-tonk Angels* soared to number one and stayed there for six weeks. The lyrics to this song answered Hank Thompson's *The Wild Side Of Life*. When Kitty sang . . .

> As I sit here tonight, the juke box playing
> A tune about the 'Wild Side of Life'
> As I listen to the words you are saying
> It brings memories when I was a trusting wife

It wasn't God who made honky-tonk angels
As you said in the words of your song
Too many times married men think they're still single
That has caused many a good girl to go wrong

It's a shame all the blame is on us women
It's not true that only you men feel the same
From the start most every heart that's ever been broken
Was because there always was a man to blame ...

(written by J.D. Miller)

... she changed country music forever.

Kitty Wells first recorded for RCA Victor in 1949, but by 1952 had retired from the music business when the 'demo' that she had cut for Owen Bradley was released by Decca and took off up the charts. She was unaware that it had even been released. The release was surrounded by many surprises, including a lawsuit by the publishers of the Hank Thompson song it answered. The suit was disregarded because the writers of the *Wild Side Of Life* had lifted their melody from two previous songs, *I'm Thinkin' Tonight Of My Blue Eyes* and *The Great Speckled Bird* — and the rest, as they say, is history.

Kitty Wells was born Muriel Ellen Deason on August 30th, 1919, in Nashville. She first performed as a member of the Deason Sisters (with sisters Wilma Mae and Mabel and their cousin Bessie Choate) on radio station WSIX. In 1937, she married up-and-coming hillbilly singer Johnny Wright, who would later team with Jack Anglin to form Johnnie & Jack. By 1943, Muriel had renamed herself Kitty Wells and was raising a family of her own. Kitty Wells did find time to sing, however, touring with Johnny & Jack and performing regularly on WBIG-Greensboro, WNOX Knoxville and both the *Grand Ole Opry* and the *Louisiana Hayride*.

Decca Records followed up the successful debut with a series of releases where Kitty Wells answered songs like Webb Pierce's *Back Street Affair* with *Paying For That Back Street Affair* and Bobby Helms' *Fraulein* with *(I'll Always Be Your) Fraulein*. These were pioneer women's songs and they struck a deep chord with female fans. When a Kitty Wells' record came on the radio, women sang along.

Kitty Wells hit the number one spot again in 1959 with *Heartbreak U.S.A.* And she had success singing duets with Red Foley, Webb Pierce, and Roy Drusky, the most memorable of which is *One By One* a 1954 number one hit for Foley and Wells. She also sang with Roy Acuff, and it was Roy's partner, Fred Rose, who named her the "Queen of Country Music." When Jack Anglin died in 1963, Kitty Wells and Johnny Wright formed a family act once again. Their children, Ruby and Bobby, both became singers, and their show has always been 100 percent family entertainment. Kitty Wells was named *Billboard* magazine's Best Female Artist from 1953 through 1965. She released more than 80 singles to radio and in 1976 was inducted into the Country Music Hall of Fame. At the 1991 Grammies Kitty Wells was awarded a Lifetime Achievement award.

ANSWER SONGS

Answer songs like *It Wasn't God Who Made Honky-tonk Angels* provided a new identity for women who sang country. For a while, they were a novelty that often proved to be a springboard for launching new careers. Some singers, like Jeanne Black, who reached number 6 with *He'll Have To Stay*, a 1960 answer to Jim Reeves' *He'll Have To Go*, would be one-hit wonders. Jo Ann Campbell reached the number 24 position with her 1962 Cameo Records release of *(I'm The Girl) On Wolverton Mountain*. It would be her only Top 40 hit, although she would marry songwriter Troy Seals and record with him as Ann & Troy. *It's Not Wrong*, one of Connie Hall's five Top 20 hits during the early 1960s, was an answer song to *Is It Wrong (For Loving You)*. Arlene Harden's *Lovin' Man (Oh, Pretty Woman)*, a female version of the Roy Orbison hit, was a number 13 charter in 1970 and the most successful of Hardin's seven Top 40 recordings, although as a member of the Harden Trio, Arlene had reached the number 2 position on the *Billboard* chart with *Tippy Toeing* in 1966.

Jody Miller kicked off a successful recording career with *Queen Of The House*, a 1965 answer to Roger Miller's *King of the Road*, hitting number 5, a chart position she only surpassed with her 1972 release of *There's A Party Going On*. Ruby Wright, Kitty Wells' daughter, hit the Top 20 with *Dern Ya*, her 1964 answer song to Roger Miller's *Dang Me*. And CMA Hall of Fame country comedienne and longtime Opry star, Minnie Pearl, had her only Top 40 hit with an answer version of Red Sovine's *Giddyup Go*. The phenomenon of answer songs petered out during the 1970s. The novelty had worn off and the male lyrics were no longer so prone to this form of parody.

Although the pre-1960s years of country music have been described as Kitty Wells and a whole lot of men, several other women made significant contributions during the era. Not the least of these was Wilma Lee Cooper. Born Wilma Lee Leary on February 7th, 1921 in Valley Head, West Virginia, Wilma Lee sang and played guitar, banjo, and piano with the Leary Family gospel group on the WWVA-Wheeling *West Virginia Jamboree* until 1940. During this time, she married one of the group's fiddlers, 'Stoney' Cooper. The two formed a duo and performed on the Opry from 1947 to 1957. When the Coopers began to record, they formed their own band, The Clinch Mountain Clan. From 1956 through 1961, Wilma Lee and Stoney charted seven records on the *Billboard* Top 40, including two number 4 hits: *Come Walk With Me* and *Big Midnight Special*. They also had a number 3 charter with Don Gibson's *There's A Big Wheel* in 1959, and their cover of Rosemary Clooney's 1954 release *This Old House* was a number 16 hit in 1960.

WILMA LEE COOPER

I recently had the pleasure of hearing Wilma Lee sing on the *Grand Ole Opry* and spoke with her backstage. I learned that she had continued on as a solo artist after she had "lost Stoney in 1977," and that she was hugely proud of the fact that her daughter, Carolee Cooper, the leader of the Carol Lee Singers, was the person in charge of the background singers on the Opry that night.

Bonnie Lou, a popular performer on the *Midwestern Hayride* for over 20 years, hit the Top 10 twice in the early 1950s, first in 1953 with her cover of Georgia Gibbs' pop hit *Seven Lonely Days* and again in the same year with *Tennessee Wig Walk*.

Another Bonnie, Bonnie Buckingham, became known as 'Bonnie Guitar'. An accomplished session guitar player, she first surfaced in L.A. recording sessions during the mid-1950s. Founder of Dolphin and Dolton Records in Seattle in 1958, she issued her own singles on Dot Records beginning with *Dark Moon*, a number 14 hit in 1957, and *Mister Fire Eyes*, a number 15 charter in 1958. Discovering and developing The Fleetwoods, who hit with *Come Softly To Me*, Buckingham was hired by Dot and ABC Paramount as director of A&R, the first woman to hold such a prestigious position. Bonnie Guitar returned to recording in 1966 and charted eight more Top 40 singles, including *A Woman In Love,* a number 4 hit in 1967.

Some relatives of famous artists like Betty Foley, daughter of Pauline and Red Foley, who had three chart hits during the period, did well with a few releases. Others, like Garth Brooks' mother, Colleen Carroll, who was signed to Capital Records in 1954 and became a regular on Red Foley' *Ozark Jubilee,* do not show up on the Top 40 charts at all. Another member of Foley's radio troupe, the tiny, blonde, sob-soaked-vocal specialist, Jean Shepard, debuted in 1953 with the number one smash *A Dear John Letter,* a duet with Ferlin Husky.

Jean Shepard was born Ollie Imogene Shepard on November 21st, 1933 in Pauls Valley, Oklahoma and raised in Visalia, California where she formed the all-girl group The Melody Ranch Girls in the late 1940s. Discovered by Hank Thompson, Jean linked up with Red Foley in the early 1950s and has been a member of the Opry since 1955. Her husband, Hawkshaw Hawkins, was killed in the same plane crash that took Patsy Cline's life in the early 1960s, but Shepard went on to record 31 charting singles, many of which were Top 10 hits, but never repeated the success of her debut release.

MYRNA LORRIE

In 1955, Myrna Lorrie became the first Canadian female singer to chart in the *Billboard* Top 40 with *Are You Mine* a Top 10 duet with fellow Canadian Buddy deVal. Lorrie was born Myrna Petrunka on August 6th, 1940 in Cloud Bay, Ontario, some 30 miles outside of Thunder Bay. In 1954, while singing at a local nightclub, the teenager was discovered by songwriter-producer Don Grashey. That same year, Don Grashey and Buddy deVal had gotten two of their songs recorded by Jim Reeves on Fabor Robison's Abbott label, and Robison was also interested in recording Buddy deVal. Sensing Myrna's potential, Grashey recorded two duets featuring Buddy and Myrna and sent them along to Robison.

When *Are You Mine* was released, it rocketed up the charts to become a Top 10 hit while Myrna Lorrie was still only 14 years of age. She was the talent Grashey wanted to promote and was credited with a co-write on the song. *Are You Mine* peaked at number 6 on *Billboard* and number 2 on *Cashbox.* Grashey took Myrna Lorrie to Nashville. The Thunder Bay teenager's first U.S. tour had her opening for many of the popular stars of the day, including Hank Snow, Johnny Cash, Kitty Wells, and Marty Robbins. Hank Snow took a shine to the teenager and featured her on his

Grand Ole Opry segment, where she was heard by the large audience tuned in to the WSM broadcast. In 1955, *Are You Mine* received the BMI Song of the Year Award. When Myrna Lorrie was barely 15, she was named Top New Female Artist in America at the annual Disc Jockey's convention in Nashville. Later that same night in the lobby of the Andrew Jackson Hotel in Nashville, the Canadian teenager was congratulated by fellow-winner Elvis Presley. It was, in many ways, the high point of her career because, although she went on to tour with the likes of Ferlin Husky and Skeeter Davis, subsequent U.S. releases by Myrna did not grace the Top 40.

On her own for a few years, Myrna Lorrie hooked back up with Grashey and his Gaeity Records chum, Chuck Williams, in Los Angeles in 1961. It was Grashey and Williams who recorded the tracks that would become a string of Canadian country hits for Myrna Lorrie during the 1960s. *Turn Down The Music* and *Your Special Day* were number one hits in Canada, and Myrna was winner of a Juno Award as Best Female Country Singer at the very first Juno Awards show in 1971. She won a second Juno in 1972 and hosted two television shows of her own before losing momentum and dropping out of the recording scene altogether. However, in 1989, Myrna Lorrie recorded what Canadian reviewer Larry Delaney deemed "a remarkable comeback album."

Drawn out of her doldrums by her brother, Dave Petrunka, who became her new manager, Myrna recorded her 1989 sides for BLUE BLUE ME with Joe Bob Barnhill at Reflections Studios in Nashville. Her original song, *Blue Blue Me*, went number one in Canada. When Myrna toured Western Canada in 1990, featured on a Grand Ole Opry tour with Porter Wagoner, Connie Smith, Stonewall Jackson, Freddie Hart, and Little Jimmy Dickens, *Country Music News* reporter Dennis Charney described her performance in glowing terms: "When she stepped on stage at Edmonton's Jubilee Auditorium 2,000 people knew that nothing had changed...except for the better! The control and emotion in her voice had been expanded and refined. When she sang *Blue Blue Me* and *Sometime* they knew her song-writing form had never been better."

In 1996, Myrna Lorrie was inducted into the Canadian Country Music Hall of Fame. In 1998, a CD compilation CHILD TO WOMAN was issued by EMI/Northern Heritage. Don Grashey supervised the restoration of the original masters. Forty-four years after he first heard Myrna sing in a nightclub in Thunder Bay, Grashey was still a Myrna Lorrie fan.

WANDA JACKSON

Wanda Jackson was the only female singer during the 1950s to exploit the rockabilly style fully. Born in Maud, Oklahoma on October 20th, 1937, Jackson was an early achiever on both guitar and piano. By the age of 13, she had her own radio show on KLPR Oklahoma City. During the early 1950s, she recorded for Decca and first had Top 10 success with *You Can't Have My Love* a 1954 duet with Billy Gray. Tours with Hank Thompson, Red Foley, and Elvis Presley increased Jackson's profile, and she was signed by Capitol Records. Wanda had caught the rockabilly fever from Elvis, and her Capitol recordings attracted airplay from pop stations where she became known as the 'Queen of Rockabilly'. When her career as a female-rocker peaked with the 1961 release of *Let's Have A Party*, she returned to country radio with *Right Or Wrong* and *In The Middle Of A Heartache*.

Wanda Jackson was one of the most prolific recording artists of her time and a huge influence on succeeding generations of honky-tonkin' angels. In the 1970s she focused on recording gospel music. In the 1980s, she continued to tour and sing both gospel and rockabilly but kept her performances out of liquor dispensing establishments. In 1995, Wanda Jackson recorded duets with Rosie Flores that were issued on Flores' High Tone Records album ROCKABILLY FILLY. The two toured together during the same year. Wanda Jackson's hundreds of recordings are available through collections issued by Rhino Records, Bear Family Records, and Capitol Records' Vintage Collection Series.

SKEETER DAVIS

Skeeter Davis, born Mary Frances Penick, struck first with a number one in 1953 as a member of the Davis Sisters with Betty Jack Davis. *I Forgot More Than You'll Ever Know* was number one for 8 weeks; however, a tragic motor vehicle accident claimed Betty Jack's life and left Skeeter severely injured. In 1956, Skeeter went solo. She toured with Eddy Arnold and Elvis Presley and joined the Grand Ole Opry in 1959. Her first solo hit was the 1958 release *Lost To A Geisha Girl*, an answer song to Hank Locklin's *Giesha Girl*. She had a number 5 hit with *Set Him Free* in 1959, and in 1960 was at number 2 for three weeks with *(I Can't Help You) I'm Falling Too*, an answer to Hank Locklin's *Please Help Me I'm Falling*.

Skeeter Davis grew up on a farm in Kentucky and got her nickname from her grandfather who said she was always buzzing around like a mosquito. At

RCA Victor for her entire solo career, Skeeter Davis charted 26 Top 40 records during the 1960s for the label, including the million-seller *The End Of The World*. She co-wrote the lyrics to Floyd Cramer's *Last Date* with Boudleaux Bryant. Skeeter Davis kept on buzzing with many of her releases crossing over to the pop charts and getting airplay in the U.K. She appeared on television with Duke Ellington and toured with The Rolling Stones. Her touring has made her popular in Canada, Europe, and the Far East, as well as at home in the United States. Skeeter Davis also had success with her duets sung with Bobby Bare, but was censured by the Opry when she became a born-again Christian and began preaching from the Opry stage.

BRENDA LEE

Brenda Lee was the second child prodigy to appear on the national country & western scene. Born Brenda Mae Tarpley on December 11th, 1944 in Lithonia, Georgia, Brenda Lee was signed to Decca Records in 1956 and became known as 'Little Miss Dynamite'. Brenda first charted with *One Step At A Time*, a number 15 country hit in 1957, but her 1960 release *Rockin' Around The Christmas Tree* was a novelty hit and her big hits like *Sweet Nothin's*, *I'm Sorry* and *I Want To Be Wanted* came as a pop artist. She returned to country in the 1970s with some 20 releases, many of them Top 10 entries like *Nobody Wins* (number 5 in 1973), *Sunday Sunrise* (number 6 in '73) and *Wrong Ideas*, *Big Four Poster Bed*, *Rock On Baby*, *He's My Rock*, and *Broken Trust* (a number 9 hit on which she was accompanied by The Oakridge Boys). Her final Top 40 chart entry came in 1985, *Hallelujah, I Love Her So*, a duet with George Jones. Brenda Lee had been in the music business four decades and sold over 100 million records. She continues to entertain to the present day.

PATSY CLINE

1957 was also the year that Patsy Cline released *Walkin' After Midnight*, her first Top 40 single. Cline was a trendsetter who got her break after being discovered on Arthur Godfrey's TV show *Talent Scouts* in January 1957. Her tragic death in a plane crash in 1963 cut short a career that might have changed the face of country & western music more quickly than did the legend she left behind. However, her renditions of *I Fall To Pieces* (number one in 1961), *She's Got You* (number one in 1962), *Leavin' On Your Mind*, *Sweet Dreams (Of You)*, and *Faded Love* created such a vivid impression on generations of young women who followed that her seven short years as a recording artist guarantee that she will never be forgotten. Patsy Cline's 1962 release of Willie Nelson's *Crazy* only went to number 2 on the charts, but remains one of the truly classic country recordings of all time.

> Crazy, crazy for feeling so lonely
> I'm crazy, crazy for feelin' so blue
> I knew you'd love me as long as you wanted,
> And then someday you'd leave me for somebody new . . .
> I'm crazy for tryin', crazy for cryin'
> And I'm crazy for lovin' you
>
> (written by Willie Nelson)

Patsy Cline brought some soul to the country music scene. Where many female vocalists had sung through their noses with a catchy accent or yodeled, Cline was a vocal stylist of the first order, one of the best singers of the entire century of recorded music, and her influence is far beyond proportion to her few radio hits.

Allegedly abused by her father and not supported by a compliant mother, Patsy emerged from her childhood into an equally hostile world where she became willing to sacrifice dignity for career opportunities. Often a victim, Patsy Cline had a foul-mouthed approach to the male bullshit of the times, never afraid to berate the beraters. Although several sensationalist biographies and a truly off-the-mark Hollywood film called *Sweet Dreams* and starring Jessica Lange portrayed Patsy and her husband Charlie Dick inaccurately, Cline's tragic life was, in reality, a continual struggle to outsmart a series of domineering males. After a compromising relationship with a married local band leader in her home town, Cline was suckered by Bill McCall at 4-Star Records into a succession of one-way-street contracts. It was not until she met Owen Bradley and her second husband, Charlie Dick, that Cline received the support she had always needed to stand up for her own rights.

Once Patsy Cline got things ironed out, she recorded quality songs by writers like Harlan Howard and Hank Cochran and became a national star. She stood by her mother, who responded by sewing Cline costumes, unique combinations of appliqué that would rival Nudie's high-dollar Hollywood creations. PATSY CLINE'S GREATEST HITS was for many years the all-time best-selling album by a female country music singer. The variety of arrangement and mood created by Owen Bradley on Patsy Cline's best cuts is only matched by her ability to rise to the occasion and deliver ultimate takes in the studio.

One of Patsy's proteges and good friends, Loretta Lynn, took up the cause when Patsy was no longer there to lead the way. **LORETTA LYNN**
Loretta Lynn was born Loretta Webb on April 14th, 1934 in Butcher Holler, Kentucky. Her story is one of the best known to country fans, many of whom have read her book *Coal Miner's Daughter* or seen the feature film of the same name starring Sissy Spacek. Loretta's biography is an entertaining read. She is no preacher, but she speaks openly and effectively when describing the conditions endured by women before women's rights organizations set out to change the situation in the 1960s.

It was Canadian Don Grashey who discovered Loretta Lynn when she showed up at a jam in a Vancouver club. "I was the one who took her to Western Recorders in Hollywood," the enigmatic Canadian manager of Carroll Baker and Myrna Lorrie declared in his gruff voice over the telephone from his Thunder Bay home. "It was me that found her in the Chickencoop in Vancouver and it was me that put out her record on Zero Records. But she forgets. It's not in her book. She forgets. She credits Norm Burley. He was there, but he was just a director." In *Coal Miner's Daughter*, Loretta does mention Grashey, saying he was the only one in the bunch who had "some business sense," but she identifies Burley as the guy who put up the money. To a greenhorn from Butcher Holler, money must have seemed the most important ingredient. If Grashey had not gone on to steer both Myrna Lorrie's career and Carroll Baker's, you might wonder if it isn't Grashey who doesn't remember how it really was. But Grashey co-wrote many of Myrna Lorrie's hits and he has been in the industry a goodly long time. He just would like it better if Loretta remembered him for what he did.

Loretta Lynn didn't exactly burst upon the scene with her first release. In fact, it took her and her husband, Mooney Lynn, getting in their car and promoting *I'm A Honky-tonk Girl* in almost every state in the union to sell 50,000 records.

Ever since you left me I've done nothing but wrong
Many nights I've lied awake and cried
We once were happy, my heart was in a whirl
But now I'm a honky-tonk girl

So turn that jukebox up high
And fill my glass up while I cry
I've lost everything in this world
And now I'm a honky-tonk girl

I just can't make a right of all my wrongs
Every evening of my life seems so long
I'm sorry and ashamed for all these things you see
But losin' him has made a fool of me . . .

(written by Loretta Lynn)

Canadian Norm Burley funded the trip, but he couldn't have put up too many dollars because Loretta says that she and Moony lived in their Mercury and ate "baloney and cheese sandwiches." To give Grashey some credit, Loretta does admit that her record was often at the stations she would visit. Sometimes, it would be in the trash can. The way it worked was that Grashey was getting the product there and Loretta would charm the disc jockeys into playing it. She would be on the air talking to the jock, and Moony would be out in the car, listening. One of the people the Lynns met along the way was Waylon Jennings who was working at that time as a disc jockey in Tucson.

When they got to Nashville, the two lived in their car until Loretta got her first break and began working clubs in the surrounding area. Loretta badgered Ott Devine to let her on the Opry and the response was so positive that he let her on again. She also met Patsy Cline during this period, when she sang a tribute to Patsy on the Opry broadcast after Patsy's near-fatal car crash, and they soon became best friends. Loretta and Mooney's method of promoting had not been the usual way to promote a career or even a record, but everything we learn about Loretta Lynn tells us that she is one of the originals, and many of the doors that were opened were only opened due to her persistence and her charm.

In her book, we get graphic details of the plight of a young girl plunged into the complexities of marriage and sex. She was real young, only 13, when she married Mooney Lynn, a war veteran seven years her senior. She speaks quite plainly about her lack of sex education and the fact that for most women back in Butcher Holler nursing a new-born was the only form of birth control used. And the lyrics to *The Pill*, a number 5 hit for Loretta in 1975, were considered controversial at the time. Loretta is a straight-shooter when she says: "I don't believe in double standards where men can get away with things women can't. There's no double-standard in God's eyes."

Her songs convey similar themes. *Fist City* delivers the message that she is ready to protect her marriage and deliver a knuckle sandwich to anyone who comes after her husband. *Don't Come Home A-Drinkin' (With Lovin' On Your Mind)* was a song lyric far ahead of it's time, yet long overdue, especially in the world of people who lived the country way of life. Based on an idea provided to Loretta by her sister, Peggy Sue, this 1966 release was Loretta's first number one hit. People were ready to hear what she had to say.

> Well, you thought I'd be waitin' up
> When you came home last night
> You'd been out with all the boys
> And you ended up half tight
> But liquor and love they just don't mix
> Leave the bottle or me behind
> And don't come home a drinkin'
> With lovin' on your mind ...

(written by Loretta Lynn/ Peggy Sue Wells)

In Kentucky, Mooney, when he came courting Loretta, had driven the first automobile, a jeep, to ever appear in Butcher Holler. When the young married couple moved to Custer, Washington, Loretta had four children before she was 18. She took in other people's laundry and picked fruit to supplement the family income. And she tells with pride the time she and another woman entered some preserves in the Lynden Fair competition and won a heap of blue ribbon prizes. She jumped three feet in the air and "hollered" so loud they took her picture and blew it up big and posted it at the gate. This unbounded enthusiasm is what got Loretta through the many years of dawn-to-dusk labor until the time that Mooney brought home a Sears Roebuck guitar. It was Mooney who encouraged Loretta to write songs and sing. When she got a band, Mooney became her first manager. His support and growing understanding of her was a reward for the times she'd reined him in when he thought he might stray during the early days of their marriage. And it is an example of the benefits that fidelity can bring, if a person is willing to work at it.

At first Loretta sang songs by her idol, Kitty Wells, but she'd made up her own songs when she was a young girl and began to do it again. Her first efforts like *Doggone Blues* weren't as successful as the ones we hear on the records, but it was a beginning. Finally, it was time to cut a record, which she did when she and Mooney went to Los Angeles. *I'm A Honky-tonk Girl* eventually peaked at number 14 on the *Billboard* c&w chart.

In Nashville, Patsy provided valuable advice to Loretta about how to entertain a large audience, how to walk on, and how to walk off. Cline was happy to oblige. She liked Loretta. Patsy even helped out a bit with wardrobe now and then while Loretta and Mooney were still struggling to make ends meet. And in 1962, Loretta began to record with Patsy's producer, Owen Bradley, who had the magic touch when it came to making records. Loretta sometimes toured with Patsy Cline until Patsy's tragic death. After that it wasn't long before Loretta was regarded as the top female country singer in America. Loretta and Kitty and Patsy were the first female country entertainers to gain a large audience with female fans.

Success, Loretta's first record on the Decca label, went to number 6 on the c&w charts when it was released in 1962. She went on to record 16 number one solo hits, including *Fist City (1968)*, *Woman Of The World Leave My Man Alone (1969)* and *Coal Miner's Daughter (1970)*. In 1970 Loretta began touring regularly with Conway Twitty. Together, Loretta and Conway had a string of number one duet releases, beginning with *After The Fire Is Gone* and *Lead Me On* in 1971. In 1973, the two hit the top of the chart again with *Louisiana Woman, Mississippi Man*. They hit the number one position twice more with *As Soon As I Hang Up The Phone (1974)* and *Feelin's* in 1975.

Loretta Lynn was the first woman to be named CMA Entertainer of the Year and the first to be inducted into the Country Music Hall of Fame.

She headlined on the country circuit for more than 20 years, but the many years of child-bearing (she had six children in all), farm-laboring, and touring finally caught up with her workaholic drive. Anne Janette Johnson writes in the December 1989 issue of *Contemporary Musicians* that Loretta "suffered from insomnia, depression, migraine headaches, bleeding ulcers, seizures, and exhaustion and more than once collapsed on stage in the middle of a performance . . . the punishing pace Loretta set, two shows per night for as many 300 nights per year — began to take their toll." Loretta finally came off the road in 1984 when she received the news of her son's death. The tragedy of Jack Benny Lynn's horseback riding accident kept her off the road for a while, and when she went back to recording and touring, she set herself a more leisurely pace.

Sissy Spacek had two charting singles from the soundtrack of the feature film. When Sissy and Loretta appeared on *Nashville Now* with Ralph Emery in 1999, the two seemed to be twins, two peas from the same pod.

Loretta's awards include a Grammy in 1971; CMA Female Vocalist of the Year in 1967, 1972, and 1973; CMA Duo of the Year with Conway Twitty 1972 through 1975, and an American Music Award in 1978. She was named Entertainer of the Decade in 1980 by the Academy of Country Music. Altogether, she recorded 53 Top 10 singles and 16 number one albums, including the first country album by a female vocalist to be certified gold. Profiled in *McCall's* magazine, Loretta's own words sum up her success better than any ever written about her: "You either had to be first, best or different. I was just the first to say what I thought. The rest of country music's women stars didn't write. I wrote it like it was."

For Loretta, the brightest female country star to shine during the 1960s, this was the 'real thing'. She influenced a whole generation of women who followed her to write and sing it like it is.

QUEENS
OF COUNTRY
MUSIC

☆☆☆

During the 1960s, the number of country female vocalists signed to major labels continued to build. In addition to Tammy Wynette and Loretta Lynn, there were many singers who vied for the right to succeed Kitty Wells as the 'Queen of Country Music'.

CONNIE SMITH

Indiana-born Connie Smith was raised in Ohio and West Virginia. One of 14 children, Smith was already married when she was discovered by Bill Anderson who encouraged Connie to come with him to Nashville. Anderson was instrumental in getting Connie signed to RCA and wrote her debut single *Once A Day*, which immediately rocketed to number one on the *Billboard* country chart where it stayed for eight weeks. Connie followed her debut with a string of Top 10 hits like *Then And Only Then, I Can't Remember, If I Talk To Him*, and *Nobody But A Fool (Would Love You)*. Her debut album, CONNIE SMITH, spent seven weeks at number one on the country album charts in 1965. A genuine contender for the title of the 'Queen Of Country Music', Connie was also known as the 'Rolls Royce of Female Country Vocalists.' Dolly Parton once said, "There's really only three female singers in the world: Streisand, Ronstadt, and Connie Smith. The rest of us are only pretending."

Twelve of Connie Smith's 50 album releases charted in the Top 20. Twenty of her singles made the Top 10. She appeared in two feature films, *Second Fiddle To A Steel Guitar* and *Road To Nashville*, before retiring from the touring and recording scene to raise her family. During the 1970s,

Connie ventured into gospel music. Her 1975 album CONNIE SMITH SINGS HANK WILLIAMS resulted in   tenth Grammy nomination.

A petite blonde wh   put her family before her career, Connie Smith wrote some of her   nits, like *I'll Come Runnin'* and *You Got Me Right Where You W*   During the 1970s, she formed a music publishing company   rge Jones, one of the first women to venture into what was us   ded in the 1960s and 1970s as a male domain. Perhaps the big   prise of the late 1990s was the announcement of an upcoming   bel album by Connie Smith, her first new release in over 20   rking with Harlan Howard and her new husband Marty Stuart to   nd record her new songs, Connie appeared to have drunk from the   ntain of youth when she began to make public appearances to promote the album. She was living proof that age does not diminish true beauty. Connie co-wrote nine of the 10 new songs. CONNIE SMITH is an album filled with songs that demonstrate that country music is an idiom best addressed by those who have experienced enough living to know their heartache and joy. Songs like *You Can't Take Back A Teardrop* and *Your Light* are the real deal.

N ot all of the women who hit big with their early releases were to enjoy such lucrative and lengthy careers. Jeannie C. Riley hit the top of the charts in 1968 with *Harper Valley P.T.A.*, a song written by Tom T. Hall that parodied small town hypocrisy. The song also announced the new spirit of female spunk which marked the 'liberated' 1960s , even though it was written by a man.

JEANNIE C. RILEY

> I want to tell you all a story 'bout a Harper Valley widowed wife
> Who had a teenage daughter who attended Harper Valley Junior High
> Well her daughter came home one afternoon and didn't even stop to play
> She said, 'Mom I got a note here from the Harper Valley P.T.A.'
> The note said, 'Mrs Johnson, you're wearing your dresses way too high
> It's reported you've been drinking and runnin' round with men and goin' wild
> And we don't believe you ought to be bringing up your little girl this way'
> It was signed, Harper Valley P.T.A.

(written by Tom T. Hall)

Of course, Mrs Johnson turns the table, exposing the dalliances and boozing of the members of the P.T.A., ending the song, "Then you have the nerve to tell me you think that as a mother I'm not fit / Well this is just a little Peyton Place and you're all Harper Valley hypocrites."

Riley, who had been working as a secretary on Music Row at the time she was selected to sing Hall's song, was in the right place at the right time and became the appropriate voice selected by Plantation Records impresario Shelby Singleton, who also developed the Cowsills, the real life prototypes for *The Partridge Family* television show, during this same period. The extent to which Shelby Singleton went to groom his protege was often brutal. For example, when Riley was nominated for the 1968 CMA Single of the Year, she had her dressmaker sew a full-length formal gown for the occasion. Hours before the CMA show, Singleton ordered it cut to a mini-skirt length. Riley was not happy. In her biography *From Harper Valley to the Mountain*, she recalls that Singleton said, "You don't understand. *Harper Valley P.T.A.* just can't be sung by a girl in a long dress. The world knows you as a sassy, sexy, sock-it-to-'em girl. If you show up in an old-fashioned dress, it will kill the whole thing." When Riley continued to protest, saying she was an artist who had rights, Singleton interrupted her: "You're not an artist, baby. You're a commodity — a miniskirted, silver-booted commodity. Now be there early. We've got a show to rehearse."

Jeannie was humiliated that night, forced to appear wearing the cut-off dress while everyone else at the CMA show wore formal gowns and tuxedos. It was just one incident in a continuing battle between the inexperienced singer and the insensitive record exec. A concept album, HARPER VALLEY P.T.A., was Top 20 on the pop charts in 1968. Five of Jeannie's 13 Top 40 singles landed in the Top 10, but by 1972 her records no longer charted in the Top 40. Divorced from her husband Mickey Riley, and under stress from the whole experience, Jeannie had turned to booze. By mid-decade, with her Christian faith rekindled, she had rehabilitated herself and reclaimed her marriage to Mickey. Barbara Eden starred in the film and television series that were spun-off from the hit single, and Jeannie C. Riley continued to record and entertain, though she refused to sing in venues where liquor was served.

When Sammi Smith hit Nashville, she was a more soulful and experienced vocalist than Jeannie C. Riley. Born Jewel Fay Smith in Orange, California in 1943, Sammi Smith was raised in Oklahoma. From the age of 12, she sang pop standards in local clubs. In 1967 she was discovered by Tennessee Two bassist Marshall Grant. After a couple of minor hits for Columbia in the late 1960s, Sammi Smith was signed to the new Mega Records label. Her second Mega release, Kris Kristofferson's *Help Me Make It Through The Night*, shot right to the top of the country charts, becoming the label's first gold single and eventually selling two million copies when it crossed over and climbed into the Top 10 on the pop charts. The cut was deemed the CMA Single of the Year, but she found it was difficult to follow up on that success. After albums for Elektra, Zodiac, Cyclone, and Sound Factory, Sammi focused on her Apache heritage, forming the all-Indian band, Apache, and adopting two Apache children.

SAMMI SMITH

Margo Smith's approach to the top of the country charts was more cautious. A diminutive school teacher from Dayton, Ohio, Smith recorded demo tapes of the songs she was writing and pitched them in Nashville where she secured a recording contract with Chart Records. After some minor success, she moved to 20th Century Records in 1975. Her first release for her new label was her own composition, *There I Said It*, a Top 10 hit that convinced Margo to quit her job as a school teacher. Signed to Warner Nashville in 1976, Margo hit the top of the *Billboard* country chart with *Don't Break The Heart That Loves You* and followed that up with her second chart-topper, *It Only Hurts For A Little While*. Margo continued to chart in the Top 40 until 1981 when the bottom fell out of the country market and many artists lost their record deals.

Donna Fargo adopted her stage name in order to conceal her career as a singer in Los Angeles clubs from those who knew her as a school teacher in the nearby Covina, California area. Born Yvonne Vaughn on November 10th, 1949 in Mount Airy, North Carolina, Fargo grew up in a family of tobacco farmers. She attended High Point, North Carolina Teachers College and the University of Southern California.

DONNA FARGO

Torn between a love of the stage and her more practical day-job,

Fargo did not make a decision to get serious about her singing until she met and married record producer Stan Silver. Fargo took up guitar and began to write songs, but her early releases on Ramco Records failed to convince her to quit the teaching profession. When Donna was signed by Dot Records, her self-penned debut single, *The Happiest Girl In The Whole U.S.A.*, went right to the top of the country charts and stayed there for three weeks. *Funny Face, Superman,* and *You Were Always There* followed her debut to the number one position, establishing Donna Fargo as the first female to enter the national charts with four straight number ones. *The Happiest Girl In The Whole U.S.A.* won her a CMA award when it was named the best single of 1970, and both it and *Funny Face* were certified gold. By 1972, the singer had quit her teaching job and was into the Queen of Country sweepstakes in a serious way. She scored number ones with *(You Can't Be A Beacon) If Your Light Don't Shine* in 1974 and *That Was Yesterday* in 1977.

A brilliant career was scaled back in 1979 when it was discovered that Donna Fargo was suffering from multiple sclerosis. The singer has fought the crippling disease with immense courage, recording a gospel album, BROTHERLY LOVE, and hitting the charts briefly with her 1988 duet of *Members Only* with Billy Joe Royal. She also recorded a version of the Shirelles' *Soldier Boy* to encourage U.S. service personnel during the Gulf War. In the fall of 1998, her MS in remission, Donna Fargo was still involved in songwriting. She told *Country Weekly* reporter Pat Mandia, "I think if I contributed anything to music, it would be a sort of positivism, the message that life is good, and we need to help each other."

CRYSTAL GAYLE

Crystal Gayle first sang in her sister's, Loretta Lynn's, touring band. She was born Brenda Gail Webb in 1951, but changed her name to Crystal Gayle when she began her solo career. Crystal Gayle excels at singing ballads. Possessed of a truly unique voice, she was able to mesmerise her early audiences with her beauty and a mane of hair that swept down her back almost to her heels. Crystal Gayle's accomplishments place her among the top forty country singers of all-time, the seventh most-played female vocalist on country radio.

Crystal Gayle had already logged nine Top 40 hits, including two number ones, when she recorded her signature tune, Richard Leigh's *Don't*

It Make Your Brown Eyes Blue. This 1977 hit held at the top position for four weeks and was certified gold, driving sales of Gayle's WE MUST BELIEVE IN MAGIC album over the million-seller mark. Too pop to be seriously considered as a Queen of Country, Gayle had 18 number ones in all before her popularity waned in the late 1980s. As several commentators have stated, only her hair was longer than the list of her millions of records sold.

Crystal Gayle's first releases were on Decca, but she hit her stride when she signed with United Artists and was paired with Allen Reynolds, the producer of those mellow Don Williams records every country fan knows so well. Reynolds wrote Crystal Gayle's first Top 10 hit, *Wrong Road Again*, and the Gayle-Reynolds productions grew ever more lavish as the number ones rolled off the assembly line. However, Crystal was one of few country-pop singers to survive the early 1980s country recession, hitting near the top of the charts until 1988. She continues to record on the Branson label and to please concert audiences wherever she appears. Crystal Gayle was named CMA Female Vocalist of the Year in both 1977 and 1978.

BILLIE JO SPEARS

Another country singer known for her penchant for country-pop is Billie Jo Spears. Raised on country music in Beaumont, Texas, Spears made an appearance singing *Too Old For Toys, Too Young For Boys* on the *Louisiana Hayride* when she was barely in her teens. Sales of an amateur recording of the song are said to have earned the teenager more than $4,000. However, Billie Jo was nearly 30 years old before she moved to Nashville, spurred to make the move by songwriter Jack Rhodes who thought she could be a star. *Mr. Walker, It's All Over*, Spears second single for Capitol, hit the Top 10 on the country charts in 1969. In 1975, Billie Jo's recording of Roger Bowling's *Blanket On The Ground* hit the top of the country charts. When she appeared at the gigantic Wembley festival in 1977, she secured an English fan base that would last for many years.

Billie Jo Spears only hit the Top 10 three more times during her career, with *What I've Got In Mind* and *Misty Blue* in 1976, and *If You Want Me* in 1977, but her bluesy vocals have endeared her to legions of country fans. It is scary to consider that if Billie Jo had not canceled the release of her raunchy version of *Heartbreak Hotel* in 1977, because she felt it conflicted with Elvis Presley's tragic death, she might have gone right over the top into superstardom.

**DIANA
TRASK**

Although the British Invasion bands never really affected country music during the 1960s, five female vocalists from British Commonwealth countries made their own indelible mark upon the North American country scene during this era. The first to surface was Diana Trask. Born in Melbourne, Australia in 1940, Trask was a star in her native land by the age of 16. In 1959, she decided to try her luck in America. Appearances on Don MacNeil's *Breakfast Club* and *The Jack Benny Show* led to Diana becoming a regular on Mitch Miller's *Singalong Jubilee* TV series. In the late 1960s, she toured with Hank Williams Jr. and recorded for the Dot label. Her radio hits include covers of *I Fall To Pieces* and *Oh Boy*. Her best outing came in 1974 when *Lean It All On Me* peaked at number 13 on the *Billboard* country chart. She returned to Australia in 1975.

**LUCILLE
STARR**

Lucille Starr was born Lucille Savoie in St. Boniface, Manitoba and raised in Maillardville, an equally francophone section of Port Coquitlam, British Columbia. She first surfaced singing with Bob and Keray Regan in Western Canada during the 1950s. Dave Schroeder described Lucille's early career in a 1988 story in the *Rana Review*: "Keray Regan was a major local country star (his recording of *My Home On The Fraser* had sold 100,000 copies in 1951) but playing country music in British Columbia in the Fifties generally meant playing the schoolhouse circuit ... Lucille recalls, 'We played everything, all the little halls. It was an experience of how tough things can get ... we hadn't eaten all day, we'd do the show, someone would get us a sandwich, and then we'd play for the dance.'"

After several years of touring, during which Lucille married Bob Regan, the couple began booking themselves as The Canadian Sweethearts. They had several Canadian country hits, including *Freight Train, Don't Let The Stars Get In Your Eyes, Hootenanny Express*, and *Blue Canadian Rockies*. Moving to Los Angeles, the Regans struggled at first but eventually found themselves appearing on shows with Marty Robbins and Eddy Arnold, and on Grand Ole Opry tours with Hank Snow.

The Canadian Sweethearts' first U.S. singles were a rocked-up 1961 version of the Carlisle's *No Help Wanted* and the 1962 Ditto Records release *Eeny Meeny Miny Mo*, which Dave Schroeder describes as a "rockabilly classic." In 1963 the Regans began to work with Herb Alpert, and in

1964 Lucille recorded *The French Song*, which went on to sell more than five million copies world-wide and established Jerry Moss and Herb Alpert's A&M Records label in the international market. It was the first million-seller for a Canadian female vocalist. The record went Top 10 in Canada, Holland, and South Africa. "The song was renamed because Herb Alpert couldn't handle the original title which was the first line of the song (in French)," Lucille told Larry Delaney for a January 1988 *Country Music News* cover story. "He would say, 'I know this is a hit.' And I recall Dorsey (Burnette) being so helpful in that first session. He would be in the studio helping Herb produce the session and he'd tell me, 'C'mon Lulu, you can do it.' He called me Lulu all the time . . . I was actually crying and he was settling me down . . . 'C'mon, Lulu, you can do it' . . . and out of that came a million-seller."

Starr's debut solo album yielded additional international hits like *Jolie Jacqueline*, *Yours*, and *Colinda*. She made many television appearances during the era and recorded the yodeling part attributed to Cousin Pearl on *The Beverly Hillbillies*. *The French Song* was a high point for Lucille who toured in Africa and Europe where she played many spectacular shows and shared the stage with the likes of The Supremes, The Everly Brothers, and Vera Lynn. By this time, the Regans were notoriously known as country music's answer to Ike and Tina Turner, all smiles on stage, only, and the two separated. After moving to Epic where she was produced by Billy Sherill, Lucille eventually returned to Canada where she has continued to record. In 1987 Lucille was the first female vocalist inducted into the CCMA Hall of Honour.

Another Canadian artist, Carroll Baker, hooked up with Don Grashey at the beginning of the 1970s. She had only two of **CARROLL BAKER** her records chart on *Billboard* but in Canada reigned as the 'Queen of Canadian Country' until the late-1980s. Carroll Baker was an eight-time winner of the CCMA Female Vocalist of the Year award. She won Juno awards in the same category in 1977, 1978, and 1979, and it is said that she has sold a million records during her three-decade career.

Born in Port Medway, Nova Scotia in 1949, Baker was raised in Oakville, Ontario. Her first single to chart was her 1970 debut *Memories Of Home* and her first Canadian number one was *I've Never Been This Far*

Before. Perhaps her most remarkable stat is that from 1975 through 1979 Carroll had a string of 12 consecutive number one hits in Canada. She wrote many of these chart-toppers, and Tom Jones had a U.S. hit with her *I'm An Old Rock & Roller* in 1984. Her early records were released on Don Grashey's Gaeity Records and then on Columbia. Twenty-three of those recordings have recently been made available in CD format through EMI/Northern Heritage on FROM THE BEGINNING.

When Carroll Baker toured, it was to sold-out houses in Canada and England. Along with Slim Whitman, she got a standing ovation from an audience at London's prestigious Palladium. At the world-famous Wembley Country Music Festivals, she was a repeat favorite. Carroll Baker was 100 percent country, and when she toured in the United States with David Houston and Faron Young she was a proud ambassador of Canadian country music.

ANNE MURRAY

With the release of *Snowbird* in 1970, Anne Murray became the first Canadian female vocalist to receive a gold record in the United States. Never one to miss an opportunity, Murray accepted that award on the *Merv Griffin Show* in full view of the audience that would eventually purchase 30 million of her records. From the Canadian Maritimes, where country music often took on a distinctive Celtic flavor, the Nova Scotia-born singer launched herself into an international superstar career that would see her music embraced by both country and pop music audiences.

On the strength of her national television experience in Canada as a regular performer on the CBC-TV shows *Let's Go* and *Singalong Jubilee*, Anne soon found herself a regular on the *Glen Campbell Goodtime Hour*, working, not in Nashville, but in Hollywood. A duet with Campbell from their 1971 album ANNE MURRAY / GLEN CAMPBELL was her third U.S. release to gain Top 40 airplay. In 1972 her recording of Gordon Lightfoot's *Cotton Jenny* nearly hit the *Billboard* Top 10. Her rendition of Kenny Loggins' *Danny's Song* peaked at Number 10. Then, in 1973, *Love Song* hit the number 5 position and won Anne Murray her first Grammy.

He Thinks I Still Care was Anne Murray's first number one on the U.S. country charts in 1974. In 1979, Anne had three straight chart-toppers: *I Just Fell In Love Again*, *Shadows In The Moonlight*, and *Broken Hearted Me*.

Another energetic run at the top spot began in 1983 with *A Little Good News*, which won Anne a CMA award for Single of the Year and led to a Grammy for Best Female Country Singer. She hit with a third in a row chart-topper, *Nobody Loves Me Like You Do*, a duet with Kenny Loggins that won the CMA Award for Vocal Duo of the Year in 1985. Her 10th number one would be David Foster's *Now And Forever (You And Me)* in 1986.

Anne Murray continued to live in Canada and moved from Halifax to Toronto in the mid-1970s. A stabilizing factor in her career right from the start was strong management headed by Leonard Rambeau. Rambeau was not the only Maritimer to make the move from Halifax to Toronto along with the singer. Surrounded by down-east confreres like Rambeau, Brian Ahern (who later married Emmylou Harris), Lyman MacInnes and Bill Langstroth, all men she could trust to get the job done, Murray would find her team branded the 'Maritime Mafia' by Toronto media. When Leonard Rambeau passed away, a victim of cancer, in April, 1995, Murray would begin to work with Bruce Allen, veteran West Coast manager of best-selling acts like BTO, Loverboy, and Bryan Adams, but she would sorely miss the man who had guided her career for nearly 25 years.

At the very first Juno Awards in 1971, Anne Murray and her team of songwriter Gene McClellan and producer Brian Ahern won five of the 16 trophies. At the 1972 Junos, Ahern again won the Best Produced MOR Album for Anne Murray's TALK IT OVER IN THE MORNING. Anne repeated as Female Vocalist of the Year. In 1973, the singer-producer team repeated the feat on the basis of their album ANNE MURRAY. That same year Leonard Rambeau kept his artist in the media limelight when he arranged for a photo to be taken of Anne with members from the audience at her L.A. appearance at the Troubador club. The audience members were none other than John Lennon, Harry Nilsson, Alice Cooper, and Mickey Dolenz, and the photo appeared in dozens of publications all over North America. At the same time that Rambeau was doing his promoting, Gene McLellan's song *Snowbird* was being recorded by everyone from Elvis to Chet Atkins. No less than 100 artists would eventually release their version of Anne Murray's signature tune.

1974 saw the Murray-Ahern team win a Juno for Best Produced Pop Album with their DANNY'S SONG release. Anne was, once again, named Best Female Vocalist. Anne Murray won her fifth Best Female Vocalist Juno in 1975, but in 1976 Joni Mitchell supplanted Murray as the top

Canadian female for the first time since the televised awards show presentation had begun. That year, Anne won her Juno as Best Country Female Vocalist. She was back at the top in 1979 and held the Best Female Vocalist Juno in that category until 1982. It was a remarkable run of wins. In 1983, when she was nudged from the top female spot by Rough Trade vocalist Carole Pope, Anne again won a Juno for Best Female Country Vocalist. In 1985, Anne Murray hosted the CMA Awards with Kris Kristofferson. In 1986, she hosted the Juno Awards show and won another Juno as Best Country Female Vocalist. And in 1989 she hosted the CMA show in Nashville for a second time, sharing the role with Kenny Rogers.

Through a series of CBC television specials, Anne Murray dominated record sales in the domestic market while bringing home plenty of U.S. silver dollars from her regular engagements in Vegas. In Canada, Anne Murray was associated in many viewers' minds with the warm feelings of family and Christmas and a safe place to store your money, a comforting image she promoted on a series of high-rotation Canadian Imperial Bank of Commerce TV commercials that have only been rivalled for all-time exposure on Canadian network TV by Candice Bergen's recent spate of Sprint commercials. The fact that Murray was not that much more nimble than Mary Tyler Moore when it came to dance routines in her lavish stage shows created a particularly Canadian mystique to which both Canadian and American audiences were drawn as if by an unseen magnet. People everywhere loved her and were ready and willing to pay to hear her sing.

Biographer Barry Grills, author of *Snowbird: The Story of Anne Murray*, offers an enigmatic portrait of the singer: "When Anne Murray took the stage to host the 1996 Juno Awards in Toronto in March, she was nearly 51 years old. Her gait was familiar to Canadians watching the telecast, not only because it retains a trace of the gym teacher she once was, but because it has, along with everything else about Anne Murray, infiltrated our consciousness. There are those who claim she is an institution, our ambassador to the world, even a reflection of the Canadian identity. But that's not why she seems so familiar. Not really. Rather it's just that we realized, as we have so many times before, that Anne Murray has been absorbed into our musical sense like no-one has before. Such has been the woman's power and influence on us that we don't even have to be a dedicated fan to feel that we know her and her music intimately."

Anne Murray has sold more than 30 million records during her career and made the world aware that Canada was on the map more surely than any Canadian with the exception, perhaps, of Wayne Gretzky. Still, for Canadians, it has been difficult to envision just how big an international star Anne Murray got to be. George Brothers in a 1991 column for *Country Music News* wonders aloud about this very issue: "I'm not sure if it's the sheer magnitude of her career which makes it so difficult to comprehend for Canadians and Maritimers — we're vaguely uncomfortable with the kind of success Anne Murray has achieved. . . . When we can't deal with something on our terms we find ways of reducing them."

The establishment of the Anne Murray Center in her home town, Springhill, Nova Scotia, was a first for a Canadian performer and has been imitated by a Hank Snow Center and Rita MacNeil's "Tea Room." Anne Murray's own description of her museum reveals both her pride and earnest generosity. "I just emptied my house into this building. My mother kept everything from when I was a child. Perhaps because I was the only girl with five boys. But she kept a lot of things like prom dresses, soft-ball gloves and skates and things like that. So, it's really an interesting trip through my life and my career and a lot of videos, a lot of television . . . I've done a lot of television over the years, and that's all there. And pictures of me with other celebrities, it's great. It's beautifully done. I'm very proud of it. It's a non-profit organization. All the sales of sweat shirts and t-shirts and albums, everything goes back into the running of the building. It's really nice. It's been a terrific shot in the arm for a small town that has been dwindling in numbers over the years since the coal mines closed. So it was great for me to give them something back."

One of the best Anne Murray records is the children's album THERE'S A HIPPO IN MY TUB, another Juno winner in 1979 that she recorded during a hiatus from world stages when she was being a stay-at-home mom and working with the Save The Children Fund in Canada. However, the fact that she had chosen to take this time off right on the heels of *Billboard* magazine naming her the second most popular female artist of 1975 drew criticism from the media. In her own defence, Murray has explained that: "I find it difficult to travel as much as I have to, and I travel probably less than anybody else in the business. I do the bare minimum of road work. I do 70 to 80 dates a year . . . and that kinda keeps the tools honed, the wheels oiled, and it keeps everybody eating, it just kind of keeps the machinery going. I'm able to maintain the life-style I've established. I don't have to make those other 20 million, you just give a lot of it away, anyway. So, I get to play tennis . . . The problem is my kids are at the age where I miss a lot when I'm away. They don't save up for two weeks, save up everything that's gone on when I'm away, and that's tough."

In addition to putting her family first, Murray has walked the tightrope between pop and country with style, refusing to be nailed down or reined in and standing by the quality of her musical releases. The only items on a checklist of qualities that many country singers speak about that Anne Murray *doesn't* lay claim to is being raised in poverty. Her father, Carson Murray, was a doctor and her mother, Marion, ran the town hospital. Her father, it would come out upon his death, had been more benevolent in helping locals in need than anyone knew during his lifetime. Anne Murray's own generosity has always been apparent when it comes to Canadian songwriters. She has recorded many of their songs. In November 1988 she chose to thank Nashville songwriters as well for their contributions to her career by staging a $100 per plate fund-raising dinner for the Nashville Songwriters Association.

Always willing to seek the largest audience possible for her performances and promotions, Anne has entertained sold-out audiences in Carnegie Hall and Radio City Music Hall in New York City and the Palladium in London. There was also the time Anne Murray shared the spotlight with Mickey Mouse. She was featured on the February 1991 cover of *Country Music News* holding hands with the rodent, the full-sized non-animated Mickey who often wanders about on the Disneyland and Disney World grounds. Larry Delaney's opening burst of cover story enthusiasm set the scene: "Anne Murray, Canada's most musical personality has literally done it all, seen it all, and won it all! She could easily have hung up her vocal chords a decade ago and rested on the laurels that many artists can only dream about. But that's not Anne Murray! The lady — a sure bet to be Canada's first woman Prime Minister, if she was ever so inclined (and she's not) — continues to search out and reach new plateaus in her music career."

Delaney went on to praise Murray's new release YOU WILL, which had already provided the singer with radio hits like *Feed This Fire* and *Bluebird*, and said it had brought her to the fore of country music, once again, after a brief flirtation with synthesized explorations. The new TV Special was to be *Anne Murray In Disney World* on the same network. Her guests were to include Julio Iglesias, Patti LaBelle, and comedienne Andrea Martin. Delaney wondered if there was a patriotic element involved in her consistent choice of Canadian songwriters on her albums? "I search out a lot of the Canadian material," Murray told Delaney, "and I think I have a tendency to give it a special listen and if it stands up to the other songs being considered at the time of a recording session, then I usually try to opt for the Canadian-written songs. But, you have to remember that there are some really talented songwriters here in Canada . . . so I'm not going out on a limb by recording their material."

A few years later, Anne Murray would turn to Canadian superstar Bryan Adams to once again revitalize her career. After a period during which she had not been heard on the radio at all, Anne Murray was back with a killer video, looking vital and effective singing *What Would It Take*. December 1997 brought *Anne Murray's Classic Christmas* to TNN. The all-Canadian lineup of talent featured the Bare Naked Ladies, Roch Voisine, and figure skating sensation Elvis Stoijko. A final segment featured Anne with her husband, Bill Langstroth, and children, Dawn and William, singing *Silent Night*.

Anne Murray received what may be her last Juno Award in 1993 when she was inducted into the Canadian Music Hall of Fame. It was her 31st Juno, more than any other singer had won. With her 10 number one country singles, she had surpassed Hank Snow. In 1998, Anne released her first-ever live recording, AN INTIMATE EVENING WITH ANNE MURRAY LIVE, a CD recorded as part of a PBS special that featured collaborations with Bryan Adams and Jann Arden. Later that same year, EMI Music Canada released the first of a series of boxed set collections of Anne Murray's recordings.

No longer heard in rotation on the radio, Anne Murray was typically frank when she told reporter Nancy Van Valkenburg for an October 1998 story printed in the Salt Lake City *Standard Examiner* that "It's hard to talk about this without sounding really negative. But the fact is that radio play for people over 40 is rare. There's a whole list of veterans who don't get played on radio and their hope of doing so is slim. We had our time. Now we have to find alternative ways of letting people know that we are out there. We know we have audiences, we see them at concerts. And concerts are one way of letting people know we have new music. But I have no complaints."

Anne Murray has shown heart and intelligence throughout her life, but never more than when she spoke with her daughter, Dawn Langstroth, about Dawn's eating disorder, a condition that has seen Dawn hospitalized more than once. Together, the two worked things out and discovered a new intimacy when they sang together at a benefit concert at the Elgin Theatre in Toronto to raise funds for Sheena Place, a non-profit center for people with eating disorders. Jane Stevenson, writing in the *Toronto Sun* provides this portrait of mother and daughter: "Langstroth strutted onto the stage wearing a sexy, black, floor-length evening gown and heels and shimmied her hips before belting out Bonnie Raitt's *Something To Talk About* with support from Murray's seven-piece band. . . . 'Did I water her well, or what?' joked Murray, upon returning to the stage. 'You little show-off,' she added, turning to her long-legged, red-headed daughter." Dawn and Anne then sang a duet version of *Walk Right Back*. To me, it seemed like singing together had been terrific therapy for both Anne and her daughter.

OLIVIA NEWTON-JOHN A fifth invading singer, Olivia Newton-John, caused considerably more sparks to fly when her debut MCA single *Let Me Be There* and the follow-up *If You Love Me (Let Me Know)* won the British-born, Australian-raised singer the CMA Female Vocalist of the Year Award in 1974. Traditionalists were up in arms. They said that Newton-John was 'not country', and the win heaped fuel on a controversy that resulted in the creation of ACE, the Association of Country Entertainers that was formed at the home of Tammy Wynette and George Jones when John Denver was named Entertainer of the Year in 1975. ACE was short-lived, however, as founding members Dolly Parton and Barbara Mandrell soon followed Newton-John's example and went pop themselves.

There was no doubt that the lithe Newton-John was widely popular. Her singles continued to chart in the Top 10 on the country charts for several more years, and her first five singles were all certified country gold records. More importantly in terms of hard cash earned, her first two MCA albums hit the number one position on the *Billboard* pop album chart and also went gold. Newton-John's 1977 release of a GREATEST HITS package sold three million copies and her subsequent pop album releases sold in the multiple millions. TOTALLY HOT (one million), XANADU (two million),

PHYSICAL (two million), and OLIVIA'S GREATEST HITS VOL 2 (another two million) were all palpable sales numbers to be coveted by country singers who were selling no more than a few hundred thousand units at best. The fact that Olivia Newton-John skipped over totally into the pop world and did so amid the exploding fireworks of hugely popular feature films like *Grease, Xanadu,* and *Two Of A Kind,* where she was paired with John Travolta for her dance routines and box office successes, served as an example to country singers who wanted to sell more records.

DEBBY BOONE

Debby Boone, daughter of Pat Boone and Shirley Foley, was a gospel singer who crossed over into country and pop in a big way when she recorded *You Light Up My Life,* selling a million singles and several million albums. The song was the title of a Hollywood film that Mike Curb convinced Debby to record. Her vocal efforts were rewarded with a Grammy and an Oscar. Not really a country singer, Debby hit the number one spot on the *Billboard* country chart with *Are You On The Road To Loving Me Again* in 1980 but returned to singing Christian music soon after that.

LYNN ANDERSON

Lynn Anderson was born in North Forks, Idaho in 1947. Daughter of songwriters Liz and Casey Anderson, she followed in her mother's footsteps, but not before she'd become the California Horse Show Queen as winner of equestrian events at the California State Fair. In 1966 Lynn signed with Chart Records and recorded more than 100 songs for the label many of which were chart hits. A marriage to producer-songwriter Glen Sutton resulted in a record deal with Columbia Records and Lynn's number one country smash *Rose Garden.* Although the song was penned by Joe South, the tough lyrics — "I beg your pardon / I never promised you a rose garden . . ." — were ideally suited to the growing market for women's songs. When sung by the vivacious blonde Lynn Anderson, it became a monster crossover hit, winning the singer a Grammy and a CMA award for Best Female Vocalist in 1970.

Rose Garden peaked at number 3 on the pop charts and the album of the same name sold over a million copies. It was the kind of killer song needed to spark a career as a country star, a career that was guaranteed longevity when Lynn Anderson followed up with two more number ones in 1971, hitting first with Glen Sutton's *You're My Man* and then with *How Can I Unlove You*. Sutton and Anderson divorced a few years later and the singer married Harold Stream III, a Louisiana millionaire who had made his money in oil. Another hit was *Ride, Ride, Ride*, a strident early '70s take on a leavin' theme.

> If you don't want me baby
> If you're not satisfied
> If you don't care, get on your horse
> And ride, ride, ride . . .
> You talk about me honey
> You try to tear me down
> But while you're throwin' dirt at me
> You're slowly losin' ground . . .
>
> (written by Liz Anderson)

When her singing career tapered off in the 1980s, Lynn Anderson returned to her first love, horses, and her quarter horse involvement has resulted in numerous awards. Lynn Anderson was a genuine country star of her era and logged nearly 50 Top 40 singles, including five number ones. She was listed in the Top 100 Artists (1944-96) in the *New Billboard Book Of Top 40 Country Hits* at the number 50 position, the ninth most successful country female vocalist of all time on the radio charts at that time.

QUEENS & KINGS

Duets have always appealed to country music fans, although at times some fans have mistaken duet partners for real life lovers and married couples. Probably the most well-known of these two-somes was George Jones and Tammy Wynette who *were* married for a few years and who took up singing together again years after their highly-publicized divorce. Many of the women who sang country music thrived on singing with the male stars of their day. For some singers who might have otherwise been one hit wonders, duets prolonged careers that showed early promise but may have ended much earlier if the vocalist had not linked up with a duet partner.

TAMMY WYNETTE

CONNIE SMITH

DONNA FARGO

**CARROLL
BAKER**

**ANNE
MURRAY**

**LYNN
ANDERSON**

**JEANNIE C.
RILEY**

OLIVIA NEWTON-JOHN

CRYSTAL GAYLE

**DOLLY
PARTON**

Some very popular duet partners never achieved Top 40 status with their solo releases, yet enjoyed long and successful careers as country entertainers. Lulu Belle and Scotty were a husband and wife team who sang on the WLS *National Barndance* for 25 years. Lulu Belle joined the radio show in 1932 and was first featured dueting with a young Red Foley. When Scotty joined the show, he began performing with the pig-tailed Lulu Belle. Together they were an instant hit singing Scotty's *Homecoming Time In Happy Valley*. Before they were married in 1934 they were the focus of angry fan letters from well-intentioned radio listeners who thought that Scotty had stolen Lulu Belle from Red Foley. When Lulu Belle and Scotty's career had run its course and their records on the Old Homestead and Starday labels were no longer selling briskly, they retired to their old North Carolina stomping grounds, where Scotty taught school and Lulu Belle ran successfully in state elections and served two terms in the North Carolina legislature.

Texas-born Goldie Hill, who was known as the Golden Hillbilly, hit big with her 1951 Decca release of *I Let The Stars Get In My Eyes*, an answer song to Slim Willet's *Don't Let The Stars Get In Your Eyes*. But most of her Top 40 success after that came when singing duets. In 1954, she teamed up with Justin Tubb for the number 4 hit *Looking Back To See*. A year later she and Justin hit again with *Sure Fire Kisses*, which peaked at number 11. In 1955 Goldie Hill and Red Sovine recorded Myrna Lorrie's *Are You Mine* and rode the duet to the number 14 position on the *Billboard* country & western chart.

Some 'girl singers' who joined a band and married their band leader, *never* got to sing hit duet singles. Ella Mae Evans got the worst treatment of all. She joined Spade Cooley's Orchestra in the 1940s and married the "King of Western Swing" in 1945. Sixteen years later, in 1961, Ella Mae fell victim to the bandleader's insane jealousy. For years, Cooley — who had at one time in his career entertained thousands of western swing fans during his nightly appearances at the prestigious Santa Monica Ballroom — had abused his wife. When Ella Mae confessed that she had been having an ongoing affair with Roy Rogers on Saturday afternoons while Spade was at rehearsal, Cooley beat her brutally in the presence of their daughter, Melody Cooley. Cooley was convicted of the murder and sentenced to life in jail.

When Helen Cornelius joined forces with Jim Ed Brown in 1976, their first duet, *I Don't Want To Have To Marry You*, hit the top spot on the *Billboard* country chart. The two were rewarded with a CMA award in 1977 for Vocal Duo of the Year and were featured on the TV series *Nashville On The Road*. By 1980, when she went solo, Helen was well-known to country audiences. Some duet partners *were* happily married couples like Carl and Pearl Butler who recorded 11 Top 40 duets beginning with the number one hit *Don't Let Me Cross Over*. And some singers, like Sherry Bryce, who recorded seven Top 40 duets with Mel Tillis, might not have tasted the sweetness of a Top 40 hit at all if they had never teamed up with a well-known male star.

Faking Love, Karen Brooks' 1982 collaboration with T.G. Sheppard, was the singer's only number one; it was also Matraca Berg's first-ever songwriting triumph, co-written with legendary songwriter Bobby Braddock.

Singer Jan Howard was enjoying modest success with her own releases during the 1960s, but when she hooked up with Bill Anderson the pair hit the number one spot on the *Billboard* country chart with their 1967 duet release of *For Loving You*. Anderson and Howard hit the number 2 spot in 1969 with *If It's All The Same To You* and number 4 in 1970 with *Someday We'll Be Together*. Howard toured and appeared on television shows with Bill Anderson for seven years before moving on to work with Johnny Cash and Tammy Wynette. She has since become a regular on the Grand Ole Opry.

Leona Williams (born Leona Helton in Vienna, Missouri in 1943) showed early talent as both a singer and a songwriter, but first got into the music business in 1958 playing bass in Loretta Lynn's band along with her first husband, drummer Ron Williams. Signed to a recording contract with Hickory Records in 1968, Leona had minor radio hits with cuts like *Once More* in 1969 and *Country Girl With Hot Pants On* in 1971. She began to hit the higher echelons of the charts in 1976 when she married Merle Haggard. The two recorded an album, which yielded the number 8 chart hit *The Bull And The Beaver*, and were married for five stormy years. Leona's backing vocals on Merle's 1981 number one smash, *Big City*, was to be her most played track, although her 1971 album SAN QUENTIN'S FIRST LADY was the first album to be recorded inside a prison by a female vocalist.

Long after her initial career as a member of The Maddox Brothers and Sister Rose had run its course, Rose Maddox continued to shine on duets with Buck Owens. Bonnie Owens dueted with Merle Haggard, long after *her* marriage and singing career with Buck Owens broke up. Bonnie married Merle and they recorded the award-winning album JUST BETWEEN THE TWO OF US. She was named top female vocalist by the Academy of Country Music in 1965 and 1966. In the 1970s, when Buck needed a new singing partner, Susan Raye filled the bill, recording seven Top 40 duets with Owens including the memorable 1972 Top 20 hit *Togetherness*. It was often a matter of fixin' the hurtin' with some good old harmony singing. George Jones, it seems, has sung with just about everybody. *We Must Have Been Out Of Our Minds*, the Possum's first duet with Melba Montgomery, helped Montgomery kick off a successful 15-year recording career when it landed on the number 3 spot on the *Billboard* country chart.

A fiddle player and a guitarist, Melba was first picked from a *Grand Ole Opry* performance to tour with Roy Acuff and his Smoky Mountain Boys. After three years with the 'King of Country Music', she began her solo recording career. From 1963 through 1978, Melba charted 16 records on the *Billboard* Top 40 as a solo artist and singer of duets. And, although she is best known for her duets like *Let's Invite Them Over* and *Party Pickin'* with George Jones, she issued no less than 20 albums during this same period, including several with Jones and QUEENS OF COUNTRY MUSIC with Dottie West.

Without a doubt, the eeriest duet of all time came with the 1981 pairing of Jim Reeves and Patsy Cline by RCA, who spliced the two singers' voices together electronically for the number 5 hit *Have You Ever Been Lonely (Have You Ever Been Blue)*. The best-selling duet of all time came two years later when Kenny Rogers and Dolly Parton teamed up to record the Bee Gees composition *Islands In The Stream*. Of course, Dolly often has that duet magic, and in 1991, eight years after *Islands*, her collaboration on *Rockin' Years* with Ricky Van Shelton was another number one hit and winner of the TNN/*Music City News* video award in 1992.

When Johnny Cash and June Carter began to sing together, it led to the two eventually marrying. They first tasted success together with Bob Dylan's *It Ain't Me Babe*, which reached the number 4 spot on the country charts in 1964. When two superstars collide, as was the case for Clint Black and Wynonna on the 1993 duet recording of *A Bad Goodbye*, sparks can really fly. And sometimes, when a husband and wife record together in the years just before their marriage falls apart, like the time Rodney Crowell and Rosanne Cash released *It's Such A Small World* in 1988, the fireworks can be so intense that the recording goes all the way to the top of the chart. And then there are tragic moments, such as Lorrie Morgan and Keith Whitley's 1990 duet *'Til A Tear Becomes A Rose*, recorded only months before Whitley's untimely death.

Country duets are, let us say, a proven commodity. They work. And when Barbi Benton ventured out of Hugh Hefner's *Playboy* mansion to record some country songs, she immediately teamed up with a singer with a proven track record, Mickey Gilley, for the Top 40 duet *Roll You Like A Wheel*. Most of Willie Nelson's duets have been with guys, but *Something To Brag About*, his 1977 duet with Mary Kay Place (who played Loretta Haggers on the television series *Mary Hartman, Mary Hartman*), was unique enough that it charted in the Top 10. Perhaps the rarest duet of all time was the 1993 collaboration between Reba McEntire and Linda Davis on *Does He Love You*, a Grammy winner for vocal collaboration, which resulted in former backup singer Davis being signed to a record deal with Arista and then with Steven Spielberg, Jeffrey Katzenberg, and David Geffen's Dreamworks Records.

Vince Gill, who is so downright good-hearted he will help almost anyone who shows talent, supported Sara Evans sophomore album with some background vocals. Evans had worked with Harlan Howard on her first album, the critically-acclaimed THREE CHORDS AND THE TRUTH, which had bombed at country radio. For her second album, NO PLACE THAT FAR, Sara was obliged to be less country and more contemporary. Having a popular superstar like Vince sing harmonies on your album helps, too, but it doesn't always translate into the necessary boost if the fans are not made aware of his presence. To accomplish this, Evans' video for the title track included a visual presence from Vince who is seen standing in the same frames but slightly downwind of Sara Evans and turning in a visual duet presence while singing backing vocals.

DOTTIE WEST

Dottie West, whose colorful career came to a tragic ending with a fatal car accident in 1991, did some of her best work when singing duets. She first hit the duet magic in 1964 with Jim Reeves when their rendition of *Love Is No Excuse* peaked at number 7. Later in the decade, three hits with Don Gibson included the number 2 chartbuster *Rings Of Gold*. When Dottie teamed up with Kenny Rogers for *Everytime*

Two Fools Collide, they hit the number one spot on the country chart and won the 1978 CMA award for Vocal Duo of the year. Kenny and Dottie toured together and hit the top of chart again in 1979 with a cover of Sonny & Cher's *All I Ever Need Is You* and won their second CMA award. Altogether, they had six Top 40 duets, including *What Are We Doing In Love*, a number one in 1981.

Dottie West was born Dorothy Marie Marsh on October 11th, 1932 in McMinnville, Tennessee. Her marriage to steel guitar player Bill West produced yet another country singer of duets, Shelly West, who teamed up with Lefty Frizzell's younger brother, David Frizzell, for a series of Top 10 duets beginning with the 1981 chart-topper, *You're The Reason God Made Oklahoma*. During her successful career singing duets with David, Shelley was married to Allen Frizzell, David's brother. As is so often said, country music is just one big family.

Despite these contenders and numerous other pretenders, **TAMMY WYNETTE** Tammy Wynette became the Queen of Country in this era or more correctly, the First Lady of Country, not only on the strength of her own proto-feminist songs but also her heartfelt duets with George Jones, her third husband. When she toured with George, a banner on their tour bus announced them as "Mr & Mrs Country Music." When Tammy Wynette died on April 6th, 1998 there was no lack of volunteers for the tribute album TAMMY WYNETTE . . . REMEMBERED. Even Elton John, who had befriended Wynette and sung with her a few years earlier, contributed a track. There were some raised eyebrows when it was learned that he would record Wynette's signature song *Stand By Your Man*. As usual, when Tammy Wynette was concerned, there would be a turbulent vortex that would cloud the issues of the tribute release, but John himself speculated that Tammy would have been amused, if she were still around to hear his track. Wynonna's *Woman To Woman*, also released as a number one CMT video, would soon become acknowledged as the stand-out cut on the well-meant tribute CD.

The official announcement — which stated that the 55-year-old Wynette had succumbed to a blood clot in the lung while napping on a sofa in the den of her Nashville home — was consistent with a career that had revealed the singer as a victim of violence and spousal abuse and as a brutally-beaten kidnapping victim. A survivor of five marriages, several celebrated affairs with newsmakers like Burt Reynolds, and electro-shock treatments that were meant to treat drug addiction to medicinal pain-killers, Wynette had found some degree of stability in her fifth marriage to George Richey before her untimely death.

Virginia Wynette Pugh, was born on May 5th, 1942 in rural Itawamba County, Mississippi, near Red Bay. She was already a divorcee and a single mom to three very young children when she arrived in Nashville in the mid-1960s. Her father had been a musician, but he died when she was only eight years old, and she was raised by her grandparents. Tammy learned her music from a self-study of her father's instruments.

Before Wynette met George Jones and the two became known as "Mr. and Mrs. Country Music," the ex-beautician had persisted at pitching herself in Nashville until she was discovered by producer Billy Sherrill. In 1967, Tammy's debut release, *Your Good Girl's Gonna Go Bad*, hit the number 3 position on the *Billboard* country chart. A near-perfect string of number ones followed, but the 1968 releases *D.I.V.O.R.C.E* and *Stand By Your Man* written by Sherrill, Richey, and Wynette assured Tammy of a place in the Country Music Hall of Fame. Before her recording career had run its course, she would log a total of 20 number ones and become the third most played female vocalist in the history of country radio. Of course, as far as country music fans were concerned, *D.I.V.O.R.C.E* and *Stand By Your Man* represented polar opposites, and everyone who loved country music followed Wynette's career moves and the tabloid stories written about her with fascination throughout the 1970s just to find out what calamity or controversy would be next.

George Jones stepped into the fray during a well-documented scene in which Wynette's second husband, Don Chapel, was treating the singer with very little respect. Her flight with Jones and the subsequent divorce and their marriage was the food upon which country fans fed and nourished themselves while listening to the radio and the juke boxes. The new couple toured together and their duets, such as *The Ceremony* and *Let's Build A World Together*, were hugely popular. *We're Gonna Hold On* solidified their marriage on vinyl and on the airwaves. *Golden Ring* a 1976 number one, was post factum, but the two would reunite several more times, "to help Jones out," Wynette would maintain. But the truth of the matter was that George and Tammy sounded very good when they sang together, even if they were incompatible as husband and wife. When the two reunited again in 1995 for a tour and a recording, it pleased everyone who loved country music. At the time of Wynette's death in 1998, Jones was quoted by Larry Delaney in a *Country Music News* tribute article as saying, "I am just glad that we were able to work together and tour together again. It was very important for us to close the chapter on everything that we had been through. I know that Tammy felt the same way."

More than anyone who had recorded before her, Tammy Wynette became a favorite for female fans who regarded her as a champion in their struggle for equal rights with such hits as like *Womanhood* and *Woman To Woman*.

> If you think you got your man
> In the palm of your hand
> You'd better listen
> And if you think you got it made
> And his love will never fade
> You'd better listen
>
> She's out there too
> And she's a whole lot better lookin' than me and you . . .
>
> I'm talkin' woman to woman
> Heart to heart
> I'm singin' straight at you . . .
> Woman to woman, me to you

(written by Billy Sherrill)

Although her outright feminist themes were not among her number one releases, her sob-soaked vocals on tear-jerkers like *Bedtime Story, My Man, Till I Get It Right, Another Lonely Song*, and *Till I Can Make It On My Own* have never been equalled.

The stories that surround Wynette . . . from the time she stood up to some good ole boys on a tour, had them yank their back-up band, but ended up singing her first duet with George Jones . . . to the time she told the truth about one of her husbands in her autobiography and was served with a 37 million-dollar law suit . . . portray Tammy Wynette as a rebel feminist without a cause, a figurehead for the women's rights movement, even though she maintained that she and Billy Sherrill merely looked for the best songs to record, whether they and George Richey wrote them or they came from professional songwriters.

A completely remade Wynette came back strongly after many hardships and illnesses in the late 1980s with the uplifting HIGHER GROUND. Winner of the CMA award for Best Female Vocalist in 1967, '68 and '69, the First Lady of Country Music was the first female singer to so totally capture the female audience. Although TAMMY WYNETTE'S GREATEST HITS was her only million-selling album, she is reported to have sold more than 30 million records during her four-decade career.

The fact that Wynette received her first Grammy award in 1967 for *I Don't Want To Play House* and her second in 1968 for *Stand By Your Man* should have proved to her that she could stand on her own, yet, after separating from Jones, she admitted to Alanna Nash in Nash's book *Behind Closed Doors* , "I didn't realize how much I depended on him and leaned on him until after the divorce, when I started makin' some shows on my own. And I thought, 'God, what do I say now? What would George say? What are some of the things he would say?' It was really hard to make that change. But we've been working better together since we divorced than we ever did while we were livin' together." Ironically, for that 1980s interview, Nash had to wait watching television in the singer's home until Tammy Wynette returned from a hospital where she had received treatment for injuries sustained from a fall down a flight of stairs during which she had injured her tailbone. Grotesque to the core, Wynette changed into a nightgown and called the journalist into her Vegas-hotel-style boudoir where she lowered her garment to display her bruises. These black and blue tattoos were not sustained at the hand of any man but through a karmic susceptibility to injury that existed along with everything else that Tammy Wynette accomplished and stands for. The melodrama continued when she was cast as a regular on *Capitol*, an ill-fated short-run network television soap opera that was cancelled shortly after she joined the cast. The fact that Wynette had been cast as a waitress who yearned for success as a Nashville singer elicited the yawner from Wynette that her "whole career had been a soap opera." It was the stuff that country music was built from, classic Wynette — and why not, considering that she was as revered by country music fans as the first lady in the White House (whoever that might be at the time).

After the tributes and testimonies of nearly everyone in country music had died away in 1999, Tammy was back in the tabloids. Country music fans learned that Tammy's daughters were suing George Richey and doctor Willis Marsh. They had applied for a court injunction to have her body exhumed and it had been granted. Again, country fans waited with anticipation for news about Tammy, this time for the results of the coroner's examination.

While Tammy's feminism seemed to come to her by accident, **DOLLY PARTON** so to speak, Dolly Parton took on the role of spokesperson for country women, fully conscious of the the need for sex appeal to influence an audience of men. And there lies the paradox of country women artists. When Dolly Parton graduated from high school, she packed up her guitar, three grocery sacks full of personal belongings and moved from Sevier County in the Smoky Mountains of East Tennessee to Nashville. It was not the first time Dolly had been to Music City. She had sung on the Opry, introduced by Johnny Cash, when she was barely a teenager. Her uncle, Billy Owens, a mentor and songwriting partner, had taken Dolly to Nashville many times, and the two had even had a brief deal with Buddy Killen at Tree Publishing and had cut some demos with producer Jerry Crutchfield. And Dolly's first 45 rpm record *Puppy Love* b/w *Girl Left Alone* had gotten regional airplay in 1960 when put out on the Gold Band label.

In addition to her explorative trips to Nashville, Dolly had sung for years on Cas Walker's radio and TV shows in Knoxville. But Dolly is the first to admit that she was and is very much a hillbilly girl from the hollers. Where others had striven to put their rural past behind them, Dolly made a career out of celebrating it. Like so many of the singers who have made it as country stars in Nashville, Dolly learned the taste of ketchup soup, and in her biography tells of the humbling times when her only resource was to roam the corridors of hotels and scrounge leftover meals from the hotel guests' trays. Considering that she was the fourth of 12 children and that she had lived with her family in a one-room cabin near Sevierville, Tennessee, Dolly's claim to a rags-to-riches Cinderella story has not been fabricated for her press releases.

What you do learn when you read her book *Dolly (My Life and Other*

Unfinished Business) is that she has always been both a dreamer and a realist. One of the most profound lessons she learned, was that she needed plenty of attention. She soon cottoned to the fact that one of the reasons she wanted to sing at concerts or on the radio was simply that the audience was bigger than when she sang for her two or three close girlfriends. Parton was a learner, though, and remembers with vivid clarity the feeling of nervous tension and terror she felt the first time she sang on Cas Walker's show. She would later use this memory as a resource when, faced with a similar situation, she was introduced by the man in black to an audience of 2,000 Opry fans. Two thousand people, she reminds readers of her biography, was more people than she'd ever seen in one place at the same time.

Like Tanya Tucker, Dolly was sometimes victimized by jealous schoolmates. Once, she was locked in a closet and totally humiliated. Another time, a vicious rumor was passed behind her back saying that she had been gang-raped by an unruly bunch of drunken men. That time Dolly complained to her mother that she wanted to quit school. Fortunately, for Dolly, her mom gave her sound advice, namely, that to stay away was to admit that the story had some truth. Soon, the brash blonde would-be-star-singer became immune to such rumors and hateful gossip.

In Nashville in 1964, living on her own for the first time, Dolly met Carl Dean and the two began a courtship that would eventually led to a marriage which has lasted throughout their lives. She also knocked on just about every one of those closed doors on Music Row, and she continued to sing and co-write with Billy Owens. Billy and Dolly got their first break when Fred Foster signed her to his Combine Publishing and Monument Record companies. At first, Foster wanted Parton to be a rockabilly singer. He bought her stage outfits and got her on *American Bandstand*. In her book, Dolly wonders if maybe Foster didn't want to tailor her as a "female Elvis." Billy and Dolly's second break came when *Put It Off Until Tomorrow*, a song they had written together, was pitched successfully to recording artist Bill Phillips. Dolly's first record to chart in the Top 10 was Curly Putnam's *Dumb Blonde*, but it was Billy and Dolly's *Put It Off Until Tomorrow* that won the BMI Song of the Year award in 1966. When Dolly was asked to audition for Porter Wagoner and the star of the popular *Porter Wagoner Show* offered her a job as a replacement for Norma Jean, his former co-star, and an initial offer of $60,000 per year, Dolly had arrived.

It is always interesting to read the biographies of both partners in musical or romantic relationships. For example, to hear George Jones tell the story of his marriage and divorce with Tammy Wynette you might begin to believe that Jones never did *any* of those things Tammy accused him of. To read the unflattering paragraphs written by Glen Campbell concerning his stormy relationship with Tanya Tucker, you'd think the 21-year old Tucker to have been totally responsible for all of the bad sides and bad times, perhaps even responsible for Campbell's failed marriage, although that failed marriage was only one in a string of failed marriages. When Dolly left Porter, the sparks really began to fly.

Porter Wagoner was not the only male in Dolly's life who would learn that the five-foot peroxide addict would not only stand up for her own rights when it came to business deals, she would in a very few years cut loose of the good ole boy network to form her own corporation and to build her very own Disneyland . . . Dollywood. And, yes, according to Dolly, the inspiration for the name of that theme park complex did come from the letters written on those Hollywood hills, although Alanna Nash in her 1988 book *Behind Closed Doors* alludes to further richness of image when she writes, "The name, of course, is a Dogpatch play on Parton's own name, her movie career, and the trees that line the Smokies." Dolly did not build her tourist attraction in Nashville, she built it in Sevier County, back in the Smoky Mountains where she was the most famous Dogpatcher, ever.

Signing with Wagoner precipitated a move from Foster's Monument Records to RCA where Dolly began to interact with Chet Atkins. Between 1967 and 1976, Parton and Wagoner charted 17 Top 40 duets. Dolly has pointed out in numerous interviews that Porter was a somewhat lonely single guy, with no family to speak of, and that their relationship was "unique." Of course, when it came to parting ways, Parton and Wagoner both felt the loss. She paid emotionally, and she paid in dollars, as well, learning there and then a bitter truth about the way women were regarded by the male powerbrokers in Nashville. In her biography, Dolly says, "There are basically two kinds of men you have to deal with in business: the ones who want to screw you out of money, and the ones who want to screw you, period."

If she were to step into bigger markets with her music, Dolly would have to look beyond the good ole boys who ran things. There had been examples of people stepping outside traditional boundaries. Bobbie Gentry hit on radio in 1967 with a B-side number that appealed right across the board to music lovers all over America when they heard her smouldering delivery of *Ode To Billy Joe*. Gentry had gone on to record many successful duets with Glen Campbell out in California. And it was to California that Dolly would go to escape the narrow thinking of the entrenched male controllers of country music, although, to some extent, she took the Opry spirit with her wherever she went.

Bobbie Gentry's solo album ODE TO BILLY JOE went gold and her 1968 album of duets with Campbell followed suit. It was an example that could not be ignored. Dolly could see that, if you appealed to a wider audience, you sold more records. Dolly wanted more than merely a country career. She had the success of those 17 Top 40 duet singles and the numerous albums she had cut with Wagoner, but her own releases did even better. Dolly's first number one hit was *Joshua* in 1970. Her 1973 release of *Jolene* began a five-in-a-row stretch of number ones that included *I Will Always Love You*, which would be a number one hit for Dolly again in 1982 when a new version from the soundtrack of the film *Best Little Whorehouse In Texas* was released, and, ten years after that, in 1992, a gigantic pop hit for Whitney Houston.

Dolly was a songwriter who felt that production on her records was being held back by Wagoner's imposed vision. When she began to assemble a team of professionals who could take her beyond the confines of simply being a country star, she told people she wanted to be a "superstar." It was Mac Davis who took the ex-*Porter Wagoner Show* singer under his wing and introduced her to several of the industry people with whom she would forge her superstar career.

While Dolly never quibbles with assertions that Porter Wagoner was instrumental in developing her as a star, she vehemently denies that he was the person who discovered her. During the days, weeks, and months following the breakup, she took frequent digs at the flashily dressed rhine-stone-costumed television singer, even making reference to the fact that his hair was "bigger" than she could ever get hers to be. When Wagoner sued Parton for three million dollars, the liaison was ancient history. The lawsuit was the final straw, severing whatever emotional ties Dolly felt for Porter. Parton settled out of court for a much smaller amount. Yet, by today's standards, even a thin dime seems to be extortion. Wagoner seemed to be staking claim to future revenues — claim to Dolly's life, itself.

Dolly admits that much of the conflict between her and Wagoner came from "dueling dreams." She dreamed of having her own show, her own superstar career, and the good ole guy dreamed of having her forever his on *his* show. Dolly suggests that she'd stayed two more years than her initial five-year-plan, but breaking up is always hard to do, even with a guy who you never slept with. And that point, about not sleeping with Waggoner, comes out in one of the funniest anecdotes in Parton's biography, *Dolly (My Life And Other Unfinished Business)*. Dolly and Tammy Wynette, who also worked with Porter, are chewing the fat and Tammy says something to the effect of 'what if the good ole boy lies and says we laid with him?' Dolly's answer is classic Partonese: "Half of the people will think he's lying, and the other half will just think we had bad taste."

Maria Muldaur recorded Dolly's *My Tennessee Mountain Home* on her 1974 Top 20 country-rock album MARIA MULDAUR. Along with Muldaur's Top 10 radio hit *Midnight At The Oasis*, Dolly's song was heard, too, and the release was a trigger for many country-rock fans to find out more about Dolly Parton. Dolly's early 1977 release NEW HARVEST…FIRST GATHERING swerved toward pop, but her major pop breakthrough was yet to come. One of the people Mac Davis had steered Dolly Parton toward was Sandy Gallin, a Los Angeles manager who worked with Cher and Joan Rivers. Gallin and his Katz-Gallin-Cleary firm cleared up the Porter Wagoner mess, and Gallin and Dolly formed a lifetime friendship. The two set about to record the crossover that would take Dolly beyond the 60,000 in record sales she achieved with her 1976 number one JOLENE. *Here You Come Again*, written by Barry Mann and Cynthia Weil, was the song that put Dolly into the bigger market, and the album HERE YOU COME AGAIN was her first million-seller.

When Dolly appeared in the movie *9 to 5*, co-starring with Jane Fonda and Lily Tomlin, her name became a household word and the song an women's anthem for the age.

Workin' 9 to 5
What a way to make a living
Barely getting by
It's all take and no giving
They just use your mind
And they never give you credit
It's enough to drive you crazy if you let it …

(written by Dolly Parton)

People the world over were intrigued by her feisty spirit and her open-minded lack of prejudice. There was something you just had to like about the five-foot-tall singer who played a secretary in the movie and thought nothing of hog-tying Dabney Coleman and turning the tables on her obnoxious male boss, even if it was only within the make believe of a frothy Hollywood concoction. Some in the audience, who were aware of the hassles female Nashville singers had had from time to time with some of the good old boys back in Tennessee, imagined that she might as well be trussing-up Acuff, Foley, or Wagoner.

Dolly was awarded her first Grammy in 1978 for *Here You Come Again*. She had a good small-screen relationship with both Johnny Carson and, later, David Letterman, but it was a series of shows she did with Barbara Walters that established Dolly as a sympathetic character. Walters discovered there was far more to Dolly than wigs and boobs and outlandish outfits.

During the 1980s, Dollywood flourished, and Dolly herself became such a recognizable figure that only the Pope and Madonna were photographed more often. Much of her visibility came through her Hollywood films. Feature films kept Dolly in the tabloids, too, especially since the tabs fed rumors that she was having affairs with her male co-stars like Burt Reynolds and Sylvester Stallone. By this time rumors amused her, she was no longer vulnerable as she had been in high school, and when she was referred to as 'Queen of the Tabloids,' Dolly just chocked it up as more free publicity.

In interviews, Dolly is candid about her film experiences. She consistently maintains that *9 to 5* was fun as well as a valuable learning experience. However, when asked questions about Reynolds and Stallone, Parton comes up with humorous anecdotes about the trying times both she and her male counterparts had during difficult circumstances. Of course, not everything Dolly touched turned to gold. *Best Little Whorehouse In Texas* was a commercial success, but the Stallone film, *Rhinestone*, was a financial disaster. By the time she was filming *Straight Talk* with James Woods, Dolly was contributing her homespun Dollyisms to the script and getting the recognition she was certainly due. She was a natural for *The Beverly Hillbillies*.

The 1987 TRIO album, recorded with Linda Ronstadt and Emmylou Harris, was a milestone for pure country music and won Dolly her fourth Grammy. In 1994, Dolly collaborated with Kitty Wells, Tammy Wynette, and Loretta Lynn to make the album HONKY-TONK ANGELS. Her videos, like *Romeo* — where Dolly, Tanya, Kathy Mattea, Pam Tillis, and Mary Chapin Carpenter fondle hunks like Billy Ray Cyrus in a reverse of the age-old sex-object issue — broke new ground.

By 1998, Dolly Parton had become the seventh most played artist on country radio and the number one female country artist of all time. She had 24 number one singles, more than any female, and a total of 54 Top 10 singles. She had recorded more than 100 albums and was still going strong. She had been named CMA Entertainer of the Year. She had become an ambassador for country music, and her efforts in the arena of life had served as a valuable role model for women. She was the writer of the top pop single of all time, Whitneys Houston's *I Will Always Love You*, and she'd starred in Hollywood films with Jane Fonda and Burt Reynolds. She was famous in the full and universal sense of the word, but fame had not spoiled her. People still loved to hear her sing. Dolly had pushed the envelope to the max and was respected and loved for who she was and what she had done because she had never forgotten that she was a hillbilly from the hollers who was blessed with a gift.

ALTERNATIVE COUNTRY

☆ ☆ ☆

To some extent every country record that is cut outside of Nashville is an alternative to the 'Nashville Sound', although over the years that officially-endorsed sound has become the doctrinaire meat and potatoes of Top 40 country radio playlists. The few exceptions to this have mostly come from Texas and from California where the singing cowboys recorded in the 1940s and where Buck Owens and Merle Haggard developed the 'West Coast Sound' in the 1960s.

In the beginning, all country singers were raised in the country. The original hillbilly singers and yodeling cowboys took their music with them from the countryside to urban studios where they met face to face with city-slickers and their recording equipment. In Tennessee, the hillbillies were often encouraged to compromise both their principles and their music. Saturday nights on the *Grand Ole Opry* broadcast country musicians held to the traditional roots of the string-based music as if they were testifying at the altar of country music. Come Monday morning, many of the same pickers and singers would labor on Music Row in recording studios to modernize the genre. Others would be at work in the executive offices scheduling the tours and running the record business. This was a healthy mix when the record label offices were largely run by bona fide country music makers. As time went by, the situation changed.

Over the years, country music was served up to the record-buying public in ever-increasingly diluted doses as the Nashville Sound became smoother and smoother, but there have also been times when the original spirit of the music has been resurrected and bursts of vitality have once again infused country radio. To some, it has seemed like an ongoing battle between traditionalists and modernizers. Other observers have viewed the process in economic and sociological terms: country music had come to the city, just as the children of economically-challenged farmers had been drawn to the urban centers, lured there by the lyrics of songs like Mel Tillis' *Detroit City* and Bobby Bare's *The Streets Of Baltimore*. Whether you lived in the country or the city, times were often tough, and, for a good long while, country music was effective medicine that helped everyone "make it through the night."

Country music flourished in several centers, but it was in Nashville where the politics of country endorsed one single brand of music, which was "made in Nashville country music." Nashville was where the business of country music was conducted and the city that you migrated to if you sang it or picked it. In 1958, the Country Music Association was formed to promote country music and preserve it from the threat posed when many performers began defecting to rock & roll. However, in the years that followed, this came to mean the preservation of the Nashville brand of country. It was an economic necessity. The formation of music publishing companies like Acuff-Rose, begun by Fred Rose and Roy Acuff and continued by Fred's son, Wesley, was as important to the industry there as the establishment of the early Nashville recording studios. Song publishing royalties quickly became one of the most vital sources of revenue, and it would become critical to the survival of the industry there that the hits on the radio were chosen from the catalogs of the Music Row publishers.

In the beginning, the presence of WSM Nashville and the *Grand Ole Opry* broadcast was the magnet that drew hillbilly performers to Nashville. As the years went by, WSM went from a 1,000 watt transmitter to a 50,000 watt clear-channel signal, extending the Opry broadcast fully across the American heartland. The *Grand Ole Opry* became the most significant of the many barndance-type radio shows. When the Opry moved on from the WSM studios to find a home at the Ryman Auditorium, singers like Red Foley recorded some of their records in WSM's Studio B. Soon after that, the first Nashville recording studios were built. By the time ex-WSM employee Owen Bradley and his guitarist brother, Harold, moved from their first hole-in-the-wall studio to a modern facility in 1956, Nashville had become established as a recording center and hillbilly singers no longer went elsewhere to make their records.

As important as all of these record business-related industries were, touring was where the singers and bands made their money. Opry founder and master of ceremonies George D. Hay, and his pal, James R. Denny, a long-time manager of the Opry, found themselves at the spoke of a wheel. Denny operated the largest country music talent agency and had a finger in the pie of most of the booking arrangements. After a while, the pattern developed that Opry stars no longer needed to have a continuous string of Top 40 radio hits to be a draw as far away from Nashville as Alberta and California. The recording artists themselves began to live in Nashville, and the tour buses rolled out regularly from there. By the late 1950s, Nashville was the hub of almost all country activity. With the formation of the Country Music Association, country music became more and more politicized. There were things that country singers were expected to do and things they were *not* expected to do.

Without the King and the Killer and Brenda Lee, all of whom came back to a country radio presence in the 1970s, the Nashville Sound became blander and blander. By the early 1970s, some Music Rowers had seriously begun to envision a time when country was completely rid of its rambunctiousness and the dark side of its hillbilly heritage. Out west in California, Gram Parsons, Emmylou Harris, and Linda Ronstadt began stirring those muddied waters, again. Deep in the heart of Texas, Waylon and Willie were being rangy-tangs and sounding as dangerous as Jerry Jeff Walker and the Lost Gonzo Band. And these singers were only the tip of an iceberg that was drifting onto the American soundscape and spawning a whole generation of country rockers.

When badgered with questions about being the guy responsible for creating the 'Nashville Sound', Chet Atkins would sometimes jingle the coins in his pocket and say, "*That* is the Nashville Sound." When Chet began his long, slow walk away from his position as a Music Row power-broker, he began to record some of his best records. His CHESTER & LESTER album is enlivened with raucous jokes and anecdotes that he and Les Paul swap between tracks. In the 1990s, Chet recorded with Mark Knopfler. Chet was having fun with the music, tearing off licks as if it meant something to be playing again, and his fans loved it when he and Mark sang *Poor Boy Blues*. But as the years went by, it became obvious that it was harder and harder to have fun in the studio when album budgets edged up into the hundreds of thousands of dollars and people's careers hinged on continually creating radio-friendly records.

Another thread of resistance to all of these modernizing influences ‌TRIO
had begun at a subversive meeting in Linda Ronstadt's Los Angeles
living room during the early 1970s when Ronstadt, Emmylou Harris, and
Dolly Parton first got together to pick and sing some of the mountain music
folk songs that had originally given birth to country music. In their collaboration as Trio, the three singers realized that a fourth force was sometimes
born that was more than the sum of the parts. In their efforts to bring the
lyrics and melodies to life, they somehow, sometimes, set the songs free for
a brief moment in time. Their combined voices and wills created a mysti-
cal fourth voice. It was the spirit of the song coaxed into life, an indefinable
and unmeasurable quality that did not merely show up when rote singing of
the lyric and melody was performed.

The three vocalists didn't look at themselves as subversives or as a
revolutionary movement . . . but that is exactly what they turned out to be.
It took more than a dozen years before their idea for a Trio album would
finally be mixed, pressed onto vinyl long-playing records, and available to
radio stations and the record buying public. Along the way, they recorded
each other's songs and sang on each other's records. Their first public performance together as Trio was on Dolly's syndicated TV series *Dolly!*
When Linda recorded the Carter Family's *I Never Will Marry* in 1977 and
Dolly sang the harmony vocals, the recording embraced the entire history
of country music in a brief few minutes. Several tracks toward a Trio album
were recorded in the 1970s, but the three singers worked for separate corporations and no album was released at that time. Some of the tracks, like
Emmylou's *Mr. Sandman*, were issued on solo albums, and the three
women continued to sing on each other's recordings. In 1985, all three
were heard singing "Trio" harmonies on Emmylou's BALLAD OF SALLY
ROSE. And in 1986 the three vocalists recorded the remarkable album we
know today as TRIO.

Spirits were high when it was done and before it was released the Trio
made an appearance on the 1986 CMA Awards telecast. The four hit singles from the package were *To Know Him Is To Love Him*, *Telling Me Lies*,
Those Memories Of You, and *Wildflowers*. The album TRIO sold a million
and a half copies and the Trio were awarded for their efforts with a
Grammy, a CMA award, and an ACM award.

TRIO II was recorded in 1994 in Merlin Country, California, but once
again bureaucratic entanglements meant that it was not immediately

released. Some of the songs were re-recorded and released on solo albums, but the tracks remained intact until 1999 when they were issued on Asylum Records as TRIO II. It had been a struggle for the three women to get the two collaborations out there, and no wonder — the intent of their acoustic free-spirited harmonizing went directly against the grain of the business part of the music business.

Traditional country music was often being called "retro" in 1999, as if it was something that stuck to your boot. Many of the people who had understood it best were now dead. Patsy Cline and Hank Williams were gone. Bob Wills was gone. Bill Monroe was gone. Roy Acuff was gone. Patsy Montana was gone. Doc and Sara and Maybelle Carter were gone. But the songs were still alive, especially when sung by the Trio. What Linda, Emmylou, and Dolly were doing, along with Evelyn Shriver at Asylum Records, was putting the original spirit of the music out to the people, once again.

EMMYLOU HARRIS
Emmylou Harris was born in Birmingham, Alabama on April 2nd, 1947. With a father in the Marines, Emmylou moved around quite a bit until Walter Harris was transferred to the Marine Corp Combat Development Command in Quantico, Virginia, a few miles south of the nation's capitol. As a teenager in the 1960s, Emmylou enroled in classes at the University of North Carolina and then at Boston University, but discovered her vocation in the coffeehouses of the era, becoming a folksinger and eventually moving to New York where folksingers made records in those days. Her first album, GLIDING BIRD, a folk effort on Jubilee Records, was released in 1970, just as the decade folded over and the musical tastes of a whole generation turned from folk to electric music. Jubilee Records did not survive that trend. That same year, Harris moved to Nashville along with her first husband, Tom Slocum, and their daughter, Hallie, but the marriage fell apart even faster than her career. After working as a waitress, then living on food stamps, she hit out for the refuge of her parents' Virginia home.

It was Gram Parsons' ex-Flying Burrito Brothers bandmates Kenny Wertz and Rick Roberts who stumbled upon Harris who was singing in a small club in the Washington area, dragging ex-Byrd Chris Hillman along to hear her sing the next night. Hillman spoke so poignantly of Harris to Gram Parsons that Parsons was persuaded to consider that Emmylou might be the singing partner he was looking for to begin his new recording project for Warner Bros. Meeting backstage at a club she was playing, the two got together in a friend's kitchen and sang together for the first time. Soon after that, with a plane ticket Parsons had sent her, Emmylou flew to California to record on his album. Before that record was released, they hit the road. In the liner notes for her boxed set PORTRAITS, Emmylou remembered the tour. "He did stone country stuff. He was serious about instructing his audiences in country music, but he'd also have a rock & roll medley because he knew that people need to cry but they also need to dance." Parsons' audiences were "cowboy hippies," the early aficionados of what would become known as country-rock.

It was the beginning of an education in country music for Emmylou, an education that would come to a sudden and tragic ending. Parsons was the teacher but the relationship was a two-way street. Where Harris needed a connection to the music's roots, Parsons needed what he called a "kick ass" to goad him onward. Much has been said of this relationship, but the result of their coming together is the music that we are still privileged to listen to today, tracks from GRIEVOUS ANGEL like Boudleaux Bryant's *Love Hurts*, Gram and Emmylou's own *In My Hour Of Darkness*, and the Louvin Brothers' *The Angels Rejoiced Last Night* from Parson's SLEEPLESS NIGHTS. It is music that simultaneously evokes both pain and joy, music that is rooted in the past but which in the early 1970s very much looked forward to a future where country music would appeal, not because it was bland or middle of the road, but because it really grabbed a-hold of the listener. It was the music that would inform Emmylou's country soul for three decades and more, guiding her toward a no bullshit honesty on all of her recordings from then onward, even if she had to make them without her original musical soulmate.

Gram Parsons died in the desert in September 1973, a victim of too much exploring during a lifetime in which he had emulated Hank Williams in more ways than merely having Nudie sew him the same embroidered stage jackets that ole Hank had worn. "It was like an explosion, and I was going 'round trying to pick up the pieces," Harris relays in the boxed-set liner notes. It was one thing to be taught how to sing soulful country, taught how to reach back into those hillbilly roots of the music for inspiration, but she had not needed the ultimate lesson, a lesson in how Hank had ended it *his* way.

Emmylou Harris recovered from Gram Parsons' death, at least in body, if not soul, to form her own Angel Band, doing so on the advice of a friend, back in Washington, D.C. where her own roots were. The Angel Band's first gig was at the Red Fox Inn where Warner Brothers A&R director Mary Martin brought Anne Murray's producer, Brian Ahern, back to listen after Martin had first been enlisted as a believer. Working with Brian Ahern and recording her albums in California, Emmylou never sounded like Anne Murray, nor did she want to take her music in the same direction as Ahern's other superstar client and fellow Canadian Maritimer. Fortunately, Ahern had no such designs, either, and in California the two made some remarkable albums.

Emmylou's Hot Band featured players like James Burton, Emory Gordy Jr., Rodney Crowell, Glen D. Hardin, Hank DeVito, Tony Brown, John Ware, Albert Lee, and Ricky Skaggs. And the act set standards for performance that did *not* include the wearing of spandex, the evocation of sentiment via show business shlock, or the distracting production numbers and dancers that often characterized the entertainment packages of the day. In fact, show business was never part of the equation. Emmylou Harris boldly reasserted the original concert proposition: she had music and she wanted to share it with her audiences. She was rewarded by the formation of a loyal fan-base who appreciated the fact that she laid her heart on the line every time she took the stage.

Even though Emmylou Harris has won seven Grammy awards and amassed her own impressive music biz statistics, her impact has been more emotional than an ego-driven quest to be known as one of the Queens of Country. Emmylou's longtime friend, manager, and now the man heading up her new label, Monty Hitchcock, maintains that she has never felt right about it when people have tried to hang titles on her like the 'God Mother of Country' or the 'Queen of Alternative Country'. "Emmy appreciates that people are trying to give her accolades," says Hitchcock, "but she has never felt comfortable with that. Emmy has never really understood the impact she has had on the music business. She doesn't do it for the impact it has on other people, she does it for the impact it has on her. She has never made a record *for* anything, whether it be country radio, rock radio, whatever. It just doesn't happen with her. I don't think that she would say this, but I can say it. I think that she makes a record for Emmylou. Those records that she makes for herself and that she feels very strongly about, they are the ones that move all of us."

In 1994 Emmylou recorded the second landmark Trio album with Linda Ronstadt and Dolly Parton, but the release of TRIO II was held up for five years, Monty Hitchcock explains, "because the scheduling problems wouldn't let it come out. Myself and Sandy Gallin and Peter Asher and Ira Kozlow put a lot of effort into putting a tour together in 1994. We were all working really hard for that, but at the end of the day we just couldn't pull it off. The schedules were just too erratic." Monty Hitchcock was right in the thick of things during Harris' European tour when Daniel Lanois' name was suggested as someone Emmylou might work with. Together the two created a whole new kind of alternative country music when they recorded WRECKING BALL. Monty's recollection of the situation is first-hand. "I've watched Emmy pocket songs for years, put them in her hip pocket, then they will resurface years later. She'd been pocketing songs for WRECKING BALL. She credits Daniel Lanois for giving her the blueprint to follow through on that, but in October of 1994 you could have asked her what she was going to do and she would have said, 'I don't know.' The same weekend that we contacted Daniel, he flew to Nashville and they got together. He flew in on a Saturday night, they spent some time together that night, and some more on Sunday. I was going to have dinner with them on Sunday night. I walked in the door and everybody was all smiles. Daniel said, 'We're going to do this.' I said, 'Great, let's eat.'"

When it came to marketing WRECKING BALL, a full-length video entitled *Building The Wrecking Ball* proved to be an invaluable asset. Emmylou had made several music videos beginning with *Mr. Sandman* and *I Don't Have To Crawl* in the early 1980s. Later in the decade she made another for *Wheels Of Love*. And for COWGIRLS' PRAYER she made three: *High Powered Love*, *Thanks To You*, and *Crescent City*. A full-length video had also been filmed at the Ryman Auditorium for her EMMYLOU HARRIS & THE NEW NASH RAMBLERS: LIVE AT THE RYMAN album.

When it came to marketing an artist who was fixed in many people's minds as strictly a country artist to the new Triple-A and Americana radio formats, Monty Hitchcock remembers that "the *Building The Wrecking Ball* video was very important simply because it was such a strong marketing tool for us. It was very difficult at radio in the beginning. Triple-A was so diverse at that point in 1995 that there were a lot of people who understood exactly what Emmylou Harris was about. Then there were those who had a lot of difficulty listening to WRECKING BALL. And there were those who just didn't know, who were very young, and got caught up in WRECKING BALL right away."

When Emmylou began touring to promote her new album in March 1996, she did so to enthusiastic audiences who loved what she was doing once they came out and heard her and the band she called Spyboy, a configuration that she had put together with Texan guitarist Buddy Miller, bassist Daryl Johnson, and drummer Brady Blade. Miller surprised everyone by not only successfully duplicating the quirky guitar and mandolin style laid down on the record by Daniel Lanois but taking the gothic stylings to new horizons in his solos. Daryl Johnson added bass pedals to his contribution, and Brady Blade was so much more than your usual sit-behind-the-kit-and-hit-the-skins drummer. Of course, Emmylou is one of the best acoustic guitarists on the planet. All four could sing and their harmonies had reviewers scribbling madly away.

To get the fans to purchase tickets and come out to the concerts, Monty and Emmylou decided to make a live track of *Going Back To Harlan*. "It was just to give everybody an idea of what Emmylou was doing out there on the road with this band Spyboy," Monty remembers. "People just didn't know what to expect when they came out to the shows. People liked the live track, they played it on the radio. Whether it was for a couple of weeks or a couple of months, it didn't matter to us as long as it got played for the couple of weeks when she was coming into town, and it helped promote the television show *Building The Wrecking Ball*, which was getting good ratings all over the place from the New Orleans Film Fest to the Sinking Creek Film Fest . . . all of those people were giving it accolades. We were just tickled to death. We had never done anything like that. It is something that her label at that time had a difficult time with because it was not something that they normally did. I still believe that it helped sell a lot of records. That tour was very successful. It was a difficult time and tours were dying all over the place that summer. Emmy's tour turned out to be quite successful. It had a lot to do with the live track and the full-length video, working those two things together."

Monty also admits that they kind of fluked into this marketing procedure. "We had *Building The Wrecking Ball* a full year after the release of the album and we started putting it into the PBS market place. It got noticed there, big time. We didn't film this with that idea in mind. In fact,

I had talked to Bob Lanois — who shot the majority of the footage — when he first started shooting in the studio at Woodland during those first two weeks of tracking that we did. I told Bob that I'd love to get five to ten minutes for an EPK. This was just for archival purposes. Daniel had invited him in. That was something that we had never done before because it's generally pretty uncomfortable for an artist to have a camera in the studio while they are recording. Even a photographer. But Bob was extremely unobtrusive. He became like one of the mikes. He'd been in a studio a large portion of his life and he understood how to be unobtrusive. So, Emmy was very comfortable and she was having a lot of fun and that was all exposed in that piece. I refer to it as a documentary piece, and that's kind of what it was. I think that there was so much curiosity about what Emmylou had done and what made her go in that direction — that was what sparked the curiosity for people to look at this video. Plus, people were still discovering this CD a year after its release. In fact, one year to the week after the U.K. release, we did a promotion in the U.K. and, for the first time in the history of the *Guardian*, they reviewed a record for a second time and gave it a better review the second time around than the first time. So, it was a slow build and the video helped us maintain that. We were able to go back out in 1997 and continue touring WRECKING BALL, even though we were discouraged by the record label to do so. We were able to go out and, after we'd booked the tour, put the video in each one of these market places and find a radio station whether it be Triple-A, rock, or sometimes even a country or Americana one and do cross-promotions with the television and her show and everything coming together at one time."

Another aspect of Emmylou's new touring band, Spyboy, that many reviewers, myself included, had raved about was the magic that kicked in when they tackled some of her past hits, like *Love Hurts, Wheels, Pancho & Lefty*, and *Born To Run* with its alternative feminist variation on the 'wide-open-road' rebellion theme.

> Well I never did crawl, and I never did toe that line
> No man is a master to me, I ain't that kind
> I just put on my traveling shoes
> If you wanna win you just can't lose. . . .
> And all that I wanted was to be the best

Just to feel free and be someone
I was born to be fast, I was born to run.

(written by Paul Kennerly)

"She started pulling out these songs," Monty remembers. "She gave them *Boulder To Birmingham*, *Pancho & Lefty*, and *Wheels*. At first she would just give them the record. Then she got to where she just played them the songs on the guitar. Quite frankly, Daryl and Brady weren't familiar with some of those tunes. Buddy was. They brought a whole new life to these songs. She is just so amazing. The one thing that has kept her viable and alive is creating new stuff. She could have easily fallen into a groove years ago and stayed there and made lots of money, but she couldn't do that."

When Monty Hitchcock put on a new hat, as head of Eminent Records, he and Emmylou began to think about a new album. They were treading on unexplored turf every day as Emmylou Harris was no longer a Top 40 country singer. She was being called the 'Queen of Alternative Country', a champion of the alt-country movement, even if she was not comfortable with such titles. And she was being played on all sorts of radio formats all over the world. She had broken back out of Nashville and Music Row endorsed Top 40 country, having moved there from the west coast in the early 1980s. And it was on the road that she and Spyboy recorded their next CD. Again, it wasn't something that Harris and Hitchcock had planned, not until the magic kicked in.

I had heard Emmylou and Spyboy early on at the Commodore Ballroom in Vancouver in the Spring of 1996 and had written a review that was posted at *www.wcmr.com*. I heard the act again in 1997 at the Calgary Folk Festival where they got a standing ovation for their efforts. By this time songs like *Ain't Living Long (Like This)* and *Love Hurts* had been added to the show. A few hours after her Calgary set, Emmylou was in the audience for Kieran Kane and Kevin Welch and their Dead Reckoners band during the wrap party for the festival, sitting at a table with a handful of friends and taking in the fierce madness being generated by the rebel country antics of an inspired Kane, a cigaret dangling from his lips as he leapt about the stage and out onto the dance floor while literally beating on his electric mandolin...plus an equally energetic Kevin Welch who belted his songs out as if we were all in a 1950s honky-tonk deep in the heart of Texas.

Emmylou might not like to be called the Queen of Alternative

Country, but there she was digging on the alt-country music with the rest of us. A few months later, she was in the thick of it again, releasing what would turn out to be a live album that would see her nominated, once again, for a Grammy award in 1999. "We didn't put a whole lot of thought into this," Monty Hitchcock remembers. "Emmy was looking for one song. She wanted to get a live version of *The Maker*. Once we got the gear together, I just made the call to record the whole show. It was just a matter of tape. Let's go ahead and record. It's just for archival purposes. When we began to listen to the tapes in December of 1997 and January of 1998, Emmy decided it was good enough to be a record. When it was released as an album, SPYBOY was a 14-track CD with a running time of over 62 minutes."

Encouraged by sales of the live CD, the Harris-Hitchcock team next made a move that resulted in a second release from Eminent Records. This time they taped a Nashville performance and the full-length video that resulted was called *Emmylou Harris: Spyboy, Live from the Legendary Exit-In*. Along with the live footage, statements from the artist and others provide an inside look at a career in music that continues to surprise. "It's doing surprisingly well," reported Monty Hitchcock. "It was released in the stores two weeks ago on the 16th of February. To be perfectly honest, and I'm happy to say this, I got caught with my pants down . . . I had to go back and re-manufacture because I underestimated how well it would sell. PBS has responded well to it. We have put it on TV in about 50 percent of the U.S. market places. Emmylou is not touring this year — she's in California recording with Glynn Johns and Linda Ronstadt — but when she does start to tour again, we'll do the same thing that we did with WRECKING BALL."

On the album, Buddy Miller really rips off some good old country riffs on tunes like *Ain't Livin' Long (Like This)* and Emmylou Harris has never sounded better than she does on *Deeper Well*, *Love Hurts*, and *Prayer In Open D*. When she closes in on her climactic delivery of *The Maker*, easing up to the finale with *All My Tears* and *Born To Run*, the critical acclaim reprinted from *Rolling Stone* magazine on the back of the video package, "Right now Harris is making arguably the most daring music of her thirty year career," is no lie. With the nearly simultaneous release of TRIO II and the live Spyboy video, Emmylou Harris was still at the center of the cyclone of both acoustic and alternative country as the century rushed to a final curtain call. And so was her long-time spiritual sister, Linda Ronstadt.

A lot of people know that Linda Ronstadt was in the Stone Poneys before she became a solo artist. And a lot of people know that she was in the Broadway Musical and Hollywood film productions of *The Pirates of Penzance*. But not everyone knows just how key her 1974 album release HEART LIKE A WHEEL was to the West Coast country-rock explosion of the 1970s. Before Linda Ronstadt became so popular recording fusions of country and rock that she sought new horizons and turned first to lush big band arrangements recorded with Nelson Riddle and his orchestra, then to traditional Mexican material, she inspired a whole generation of young country singers, many of them women. Where Emmylou was re-infusing country with well-delivered quality ballads like *Sweet Dreams*, which reminded everyone just how good Patsy Cline *had* been, and singing like an angel in a country choir . . . Linda Ronstadt had the ability to go from a ballad like Anna McGarrigle's *Heart Like A Wheel* to the searing scorcher *You're No Good* and the solid country-rock of Phil Everly's *When Will I Be Loved*. It was the combination of the two singers out in California, where country could be anything it wanted to be, that balanced the testosterone rich country-rock being generated by the The Byrds, The Flying Burrito Brothers, Poco, The Eagles, Commander Cody & His Lost Planet Airmen, Asleep At The Wheel, Pure Prairie League, The New Riders Of The Purple Sage, and Doug Sahm and his Texas Tornados, making the country-rock era truly an exciting time to listen to FM radio. It was a brand of music you wouldn't hear on most country radio stations. Emmylou Harris and Linda Ronstadt were the country-rock singers who *were* embraced by country radio. Ronstadt had already been at it awhile, having recorded background vocals on Neil Young's early country-rock album HARVEST in 1972.

Born in Tucson, Arizona, in 1946, Linda Ronstadt began performing with her brother and sister while still in high school. After the folk-rock group the Stone Poneys, she went solo for two albums, but began to hit a groove when she formed a backup band that would become The Eagles with Glenn Frey, Don Henley, Randy Meisner, and Bernie Leadon, all of whom would record with her on her third album, LINDA RONSTADT, establishing Ronstadt as the leading lady of the country-rock genre. When she began working with producer Peter Asher, who would collaborate on most of her projects for the next 20 years, she had found the formula for success on the radio as well as in the record stores.

Ronstadt's music had been moving toward country, but HEART LIKE A WHEEL *was* a country album, an oasis of pure intent in the midst of a career that simply took off into the stratosphere. Ronstadt, unlike The Eagles, did chart in the Top 40 on the *Billboard* country chart, hitting first with *Silver Threads And Golden Needles* and *I Can't Help It (If I'm Still In Love With You)*. In 1975, *You're No Good* went to number one. HEART LIKE A WHEEL certainly didn't sell like a country album; on the contrary, it went all the way to number one on the *Billboard 200* top-selling album chart and has sold two million copies since it was first issued in 1974. Three albums, but only two years later, Linda Ronstadt's GREATEST HITS would begin a sales history that now numbers over six million. In 1977, Ronstadt's SIMPLE DREAMS, with the Top 10 pop singles *Blue Bayou* and *It Ain't Easy*, went number one on the *Billboard 200* chart and stayed there for five weeks. LIVIN' IN THE USA followed in 1978 and MAD LOVE in 1980 yielded two more Top 10 pop hits, *How Do I Make You* and *Hurt So Bad*.

Country radio played *When Will I Be Loved* (a number one country hit in 1975), *Love Is A Rose* (a country number 5 in the same year), *The Tracks Of My Tears* (a country number 11 in 1976), and the flip-side, which featured Linda Ronstadt and Emmylou Harris singing a duet on *The Sweetest Gift*, was a number 12 country hit. *That'll Be The Day* and *Crazy* also made the country Top 10, as did *Blue Bayou* and *I Never Will Marry*. It was quite a run of Top 10 hits and, at the end of it, even Linda Ronstadt's country sales had amounted to more than a mere hill of beans. Her pop sales would put her in the top fifty best-sellers of the rock era.

Unlike Emmylou and Linda, Carlene Carter was born with a pure country pedigree. The daughter of Carl Smith and June Carter, Carlene was born in Nashville on September 6, 1955. While her mother performed as a member of The Carter Sisters & Mother Maybelle, Carlene took an early interest in music. She first took piano lessons from a local teacher and then learned guitar from Carl Perkins. When her mother divorced Smith and married Johnny Cash, Carlene was only 12. At 16 she, herself, married, but her college years lasted longer than that first liaison. She next joined the Carter Sisters and toured with Johnny Cash.

CARLENE CARTER

In the late 1970s, Carlene Carter went to England where she was influenced by a renewed British interest in rockabilly. Her first Warner album, produced by Graham Parker, rocked. Her second, made in New York studios, faltered. But her third, MUSICAL SHAPES, produced by her second husband, art-rock musician Nick Lowe, found a rockabilly groove. Pictured on the cover of the album in a white leather miniskirt and a fringed white leather jacket, Carlene is standing on a tiled floor littered with 45 records. It looks like she is about to stomp the living daylights out of those vinyl discs. Carlene Carter was the very first urban cowgirl to exude essence of 'cowpunk', way back when K.D. Lang was still bouncing volleyballs on the high school gym floor in Consort, Alberta.

Through the years, Carlene Carter has alternated between a spirit of frisky rebelliousness and a roots-rich reverence for tradition. She can be an all-out driving country-rocker with a killer instinct for catchy hooks, yet is able to perform at an almost bluegrass level of pure acoustic intent. Her finest moments include both a memorable Wembley Country Music Festival appearance with her family during the early 1980s *and* a 1990 video for her number 3 smash radio hit *I Fell In Love* that set fashion trends and editing standards for female videos and is played to this day on CMT.

"I want to have fun," Carlene told *Country Gals* author Mark Bego. "Music is fun, I mean, life is hard enough as it is. God created music to heal our souls a bit. If I can be the person who can make someone laugh or giggle or shake their butt, then, you know, I want to be that girl." During the last decade of the millennium, Carlene Carter has recorded several top notch albums. I FELL IN LOVE (Reprise, 1990) and LITTLE LOVE LETTERS (Giant, 1993) were produced by Howie Epstein in Los Angeles studios. For her 1995 Giant Records release LITTLE ACTS OF TREASON, she worked with both Epstein and James Stroud and recorded some of the basic tracks in Nashville, although the spice was added in L.A. and New York. Her fourth album of the decade was HINDSIGHT 20/20 (Giant, 1996). She has maintained her liaison with British rockers like Dave Edmunds and Kiki Dee, although she is now divorced from Nick Lowe. The Epstein-Carter collaborations pushed her into the mainstream in a big way, but she manages to mix the lush L.A. pop-country with rollicking excursions into electrified hillbilly. The combination makes for very good listening.

There are not that many 'new country' albums where you can experience unfettered joy, then despair, a dash of sorrow, then be swept away in a totally unpredictable direction, but with Carlene Carter's music, especially the first time you hear it, you are never sure of anything. With only

EMMYLOU HARRIS

TRIO

CARLENE CARTER

ROSANNE CASH

K.D. LANG

six Top 40 singles in a career that has yielded a dozen albums, you know that Carlene Carter hasn't been doing this for the money, alone. You know that the music is in her heart, bursting to be set free on tracks like *I Love You 'Cause I Want To*, a co-write with Radney Foster, and soothing to the core when she sings Benmont Tench's *Unbreakable Heart*. And when you listen to that music, you know her image is a natural expression of whom she really is, not a calculated air-brushed package. Carlene Carter has been successful in linking up with great co-writers, taking her music beyond the expectations of most singer-songwriters, especially in recent years.

Like Carlene Carter, Rosanne Cash was born into country music. Her father, Johnny Cash, has remained fiercely independent **ROSANNE CASH** throughout his legendary career and often explored alternatives to Music Row's top forty mania with his pals Willie Nelson, Waylon Jennings, and Kris Kristofferson, who were known collectively for a while as The Highwaymen. Johnny is the only person to have publicly given the finger to Music Row and the CMA when they chose to ignore his terrific achievements as a senior citizen during the Garth decade.

Rosanne has never gone quite that far, but she has never fit the Nashville cookie cutter mold either. And she doesn't tour often, so, when she came to the Commodore Ballroom in Vancouver during her 1987 tour to promote her new release KING'S RECORD SHOP, I made sure that I was comped and wrote a preview of her upcoming gig for a local tabloid. Beyond that, I wasn't expecting to write anything, just dig her music. That was enough. As it turned out, I knew the promoter personally and, after all the great music — Vince Santorini on drums, Steuart Smith on lead guitar, KING'S RECORD SHOP music live and in your face with Rosanne giving it her all on every single note and phrase — the promoter asked if I'd like to go backstage and have a few words with Rosanne. She had time to do a few short interviews.

Six or seven of us stood in line. The audience was filing out, although they were taking their time about it, finishing up their drinks and visiting in small groups at the tables. The Commodore is about the classiest venue in the whole world, refurbished from its glory days in the big band era. Ahead of me in the line were a couple of people from radio. And, of course, one or two friends of the promoter. Finally my turn came and, as I went back stage, Dave McCormick, the creator of those great *Country-mentary* syndicated radio shows, came out clutching his portable tape machine and his JR-FM mike. When I was ushered into one of the small dressing rooms, directly behind the stage, Rosanne seemed like she was just about out of meet-and-greet energy. It would be a surprise if she wasn't. She'd put on a really long, powerful set and done a couple of encores.

I stuck out my hand and said, "Hi, I'm Jim Brown, and I already wrote this up as a preview, but I just want to tell you, from all the people I know out there in the audience, that we loved your music. It was great!" Cash was surprised, taken aback, even. And I believe she said, "You don't want to ask me any questions?" Something like that. I said, "No, I just want to give you a hug to thank you for the music." We hugged, shared just a bit of energy, then I said, "See you," or "Be cool," or something equally inane, and it was over. I remember that being that close to her felt very . . . good, positive, although she seemed to be running out of positive at that late hour. I just hoped that I'd been able to give her a little something in return for the music.

Years passed. I picked up a copy of ROSANNE CASH — HITS 1979-1989 and I play that sometimes when I need some positive reinforcement. THE WHEEL is way more darkly introspective, and yet whenever I've played it, it does bring me around nearly as well as her fluffier stuff. The thing is, not many country singers read Dostoevsky or D.H. Lawrence, but I somehow knew without ever having asked Rosanne a single question that night that *she* probably did. One thing I did know for certain, she had really been influenced by The Beatles, it was part of her positive energy. Before I began to think about her music, I didn't even realize just how influential Rosanne had been during the 1980s, pushing the envelope of personal expression for female recording artists as well as expanding the horizons for country lyrics and production.

I did know that since she and Rodney Crowell had split up, Rodney hadn't recorded a song that had so caught my fancy since he'd penned *She's Crazy For Leavin'* for that great DIAMONDS AND DIRT album he put out in 1988. *She's Crazy For Leavin'* is a truly funny breaking-up song, with the woman pictured in the song climbing on a Greyhound and Rodney beating up his pickup truck on a telephone pole just for good measure. And that's how I pictured Rosanne Cash in the 1990s, riding away in a Greyhound bus, riding away from country music, really, because her subsequent albums have been of the singer-songwriter variety, a treasure to me, but I wondered if she had very many country fans, these days. I wondered how she was getting along. She was way more than a "little past Little Rock" these days, living in Paris and New York, I had heard.

Then I stumbled upon a truly wonderful book, *Solo: Women Singer-Songwriters In Their Own Words*, published by Delta Trade Paperbacks and edited by Marc Woodworth with photographs of the songwriters by Emma Dodge Hanson. I opened the book and began to read about what Rosanne Cash had to say about her life and her songwriting. I learned that she'd published a book of stories, *Bodies of Water*, in 1996, and her 20 page self-portrait read like an essay by Anais Nin. It was intelligent, self-probing, told the truth about her relationship with her father without air-brushing the details or evoking unnecessary blasts of hurt, and, yes, she had read D.H. Lawrence and Dostoevsky.

I set the book aside, put on KING'S RECORD SHOP, and listened to the wonderful production, the no-holds-barred lyrics of *Rosie Strike Back*, John Hiatt's *The Way We Make A Broken Heart*, Rosanne's own *The Real Me*, Johnny Cash's *Tennessee Flat Top Box*, and then Rodney Crowell's *I Don't Have To Crawl*. When I put on the compilation, I got as far as track 3, Rosanne's *Blue Moon With Heartache*, then sat down at my processor to write these words.

As Rosanne herself says in that singer-songwriter book, KING'S RECORD SHOP was a landmark album, a "big deal," and it *is* true that before that record no woman had had four number ones from a single country album, and true that it stayed on the charts for more than a year, even if she said it herself, again, in that book. What Rosanne didn't say, because she wasn't bragging in any way, was that those four singles were clustered around another number one, her duet with Rodney Crowell on *It's Such A Small World* from his DIAMONDS AND DIRT album ... *or* that her next single, *I Don't Want To Spoil The Party*, was also a number one, making six of them in a row!

Now happily married to John Leventhal and living in New York with her husband and children, Rosanne Cash, like Emmylou Harris, is making *her* kind of music. It could never be not-country, but she's making no real effort to produce her records for Top 40 consumption, not these days. On THE WHEEL, produced at New York City studios by Leventhal and Cash, Rosanne Cash cashes in her urban cowgirl past for a singer-songwriter approach. The vocals are still prominent and as in-your-face as the usual country vocal, but Steuart Smith is the only Nashville picker who appears here and there on the tracks. Otherwise, we find Tom Petty's pal Benmont Tench on keys, John Leventhal (guitars, electric piano, organ, harmonium, percussion), Charlie Giardano (accordion), and a variety of drummers who sometimes play hand-drums rather than a full kit. Harmony vocals by the likes of Bruce Cockburn, Marc Cohn, and Mary Chapin Carpenter keep the folk music feel alive.

From the zesty opening strains of *The Wheel* and the staring-down-on-the-madness-of-New York City thoughtfulness of *Seventh Avenue*, the music moves to classic Rosanne Cash on *Change Partners*. *Sleeping In Paris* takes us even farther from Nashville and the Opry to Europe in a search for self that reeks of the days ex-patriot existentialist Americans like Gertrude Stein, F. Scott Fitzgerald, and Ernest Hemingway sought an identity separate from the post-WW1 America they had left behind. By the time we get to *Rise From The Ashes*, we sense a progression here in the song lineup that we now hear moving steadfastly through *The Truth About You, Tears Falling Down*, and *Roses In The Fire* to land solidly on *Fire Of The Newly Alive*, which opens with Rosanne Cash singing: "We are awakened, restored and renewed / The bonds of desire have led me to you . . ." The final track, *If There Is A God On My Side*, is long and dwells on the singer's relationship with the deity. The only twist is that if there is a god on this singer's mind . . . that god is a "She" and not a "He."

> If there is a God on my side
> Why don't She show me Her face?
> If there is a God on my side
> Could She live in this place?
> If there is a God on my side
> Is She inside these walls?
> If there is a God on my side
> Could She not hear me call?

(written by Rosanne Cash)

No reference to Lilith is included, and Cash, along with many of the songwriters like Joan Osborne in that singer-songwriter book, speaks not of replacing a male god with a female one so much as not genderizing the deity at all, not distancing oneself from the continual everpresent process of creation and re-creation that God is.

K.D. Lang is another alternative artist, an angel with a lariat, who tried country on for size, but found the politics too confining. She showed immense early potential to be a really big country star in anybody's world, but foundered when her jokes about the "tall hair crowd" in Nashville fell flat in the wrong circles. She has gone on to less troubled waters with her Euro-pop releases like *Ingenue* and *All You Can Eat*. Her problems with the Nashville establishment had often stemmed from the fact that, although she saw her music as an evolving career and country music as a vehicle by which she could express herself, others saw her as someone whose rough edges were being gradually worn off to fit the cookie cutter mold of becoming a "country music star."

K.D. LANG

Kathryn Dawn Lang was born in Consort, Alberta, a farming community with a population of 650. When Lang went to college, she strayed from early interest in music to an involvement in performance art. When she came back to music, spurred on by her discovery of the music of Patsy Cline, she had already become so *outside* that she immediately drew interest with her first recordings and performances. Surfacing first in Edmonton, where she linked up with her manager, Larry Wanagas, Lang put out the rockabilly album A TRULY WESTERN EXPERIENCE on Bumstead Records in 1984. Her penchant for off-the-wall performance was evident as early as a 1982 Edmonton audition for a western swing band patterned after Bob Wills & His Texas Playboys. An early Lang bio quotes an observer at that audition as saying, "Mind you, anyone who can sing that good lying on the studio floor or draped over the grand piano should be incredible standing up."

When she began appearing with her band, the Reclines, at Edmonton's Side Track Cafe, Lang caused quite a commotion. Although she called her unique style "torch and twang," it was to be dubbed both "punkabilly" and "cowpunk" by the media, phrases reporters were unwilling to part with, even when the SHADOWLAND and TORCH & TWANG albums convinced most K.D. Lang fans that the singer was much more than a cowpunker. *Friday Dance Promenade* was not exactly a radio hit, but it was the first track to gain notice from A TRULY WESTERN EXPERIENCE. Lang and Wanagas showed no hesitation when they took their music straight to New York City, and their instincts served them well when K.D. Lang & the Reclines became instantly popular with their live performances at the Bottom Line club. One of the people to catch their act was Seymour Stein, president of Sire Records. Right from the get-go, Lang does not seem to have possessed much patience when it came to record executives and music business types, saying, "I'd talked to a lot of record executives, and was getting a little weary of it. But when I met Seymour, I knew that I'd met someone who really understood what I was after."

Paired with famed British rockabilly artist Dave Edmonds as producer, K.D. cut her second album, ANGEL WITH A LARIAT, in London. Although production values were smoother than on her Edmonton debut, the match was not the best. Five months of touring in America followed the April 1987 release. K.D. Lang & the Reclines gained notoriety for their performance everywhere they appeared. Where some bands struggle in obscure clubs for years, Larry Wanagas was successful in getting national television exposure for his singer and her band. K.D. Lang appeared on Johnny Carson's *Tonight Show* a total of six times during the formative years of her country career.

In 1987, Lang was featured on the first live CTV-CCMA Awards Show wearing a white stetson and looking very much the urban cowgirl alongside fellow winner of several awards, Ian Tyson. K.D. won both the CCMA Vista Rising Star Award *and* the Entertainer of the Year Award that year and set the Canadian country music industry on its ear. The following year, 1988, she would win CCMA Entertainer, Female Vocalist *and* Album of the Year for SHADOWLAND, a feat she would repeat in 1989 in all three categories. In 1990, Lang won her fourth CCMA Entertainer of the Year Award and received the Album of the Year Award for TORCH & TWANG.

The release of INGENUE in 1992 ended Lang's five-year love-hate relationship with the country media. Many of the reviewers of Lang's early performances had been quick to cite her unique vision. Writing in the Saturday, April 4, 1987 edition of the *Los Angeles Herald Examiner*, Marc Weiss praised Lang's talent: "On stage, Lang's coltish energy, which has her dashing about the stage when she isn't do-si-do-ing with the fiddler, is leavened with a trembling intensity that teeters between despair and rage. . . . K.D. Lang is that rarity in popular music: a woman with a unique vision and the intelligence, wit, and talent to bring that vision to life."

John Pareles writing in the Sunday, May 10th, 1987, edition of the *New York Times* wondered aloud about Lang's future in country: "Ms. Lang, who is Canadian, came to country music from performance art — and it shows, because she works the stage with unabashed freneticism. Her affection for the music sounds real, but she takes the lyrics with a grain of salt, revealing their comic undertones by acting them out literally, as when she added and removed cigarets from an ashtray during the weeper *Three Cigarets in an Ashtray*. She also square-danced for *Turn Me Around*, played her microphone stand like a bass fiddle in *Honky-tonk Heart* and barked and sniffed and scratched with her toes in a countrified version of the Roches' *Damned Old Dog* which also brought out the song's genuine pain. Ms. Lang's point seems to be that in the current decade, old-fashioned sentiments need an extra, self-conscious jolt — that romance is hard to take seriously and harder not to. As she grows into country singing, she may well learn to fine-tune her heart-felt parodies." A refusal to fine-tune either her performances or her desire to push the envelope to the max placed her in conflict with everyone who had come along claiming to be a country singer before her.

K.D. Lang first found acceptance for her efforts from country audiences when she recorded *Crying* with Roy Orbison. The fact that she cut off the tops of her western boots and wore costumes that parodied the urban cowgirl outfits could be ignored as long as she sang like an angel, with or without a lariat. However, journalists continued to ponder her career as if it were a puzzle to be fitted together in order to make some sense that she had not explained. Writing a preview of Lang's April 2, 1987 appearance at the Roxy in the *Los Angeles Times*, Robert Hilburn was one of the first: "Imagine a cross between Laurie Anderson and Minnie Pearl. Or how about a mixture of Elvis Costello and Patsy Cline? Somewhere in that puzzle of images, you'll find the real K.D. Lang." In his article entitled "Did Lang Come To Praise Or Parody?" Hilburn addresses an issue that would become a crisis in a few short years: "Lang is pleased that her shows have attracted both young rock fans and older country ones. But she admits the country music establishment is sometimes confused by the colorful, almost manic nature of her concerts."

"Sometimes people feel it is great," Lang told Hilburn, "but others think I'm just making fun, and I can understand that because change is a scary thing, but it is also the essence of growth." For her acceptance of her 1985 Juno Award as Most Promising Female Artist, Lang had worn a wedding dress. A few weeks later, she had appeared with the Edmonton Symphony Orchestra. When she showed up on the cover of *Chatelaine*, the Canadian fashion magazine airbrushed her image, and Lang responded with comments that seemed to some inappropriate. It was not enough to get her picture on the cover, but she wanted to be represented as she was, not as the glamor magazine had, with lipstick added. A later Lang song, *Miss Chatelaine*, written in collaboration with Ben Mink, would parody even her covergirl image: "Just a kiss, just a kiss, I have lived just for this / I can't explain why I've become Miss Chatelaine."

Nashville Banner writer Michael McCall, writing in his "Fast Tracks" column on March 26, 1987, had warned Nashville readers that Lang's quirky country stance might be the future of the industry: "The startlingly original debut by K.D. Lang & the Reclines gives country music a tornado of a twirl that could send a few rhinestones flying into the 21st century. Put away the telescopes, Music Row. This angel from left field just tossed a lariat around the future and pulled it into view." Fine, but was this the future the execs on Music Row wanted for country music? Of course there were many articles that would declare that K.D. Lang had mellowed, that she'd matured, that she'd done this that and every other thing that fitted her more into the expected and accepted mold. The fact remained that Lang, herself, never did any of those things. The writers may have wanted her to, some of her fans may have wanted her to, but the key word in most of Lang's interviews, which most writers ignored, was "progress."

In fact, throughout most of K.D. Lang's life, one of her problems had been that people didn't always listen to what she was saying. Enroled at Red Deer College in the early 1980s, Lang had come to the college as a promising volleyball athlete but came into conflict with an authoritarian coach who would not let her cut a half hour from one of the team practices so that she could fulfil an obligation to a singing class that was part of her academic curriculum. Lang chose music. This, according to Lang biographer Victoria Starr, rang alarm bells back in Consort where Lang's mother, Audrey, became concerned that her daughter had forsaken athletics for the life of a singer. As both Heather Ostertag and Anya Wilson have pointed out, the idea of a woman choosing to become an entertainer was often viewed by past generations of Canadian women as an announcement that they had chosen a life that would lead to immoral pursuits. Alberta is as bible-belt as the hillbilly environs east of Nashville, a Canadian province where a career in rodeo is considered normal. For a woman at that time, a secretary in a typing pool or a stay-at-home housewife was probably the preferred type-cast role for a woman. So, from the beginning, Kathy Lang chose the road never traveled, but only did so when she ran into opposition from control-freak personalities.

As Lang's identification with Patsy Cline grew in intensity, she would face opposition from those who had fixed Patsy in their minds to fit their own agendas. When Lang let it be known that she consulted Patsy's spirit, few Cline fans were amused. Nevertheless, a possessed Lang continued to pursue the identification. She had learned who Owen Bradley was and had sent overtures to Bradley that had not been answered. When Bradley, in a hospital bed recovering from a heart attack, spotted her on *The Tonight Show, he* made the overture, came out of retirement, and the two sat down at the piano and began playing jazz together. Out of this instant like for each other came the lushly produced and jazz-influenced country music of SHADOWLAND: THE OWEN BRADLEY SESSIONS, a hit album in anybody's ears. For the finale, Bradley brought K.D. Lang together with Loretta Lynn, Brenda Lee, and Kitty Wells to sing a medley of songs culminating with Wells' first hit. The track became known as the *Honky-tonk Angels Medley*. Lang was pumped for the session. These women were her inspirations, especially Loretta. Biographer Victoria Starr quotes Lang as saying: "Brenda is a very technical singer, Kitty is so serene and maternal, and Loretta is exactly what you thought she'd be like. She came into the studio with a pound of bologna and a loaf of bread, and everybody had bologna sandwiches. I'm a vegetarian, but I almost ate one. I thought it was blessed food."

Bradley had the press included on the recording session. During the subsequent video shoot, the three senior country divas returned the compliments Lang had tossed their way. It was a moment in country music history. And, although at the present time it seems unlikely that such warm Nashville embracing of Lang will be repeated, you never can tell. The music was a wonder to all.

On the strength of SHADOWLAND, Lang was nominated for three Grammies and accepted by even the most fervent lovers of traditional country music during her performance at Fan Fair that June. But when she won her Grammy for her duet with Orbison, we heard the first public grumblings from the country music establishment in Tennessee. To tour the SHADOWLAND material, Lang was forced by the musicians union to employ American musicians, a move which further distanced her from her band, the Reclines, who had been waiting in the wings in Canada. Having already promised her band that she would record with them, Lang had put them off an additional year recording with Bradley. Still in America, she appeared on an HBO special that united the new wave with the old, bringing K.D. Lang, Rosanne Cash, and the Judds together with some of the legendary acts. Reviewers raved about Lang's performance of *Lock, Stock and Teardrops* and her duet with Loretta Lynn.

K.D. Lang came back to Canada to awards show appearances and a short stint on the Amnesty International tour with Peter Gabriel and Tracy Chapman. She did not immediately return to Nashville. Instead, she recorded the TORCH & TWANG album in a Vancouver studio, this time following up on her promise to record with her band. Next she recorded a duet version of *Sin City* with Nashville outcast Dwight Yoakam, a blistering rendition of the early Gram Parsons-Chris Hillman classic from the 1969 Flying Burrito Brothers rebel country album GUILDED PALACE OF SIN, and when she invited Yoakam to Red Deer, Alberta for the taping of *kd lang's Buffalo Cafe*, her first CBC special, the two singers looked like two rebels when they sang *Sin City*, evoking more the spirit of Gram Parsons and Emmylou than Loretta and Conway. It was solid "new country," but it was hardly a career move designed to endear oneself with the Nashville establishment.

In her praise of her three SHADOWLAND singing partners, K.D. Lang had brought up an issue that would soon balloon into a crisis. That casually mentioned word, vegetarian, would take on a new meaning when Lang endorsed PETA, the People For Ethical Treatment of Animals. Recruited by Dan Mathews, a special projects guy who had staged many media events during the 1980s for the 300,000-strong organization, Lang participated in a televised media event hugging a cow and saying to the TV audience: "We all love animals. But why do we call some pets and some dinner?" It was the first-ever TV "vegetarian commercial," and PETA exploited their media star to the max. News cameras were rolling during the video shoot and Lang was on the evening news.

Lang's vegetarian endorsement and the kick off of the "Meat Stinks" campaign was blasted out on early morning radio across the United States and Canada and heard by people as far away as Consort, Alberta, where angered ranchers would deface the "Welcome to Consort, Alberta, The Home of K.D. Lang" sign that well-wishers had erected on the highway where visitors would see it as they drove into town. When the issue hit the airwaves, rumor had it that the sign had first sustained bullet holes or blasts from a shot-gun before it was torn down or burned down. Whether or not any of this was true, and it later turned out that the sign had been less seriously damaged, the rumor was what people heard, and K.D. Lang became the butt of tasteless jokes fabricated by both meat-eaters and country music fans. Lang had shot herself in the foot as far as country music went. The country radio airplay demographic for activist vegetarians did not exist. Playing Lang cuts on a country station amounted to supporting her endorsement — at least that's the way the issue was perceived by country radio advertisers.

At first, however, mainstream public reaction was on Lang's side and album sales, which had not been a huge area of success for the singer, increased as never before. The fact that most of the people who were now buying her albums were not country music fans only widened the gap between Lang and Nashville. Of course, all along Kathy Lang had maintained that she was not singing country music with any aim to become a country star. She had chosen the music as a vehicle for self expression. In Canada, she was honored by the Juno organization, C.A.R.A.S., the Canadian Association of Recording Arts and Sciences, as the Female Singer of the Decade. And, although often faced by hostile interviewers, she is quoted by her biographer, Victoria Starr, as telling one reporter, "Do I regret it? The only thing I regret is that it affected my mother in a negative way. I don't regret it on a spiritual level, let's face it, I sold more records during that period than I did at any other time. But the fact that it hurt my mother really made me mad."

She would take to wearing rubber boots when confronted on the questioned purity of her feelings toward animals. And very soon, she would put country music and the whole politicizing of her music behind her when she released in 1992 what many feel may be a career album, INGENUE. It was her first album to chart in the Top 40 regions of the *Billboard* Top 200 and became her first million-seller. SHADOWLAND and TORCH & TWANG had charted well on the *Billboard* country chart, but sales had been the missing ingredient in a stormy and brilliant career in country music. Had K.D. Lang come along just a few years later, she might have sold as many country albums as Shania Twain, who is also a vegetarian. But Lang's country career had almost run its course by the time Garth Brooks was introducing pyrotechnics and laser lights to his stadium shows and on his way to realizing his goal of selling 100 million albums in one decade.

The additional issue of sexual orientation would have been accepted, if Kathy Lang had not been an activist vegetarian, if she had not ever met Dan Mathews and taped that "Meat Stinks" commercial. But, in the long run, K.D. Lang's music was not to be bound in by any politics or prejudices. Basically, K.D. Lang's country years were an interlude in the career of a singer whose music would ultimately acknowledge no boundaries.

During the late 1980s, K.D. Lang was not the only woman to sing rockabilly and to yuk it up onstage while paying homage to the roots of country music. A rallying point for West Coast alt-country females was the Railway Club in Vancouver, where acts like the Dots, Terilyn Ryan & the Hen Pals, Sue Medley, Beverley Elliott, and Babe Gurr performed. Terilyn Ryan hosted monthly events she called Hen Nights. Singer-songwriters like Shari Ulrich, Cori Brewster, Lyndia Scott, Linda Kidder, and Sue Leonard often shared the stage with the budding pop divas of the day. All of these talents were bubbling up on a scene that would eventually see Sarah McLachlan emerge as a spokeswoman for female entertainers when she created Lilith Fair, which was sort of like 'Hen Nights Hit The Road'.

The key to understanding just what went on when women first banded together to celebrate their music and their womanhood is the word "celebrate." Celebration is key to the font of creative energy women have tapped into in the 1990s, and, fortunately for the human species, women have not been fazed by opposition to their musical success. They have simply celebrated louder, hoping, I suppose, that eventually the world at large would hear what the fuss is all about. Both Cindi Lauper's *Girls Just Want To Have Fun* with its catchy hook and bubbly innocence and the more impassioned plea of Janis Joplin's lyric "Just give me another little *Piece Of Your Heart* now, baby," seem crucial to an understanding of the phenomenon. Of course, you can deride such lyrics and hooks. You can dismiss Janis Joplin as merely a loud drunk and Cindi Lauper as a overage bubblegummer. But there is so much more to both singers' lyrics ... if you are willing to clean out your ears and hear the sense of openness and freedom celebrated in their music.

When mainstream female country singers turned their skills to celebrating their womanhood, they were surprisingly adroit when addressing specific issues in their lyrics. Dolly Parton's 9 To 5 and K.T. Oslin's 80's Ladies were early rallying points. But in the 1990s singers like Pam Tillis and Shania Twain would make whole albums that were informed with the intelligence introduced into the popular idiom first by Loretta Lynn and Tammy Wynette and developed by Parton, Oslin, and Rosanne Cash. Pam Tillis and Shania Twain have become hugely popular *because* they put out songs and videos like *Cleopatra, Queen Of Denial* and *Any Man Of Mine*, not *despite* the fact that they have done so. The women's revolution in music simply came about because women got in touch with other women and made music together at venues, like the Railway Club, all over North America. When they met at festivals, conventions, or awards shows, they felt a solidarity, where in years past they might have merely felt competition with each other.

The quality of entertainment was high at these all-female events at the Railway Club. Local songwriters were joined by out-of-towners like Sharon Anderson, a singer-songwriter from Calahoo, Alberta who was a member of Trinity Lane and had a solo album out on Capitol Nashville. Pam Tillis and her Women In The Round configuration of Ashley Cleveland, Trish Walker, and Karen Staley brought the spirit of Nashville's Bluebird Cafe to the local scene.

Across town, I spent a couple of years as host and talent coordinator for 22 TV shows taped for Rogers Cable in Kitsilano at the Taverna Corfu restaurant. These *Intimate Evenings With Songwriters* were produced by Bullfrog Studios' Fred Koch, directed by Tony Irraci, and featured the likes of Willie P. Bennett, Gary Fjellgaard, and Dick Damron alongside women like Lisa Brokop, Patricia Conroy, Sue Medley, Holly Arntzen, Colette Wise, Heidi Marlaine, Laurie Thain, and Tami Greer. Some of these unplugged shows, like a Conroy-Fjellgaard night, were syndicated to cable outlets as far away as Toronto. Key to my initial interest in what has become an explosion of female musical talent in the 1990s was my early involvement with Patricia Conroy's publicity campaigns and a friendship with the lead singer of the group who called themselves the Dots. The second article that I contributed to Canada's national country newspaper, *Country Music News*, was titled "West Coast Ladies."

THE DOTS

The original Dots were an all-female quintette led by Vancouver singer-songwriter Tami Greer featuring the guitar stylings of Sue Foley. They performed Greer's rockabilly-flavored originals and covered a lot of really obscure jump and swing records from the 1940s and '50s. Foley, a remarkable lead guitarist, especially when she sang the blues, graduated from the group to go on to a solo career in Austin, Texas, where she recorded for Antones Records and issued critically acclaimed albums like her 1992 release YOUNG GIRL BLUES and the 1995 BIG CITY BLUES. The Dots' lead singer, Greer, was joined in harmony and on rhythm electric guitar by Reg MacDonald. The rhythm section was veteran rockabilly aficionado Joanie Kepler on doghouse bass and Lisa Lambert on drums. When Lambert left the group, not that long after Foley, she was replaced by Revellie Nixon. Jimmie Roy (aka Jamie Kinlock) took over the guitar playing and stayed for the duration.

The Dots played the Railway Club on a regular basis and performed at Festivals all over British Columbia, Washington, Oregon, and Alberta. Their February 1989 appearance at Edmonton's Side Track Cafe drew notice from *Edmonton Journal* writer Helen Metella who wrote, "as a predominantly female outfit . . . the vivacious act plays uptempo rockabilly and country tunes without any of the usual and distracting macho overtones. . . . Lead singer Tami Greer isn't a powerhouse crooner, but she skips lithely from the vulnerable ache of Patsy Cline's *Write Me In Care Of The Blues* to the jaunty bop-shoo-wop of *It's Raining Outside Tonight*. She can also do this dance rapidly, as she demonstrated on Lucille Starr and Bob Regan's late 1950s hit *Eenie Meenie*. . . . The Dots definitely make happy dance music." When Pam Tillis heard the Dots at the Vancouver Folk Festival in 1989, she was moved to tell *Province* reporter Bruce Mason, "They have a love and understanding of the tradition and roots of country music."

The Dots recorded an album for Dave Schroeder's Eastside Records, a Vancouver indie label that specializes in roots and rockabilly music. It featured some tracks with Foley on guitar as well as some with Kinlock on guitar and pedal steel. This was a cassette only release, but several of the tracks were included on the British CD compilation BOPPIN' IN CANADA issued by Nervous Records. The best Dots cuts would have to be the LaVern Baker standard *Jim Dandy*, a cover of the Canadian Sweethearts' *Eenie Meeny Miny Mo*, and Greer originals like *Swingin' On The Gate*. In the 1990s, Tami Greer, like her mentor K.D. Lang, went on to a solo career in alternative-pop music, recording a solo CD and basing her career out of Portland, Oregon. In 1998, she returned to Vancouver to perform as part of Lilith Fair.

T he all-female configuration known as Ranch Romance record- **RANCH** ed several CDs in the Seattle area and toured with K.D. Lang **ROMANCE** for a time in both Canada and the United States. Ranch Romance was an acoustic group featuring the lead vocals and guitar of Jo Miller; the lead vocals, yodeling, and mandolin of Lisa Theo; the fiddle and vocals of Barbara Lamb; and string bass and vocals of Nancy Katz. Lamb would go on to play with Asleep At The Wheel and Jo Miller with Laura Love. Their debut CD was WESTERN DREAM, and the first track leapt into your speakers, a zesty acoustic western swing version of Fred Howard's *When It's Roundup Time In Texas* with a yodeling chorus, a hot licks mandolin solo, and a zesty fiddle solo. Next, we heard a hiccup yodel version of *Lovesick Blues*: both the hot fiddle and the group harmonies on the chorus are the kind of performance that endeared this act to audiences when the group opened for Lang. Jo Miller's bluesy original *Baby's On The Town* took on double entendre meanings under the circumstances. At times, this four-some could be even hotter than Dan Hicks and his Hot Licks on numbers like their uptempo arrangement of W.C. Handy's *St. Louis Blues*. Subsequent releases on the group's own Ranch Hands Records label featured an added "guy," but the immediate appeal of Ranch Romance had been their all-female presence in a world still dominated by male singers and pickers. Their early popularity foreshadowed the success that would come to the Dixie Chicks when Natalie Maines joined that group in 1995, bringing a focused vocal presence to an all-female bluegrass trio who wanted to make Top 40 country records.

T he band Lone Justice surfaced in the Los Angeles alternative **MARIA** music club scene during the early 1980s, featuring lead vocalist **McKEE** Maria McKee and guitarist Ryan Hedgecock. Their 1985 album LONE JUS-TICE brought the group instant notoriety. The tracks were produced by Jimmy Iovine and blended country, rock, and gospel in a roots-rich yet defi-ant package. Maria McKee's vocals were likened to a cross between Janis

Joplin and Dolly Parton. A record contract from Geffen, and a sophomore album, SHELTER, plus the considerable local reputation the band had built, failed to translate into record sales and Maria McKee soon embarked on a solo recording project that attracted the likes of guitarists Robbie Robertson and Richard Thompson who contributed tracks to the recording sessions. The album MARIE McKEE, a Geffen release, and the 1993 indie release YOU GOTTA SIN TO BE SAVED were further derivations of the original excitement Lone Justice stirred up when they first gigged together.

Dwight Yoakam sometimes opened for Lone Justice and Maria McKee sang on the original EP version of Yoakam's GUITARS, CADILLACS, ETC, ETC. The two were appealing together on Yoakam's *Bury Me*, and this song was also included on the full-length album of the same name when it was released by Reprise Nashville in 1986. Yoakam had McKee back on his 1988 album BUENAS NOCHES FROM A LONELY ROOM, which includes their version of Hank Locklin's *Send Me The Pillow*. In 1999 Geffen reissued the best of Lone Justice on a 17-song retrospective, THIS WORLD IS NOT MY HOME.

Nashville columnist Charles Earle, writing in the March 2, 1999 issue of Nashville's City Weekly *In Review*, praised the act saying, "I would dare say that our current alt-country movement actually began many years ago when stunningly talented vocalist Maria McKee hooked up for a brief time with some Merle Haggard-worshipping club musicians to form this wonderful band. In 1984, when synthesizers ruled the day, Lone Justice became the subject of a bidding war between most every one of the major labels thanks to their high-energy, guitar-based hybrid of twangy country and rock."

That not a few of these alt-country progeny of Trio are Canadian is not surprising given that there is a long-tradition of women artists making music and reputations outside of Nashville in 'Nashville North', as Canada's indigenous country music recording industry has been called, where Nashville values have often been imposed on young Canadian women artists when they trekked to the head offices of the major labels in Toronto. Out West, where most of the alternative activity took place, there are a lot more wide open spaces.

SNOWBIRDS

☆ ☆ ☆

Besides California and Texas, another 'alternative' Nashville developed in Canada during the 1980s and '90s, following the path of Anne Murray and K.D. Lang, leading to Terri Clark and Shania Twain. The Canadian country music tradition is long, dating back to Hank Snow and Wilf Carter, with its own music industry and charts, including the Canadian Country Music Association and such trade magazines as *Country Music News*.

Even before Shania Twain and Terri Clark burst upon the international scene, a growing number of female country singers had created a whole lot of excitement on Canadian country radio in the late 1980s and early 1990s. Anita Perras and Joan Kennedy were major achievers in Canada with numerous turn-table hits. Perras was a three-time winner of the CCMA Female Vocalist of the Year award while still a member of a duo with her songwriter husband Tim Taylor. Joan Kennedy won a 1982 talent contest, and when she began to issue her own recordings, consistently hit the Canadian Top 10 with her releases, becoming accepted as a country star by Canadian fans along with Carroll Baker, Lucille Starr, and Myrna Lorrie. By the 1990s, a number of talented new Canadian females were vying for recognition with the top-achiever of the day, K.D. Lang. Some of them, like Cassandra Vasik, who sang songs written for her by Much Music network VJ, Erica Ehm, were renegade folkies. But others, like Lori Yates, were genuine country singers who were signed to major labels but failed to make a serious dent in the U.S. market when their successful Canadian singles were released south of the border. Few made the commitment to move to Nashville as did Michelle Wright, Lisa Brokop, and Patricia Conroy, who all had serious runs at international success in the 1990s. Wright was the singer who had the most success and opened the doors through which Terri Clark and Shania Twain have two-stepped onto the country scene in the United States. While all of these hopefuls plotted to head south with their music, veteran singers Tracey Brown, Sylvia Tyson, and Cindy Church continued to be major musical voices on the Canadian country music scene.

At the age of nine, Tracey Brown became the youngest member of what would turn out to be Canada's all-time favorite country band. "Papa" Joe Brown, Tracey's father, was already a Canadian country legend in 1967 when he formed Family Brown. Joe and his sister Vivian first became known as The Hillbilly Jewels when they played dates in the Nova Scotia area. Then they got a call from Wilf Carter. As Tracey explains, "I don't know how Wilf Carter heard about them, but he heard that they put on really good shows and they were really entertaining, and he hired them as his back-up band." The Hillbilly Jewels toured with Wilf Carter for eight years, off and on, across Canada. When she speaks of her father, Tracey's voice fills with obvious pride. "Dad would tell us stories . . . They played in Newfoundland before it was part of Canada and before there were a lot of roads. They had to put their car on trains or take it around by boats. There were coal oil lanterns in the halls and the people wouldn't let them go. People would come, and it was probably the first show they'd ever seen in some of these outposts, and they'd take them in and feed them and watch all five one-hour sets, and they'd sing and sing and sing . . . It must have been amazing and, for my aunt Viv back then, it must have been tough. They all drove in a car with a stand-up bass on the top. If it was rainin', the bass came in the car. That's before you had all those coffee shops and bathroom stops, I'm sure. So, for a woman on the road, it must have been really tough. There wasn't that many doing it." Although she was only a child when she started singing in the family band, Tracey recalls the patriarchal and chauvinist world of country music then. "I was the youngest in the group. Lawanda was older. I would hear stories of what women who were on their own would go through. They would have to go through all sorts of crap backstage to get their money, or people coming on to them, or people in the audience being really rude and crude. But, I guess, because my dad and my brother Barry were there, Lawanda and I never . . . we got the respect. Even if we played in the worst places, and we did play a lot of crummy places."

The first Family Brown album appeared in 1970 and since then they have received the most awards for a group in the history of the Canadian Country Music Association, winning CCMA Group of the Year honors 13 times during a 23-year career that began in 1967 and came to an end with a final performance on the *Tommy Hunter Show* in October 1990. As a member of Family Brown along with Barry, Lawanda, and her father Papa Joe, Tracey Brown had logged thousands of hours on stage, hundreds of hours in front of television cameras on the group's syndicated TV show, and recorded hundreds of tracks in studio sessions that yielded 14 albums on RCA and more than 40 Top 10 hits. On May 30, 1986, Tracey's father died shortly after coming off the stage, but his children carried on, and with Tracey singing lead on most of the group's hit singles, she took the Family Brown to even loftier heights when she sang with renewed strength on the award-winning 1988 album THESE DAYS. The dissolution of Family Brown coincided with the end of the vinyl era, but what an era it had been for Tracey Brown. In addition to the 13 CCMA Group of the Year Awards and four CCMA Entertainer of the Year Awards, there were CCMA Album of the Year wins in 1982 and 1983 for RAISED ON COUNTRY, 1984 for REPEAT AFTER ME, and 1986 for FEEL THE FIRE.

In 1988 and early 1989, Family Brown swept *all* of the major Canadian award shows: the CCMAs, the Junos, and *RPM* magazine's Big Country Awards. "The single sweep of all three awards is likely a first in Canadian country music," declared *Country Music News* editor Larry Delaney. "The awards came on the strength of three successive number one singles: *Til I Find My Love, Let's Build A Life Together* and *Town Of Tears* from their hit BMG album THESE DAYS." Tracey's husband, Randall Prescott, the harmonica and banjo player in Family Brown and father of their two children, had taken over the Family Brown production duties in 1988 and begun what would be a continuous run as CCMA Producer of the Year that runs to the present day. Of course, he was only adding to a clutter of award trophies that was becoming a storage problem at the couple's Clayton, Ontario home.

Tracey's 1990 duet with Terry Carisse was the Number 2 song on the *Country Music News* Top 100 Hits of 1990. She would next form Tracey Prescott & Lonesome Daddy with Randall and her brother, Barry. The trio won a Juno Award as top Canadian country group in 1993 on the basis of their debut album. This band name was changed to Prescott-Brown largely because Tracey herself didn't feel comfortable having her name more prominently displayed than Barry or Randall. Eventually, Barry would leave the group and Prescott-Brown's 1994 CD ALREADY RESTLESS was their last under that banner. Once again, there were radio hits, including *There Ain't Much You Can Do About Love, Broken String Of Pearls*, and *39 Days*.

Most of these hits were on the Canadian charts, but during the mid-1980s several efforts were made to get the Ottawa-based group on the U.S. charts. Larry Delaney describes the process in a May 1994 cover story: "As part of the Family Brown contingent, Tracey was able to chart seven singles, including the Top 30 *But It's Cheating*, in the early and mid-1980s on *Billboard's* country charts. There was also the much-acclaimed duet with Willie Nelson . . . but never a major breakthrough." Tracey recalls that duet, fondly. "We were in Texas. The two producers that we had at that time liked the studio down there and one of them, Neil Wilburn, liked to golf. Willie had bought this whole complex right next to the golf course, Pedernales Studios, and he just happened to be around that weekend. Randall ran into Willie in the washroom and Willie said, 'Oh, are you all from Canada?' And Randall said he should come into the studio and listen, and he did. We didn't even ask. Willie just said, 'I'd like to play along with that song, *Would You Love Us Together*.' And he did. We were just sitting there with our mouths hangin' open. It was a huge thrill." Through the weekly Family Brown television show, Tracey met many other country stars. "We had a lot of wonderful guests over the years. We had the Judds, just when they were breaking in. It was only a few months later that *Mama He's Crazy* took off like wildfire. We had Ronnie Milsap do the show. Harlan Howard did the show. He's an amazing songwriter and he's *so* humble."

The transition from Tracey Prescott & Lonesome Daddy to Prescott-Brown had brought up an issue concerning humility for Tracey. "The way that we were raised and brought up in the business was that nobody was better than anybody else. I guess there's up and down sides of that. If I got too much attention, I felt guilty, you know, or I felt that it was kind of weird. And because I was the youngest, I got a lot of attention. I always thought it was kind of hard on my sister. So, I tried to downplay it. A lot of people would ask, 'Are you ever going to do your own album?' And for years I didn't want to. I liked being a team player. I liked being part of a process, a team."

When push finally came to shove and Tracey took the plunge, it was her husband, Randall, who found the song that would kick her solo project off. "It's funny," says Tracey, "because Randall heard that song when Sherri Jeacocke, one of the co-writers of *Woman's Work*, released it as a pop single in the 1980s. He thought the song would make a great country record and he played it for me. I didn't share his enthusiasm. He had to keep persuading me. A few years later, I went into the studio reluctantly to do that song. The band started clicking on it and I said, 'I still don't know if it's my kind of song.' And my son said, 'Would you lighten up and relax and have fun with it?' He was so right!" When she had nailed her vocal and the mix was done, Tracey got into her album project with renewed enthusiasm. "The video for *Woman's Work* was filmed in Puerto Vallarta in March 1998. We have tortilla makers in it. We have women washing clothes in the river. And we used some old footage from the Canadian mint where women are making money, dollar bills. Women making money. Women in the work-force back in the 1950s. . . . Even though it's drudgery for the women doing the same work over and over, there's a real community. The women are all really tight with each other. And the families are really tight. As you know, in Mexico, family is number one. In the third video we shot down there our own kids are in it. My daughter is 12 and she sings. My boy is 15 and he plays percussion with us. . . . We own our own studio (Lakeside Studios), and during the time where I haven't been performing, we shot 33 videos. We did everything from finding video locations to catering the video shoots. And I got into editing videos. I did all the rough editing on *Woman's Work*. I got into that. It was really fun." *Woman's Work* became Tracey Brown's signature song.

A woman's work is never done
I don't stop (I take care of everyone)
A woman's work is never, never done

Stayin' home ain't easy and who's to say
It don't count if the job don't pay
Working double duty doing overtime
All I need is what I'm getting from you . . .
All I need is some affection
Coming in my direction . . .

(written by Sheree Jeacocke/Lou Pomanti/BJ Cooke)

SYLVIA TYSON & QUARTETTE

Sylvia Fricker was born on September 19, 1940 in Chatham, Ontario and began her professional career in the late 1950s singing in Toronto folk music clubs, where she met her future husband, Ian Tyson, and formed the duo, Ian & Sylvia, now widely known through their signature tune *Four Strong Winds*. Ian & Sylvia introduced the songs of Gordon Lightfoot to a world-wide audience when his *Early Morning Rain* became the title of their third album. When Ian & Sylvia played the Newport Folk

Festival in 1963, they had hit the big time and were in demand to play the lucrative college circuit where folksingers like Joan Baez and jazzers like Dave Brubeck were hugely popular in the 1960s.

Syvia remembers writing her first hit song. "*You Were On My Mind* was the first song I ever wrote," Sylvia remembers. "My accountant has been asking me to write another that big ever since. *Four Strong Winds* wasn't an immediate hit. It was a slow build. Vanguard Records was not into putting out singles. We sold a lot of albums. Our second album even charted, which surprised everybody. Joan Baez charted, but other than that . . . Vanguard's records didn't chart. Their big idea for promotion was to put an ad in *Evergreen Review*. So, we weren't exactly putting out singles. *You Were On My Mind* had been out on one of our albums for a couple of years and we were driving along the coast highway when we heard We Five singing it. It was a surprise!"

In 1967, at the height of their folk music success, Ian & Sylvia played Carnegie Hall as an acoustic act. But in 1968 they began adding musicians to their act for their Cafe Au Go Go appearance in New York before launching another campus tour. Their backup band would become known as The Great Speckled Bird and the addition of pedal steel and a rhythm section would begin their move toward country music. "We had reached a point where we felt we'd carried that traditional thing about as far as we could carry it," Sylvia remembers. "We decided that we wanted to record in Nashville. We tried several different studios, just to sort of see what we wanted to do. We got to know some of the players down there and really enjoyed recording there. We had an album that was quite different from anything we'd ever done."

In 1970, Ian & Sylvia were featured on *Nashville North* a CBC-TV show, which would be re-named *The Ian Tyson Show*, for several years, but by 1974 Ian and Sylvia were divorced, and in 1975 the two made their last regular appearance together at The Horseshoe Tavern in Toronto. Beginning in 1974, Sylvia hosted a series of CBC radio and television programs that established her as a respected and knowledgeable authority on Canadian music. In 1975, Sylvia issued her first solo album on Capitol Records, WOMAN'S WORLD, thus announcing her woman's way with music, even though Ian produced the sessions. WIND FROM THE NORTH was her second Capitol release. She then formed her own Salt Records and had more radio hits with *Denim Blue Eyes* in 1987, *Too Short A Ride* in 1988, a duet with Lucille Starr, *Pepere's Mill*, in 1989, and *You Were On My Mind* in 1990. Her album releases included SATIN ON STONE, 1978; SUGAR FOR SUGAR, SALT FOR SALT, 1979; BIG SPOTLIGHT, 1986; YOU WERE ON MY MIND, 1989, and GYPSY CADILLAC in 1992.

In Canada, as a solo artist, Sylvia was regarded as a country singer. She agrees with the designation. "I had a strong grounding in country. The roots of the original material that Ian and I did was Appalachian, which is partly the roots of country music, too."

A 1986 CBC-TV Special marked the first Ian & Sylvia reunion. Taped on August 16th at the Kingswood Theatre in Maple, Ontario, the show featured Emmylou Harris, Judy Collins, Gordon Lightfoot and Murray McLauchlan. At the 1992 Juno Awards, Ian & Sylvia were inducted into the Canadian Music Hall of Fame. In the 1990s, Sylvia worked with Tom Russell on a book featuring the lyrics of songwriters and the two released a duet *Thrown To The Wolves* in 1991.

In 1993, after being a major player on the Canadian music scene for more than thirty years, Sylvia Tyson literally lucked into what many view as her most endearing project when a one-time songwriters appearance with Caitlin Hanford, Cindy Church, and Colleen Peterson resulted in the formation of Quartette, an act which has gone on to record four CDs and regularly tours the country from coast to coast. I first heard the foursome at a CCMA showcase set in 1993 and instantly fell for the clear, rich harmonies and the unfettered freedom of an acoustic act of songwriters just letting it all hang out without any thoughts in their mind about what music you should be making to win grants or gain airplay. It was my kind of country. Contrary to all the rules, Quartette tracks like *Red Hot Blues* and *Runaway Heart* received a surprising amount of airplay on 'new country' radio stations. During the summer of 1994 the four women played the Edmonton Folk Festival where they appeared on stage with Canadian folk legend Joni Mitchell performing Mitchell's classic song *The Circle Game*. When Colleen Peterson was lost to the group in 1996, she was replaced by Gwen Swick.

In 1993, after that initial songwriters night, the four women set out to record their debut album in a unique manner. They had been through the wringer, so to speak, in the past, often held ransom by males in the music business. This time, they wanted artistic control over the music they would make on record. "We approached the various funding agencies," says Sylvia, "but those kinds of things take time, so we thought we would become adventurous and we approached some investors. Quartette has been very successful for our investors. It has worked out very well. We just do what we want to do. Nobody tells us what to do."

I also had the good fortune to hear Quartette at the Centennial Theatre in North Vancouver during their Christmas touring schedule in 1998. Sylvia, Cindy, Caitlin, and Gwen held the audience in thrall for a full two hours. Sylvia seems to enter a trance when performing with this act, picking up various hand drums, shakers or an accordion to provide just enough percussion or melodic color to augment the other's guitars. The four singers' harmonies either chill you to the bone or warm your heart.

CINDY CHURCH   Cindy Church was born in Bible Hill, Nova Scotia where, she has said, her early musical influences included Wilf Carter, Hank Snow, Kitty Wells, and Ian & Sylvia. When she was 18, Cindy moved west to Vancouver Island where she gradually worked her way into a singing career. Along the way, she learned how to play the electric bass. Meeting Nathan Tinkham in 1984 led to a full-time career in music, and she moved to Turner Valley, Alberta, a Rocky Mountain foothills community that was already a hot-bed of independent-minded musicians like David Wilkie and Amos Garrett. Just a few miles down Highway 22 from Turner Valley, in Longview, Alberta, Ian Tyson had settled down to raising quarterhorses. Cindy was soon to be on stage with one of her childhood heroes.

Ian Tyson was quick to recognize Cindy's unique vocal talents. She sang harmony vocals on the former folksinger's definitive cowboy music albums COWBOYOGRAPHY, I OUTGREW THE WAGON, and AND STOOD THERE AMAZED. After four years touring in Tyson's road band, Cindy banded together with Nathan Tinkham and Turner Valley mandolin whiz, David Wilkie, to form an acoustic trio they called the Great Western Orchestra. "Ian was always really great at exposing what I did to his audiences," Cindy says, "but The Great Western Orchestra was the first time that my voice was being heard on record, really." In 1989 the first single from the trio's self-titled album, GREAT WESTERN ORCHESTRA, featured Cindy singing Roger Miller's *Train Of Life*. Canadian country radio eagerly playlisted this fresh new vocalist with the jazzy acoustic cowgirl approach. "It was really embraced," says Church, "and you know, when we originally put that album out, we did it just to sell off the stage. We wanted to do something that was a cross-section, a real representation of what we sounded like live. It was a big surprise to us when it took on a life of its own."

Where Tyson had created a cowboy mystique with his new traditionalist recordings during the 1980s, evoking vivid pictures of the Old West and painting Charlie Russell-esque musical portraits of the fading realm of the cowboy, Cindy Church evoked equally vivid portraits made even more poignant when a female vocalist tackled songs like Marty Robbins' *Big Iron*, a classic cut from Robbins' 1959 album GUN FIGHTER BALLADS (AND TRAIL SONGS). People heard the same sort of individualism in Cindy's unique, haunting vocals that they had earlier identified and cherished when Emmylou Harris first began recording, but Cindy didn't exactly sound like Emmylou. She stood alone on the Canadian horizon.

Nathan and Cindy's original song *Ride On* and Billy Cowsill's *Vagabond* followed *Train of Life* up the charts. When the trio disbanded, Cindy began to issue her own CDs on Canada's top independent label, Stony Plain Records, again distinguishing herself with a bravely acoustic cowgirl approach on LOVE ON THE RANGE and JUST A LITTLE RAIN. *Trying To Rope The Wind*, from her second album, written by Tim Williams and Laurie Thain, would be much heard on the radio in 1996, but there were many good songs on that album. "*Radiates*," Cindy once told me, "which is *my* favorite cut on the album, was written by Chris Whitely who is Caitlin Hanford's husband and a wonderful musician. I think a lot of people don't realize how much Chris writes, how many wonderful songs he has written. Every now and then he comes out with these little gems. *Radiates* is a little gem, it is beautiful. So, the album is kind of an eclectic mix." She would reap benefits later from a session she did with a young Calgary singer named Paul Brandt. Cindy sang harmonies on the tracks that got Paul his major label deal in the United States. A year later, hot new Nashville star, Brandt, would employ Cindy Church to open for him on a 20-city Canadian tour.

Michelle Wright was born in Sylvia Tyson's home town, Chatham, Ontario, but raised in Merlin, a small farming community near **MICHELLE WRIGHT** the city of Windsor and not far from the Ontario-Michigan border. At age 13, Michelle took up the guitar and was soon singing in a band called the Marquis. Her early influences were country, which she heard on Hamilton station CHAM, and rhythm & blues, which she listened to on Detroit stations. She would later refer to her distinctive 'new country' sound as "cruise music," citing a blend of country and Motown as her influences.

In college, she continued to perform with local bands and was spotted by an American agent who offered her a job fronting a traveling band. She toured for three years working for that agent in both the United States and Canada before forming her own band. The move caught the ear and eye of Brian Ferriman, who signed her to his Toronto-based Savannah Music Group.

Michelle lucked out when she met one-half of the Nashville-based songwriting team of Rick Giles and Steve Bogard after performing at a regional country music festival. In January 1986, Giles and Bogard invited Wright to Nashville where they began putting together the material for her first album. Wright came up with a $9,600 cash prize from a talent contest in London, Ontario and used the money to record her first three Giles-Bogard tracks. "Everything was in place," she told Delaney. "I had experience, a band, a manager, and songwriter-producers, all I needed was the money, and there it was!"

Michelle Wright's first single *I Want To Count On You* resulted in a CCMA Vista Rising Star nomination. Her next release *New Fool At An Old Game* did even better at radio and resulted in a 1987 CCMA nomination as best Female Vocalist. The following year, her cruise music recording of Andy Kim's *Rock Me Gently* was a crossover hit in Canada. Michelle's first album, DO RIGHT BY ME, was released on the Savannah label, one of the last vinyl albums pressed in Canada, and Michelle's *I Wish I Were Only Lonely, The Rhythm of Romance*, and *Do Right By Me* were all listed in the Top 50 of the *Country Music News* Top 100 Cancountry hits of 1989. By then she'd been nominated for several CCMAs, two Juno awards, and had won the *RPM* Big Country award as top Female Country Vocalist. Michelle was moving on up: Reba covered three of the songs Michelle had recorded, including *New Fool At An Old Game*, and in 1989 Michelle toured as an opening act for Randy Travis.

The recording of Michelle's hits by Reba caused a minor controversy, reported in *Country Music News* by Larry Delaney, who in a split-feature interview with Reba and Michelle posed the questions about this odd circumstance. Had Michelle's singles been used to pitch the songs to Reba? Was that ethical? Reba told Delaney, "I wasn't aware of it until now! When the songs were pitched to me they were presented as being totally new material, not previously recorded. I suppose that meant not previously recorded by an American artist. In any case, I choose the songs I want to record on the strength of the songs themselves and how they would fit my style and what I want to present in an album. These are certainly top-notch songs, and I'm glad to see that some other people thought so highly of them, as well. In fact, my next single is scheduled to be *New Fool At An Old Game* and I see that this was a number one hit in Canada last year for this artist. Let's see if I can make it happen again for that song!" Reba McEntire's *New Fool At An Old Game* was released on January 14, 1989 and climbed to the number one position on the *Billboard* Hot Country Singles chart. Wright told Delaney, "I'm just tickled to learn that Reba saw fit to record these songs. We all know that Reba must receive a busload of songs to choose from and if she picked three of the same songs I happened to have recorded, too, then they must be really good tunes."

Michelle Wright next caught the fancy of Arista Records' Tim Dubois, and *New Kind Of Love* from her Arista debut album MICHELLE WRIGHT was a Top 40 hit on the *Billboard* Hot Country Singles chart. At the Edmonton CCMAs in 1990, Michelle was named CCMA Female Vocalist of the Year, ending K.D. Lang's two-year grip on the award. One year later, at the 1991 CCMAs, Michelle would again be named Female Vocalist of the Year. *New Kind Of Love* was the Single of the Year and MICHELLE WRIGHT was the CCMA Album of the Year. Her distinctive videos were in heavy rotation on CMT. In Nashville, Michelle showcased at Fan Fair before heading off to the North Dakota State Fair with Lyle Lovett and Dan Seals. The city of Chatham would declare Monday, May 27, 1991 as Michelle Wright Day.

The release of her second Arista CD NOW AND THEN in 1991 began a massive assault on charts all over North America with *Take It Like A Man*, which went right up the *Billboard* country chart to the Top 10, while the video hit the top of the CMT chart.

> I met someone the other night
> Started thinking he was Mr Right . . . wrong! . . .
> He's got a wife he forgot to mention . . .
> Girl, leave that fool alone
> Well, I keep hoping and telling myself
> Somewhere there's one good one left
> Cause my poor heart needs somebody who can
>
> Take it like a man, steady and strong . . .
> Someone wise enough to understand
> If you want this woman's heart
> Take it like a man

(written by Tony Haselden)

By June 1992, all three Canadian trades — *Country Music News*, *The Record*, and *RPM* magazine — had Michelle at number one. At the 1992 CCMAs in Calgary, Michelle Wright would haul in her third straight CCMA Female Vocalist of the Year Award and her single and video for *Take It Like A Man* would win awards, too. This was the year Garth Brooks finally knocked Rita MacNeil from the top selling album foreign or domestic category with his Capitol/EMI release ROPE THE WIND. Garth flew into Calgary and made an on-camera appearance to accept his award in person. It was a wholesome moment in which the man who had taken sales of country music to unprecedented heights mingled with his peers. Garth was charming, saying he'd discovered there was a whole lot of Canadian talent he'd just found out about. When a pre-arranged fire bell rang during his acceptance speech, Brooks quipped, "the school bus is waiting, I gotta go . . . " That night Michelle Wright was front and center, the leader of the new pantheon of Canadian country women music stars.

The follow-up release to *Take It Like A Man* was a song that touched on the topic of adoption and teenage pregnancy, a song imagining what an adopted child from an unwanted teenage pregnancy would be doing 16 years after the whole mess had been shifted from the teenage mother's shoulders. It was the road never traveled by country singers. *He Would Be Sixteen* would be the last Michelle Wright release to make it into the Top 40 regions of the *Billboard* Hot Country Singles chart during the 1990s, although Michelle's fortunes were still seemed to be on the rise in 1993 when she was named the Top New Female Artist by the Academy of Country Music in Los Angeles and became the first Canadian winner of a major U.S. country award in the 1990s.

During this time, there was another controversy brewing back in Canada that would begin to affect all Canadian country recording artists both in Canada and in the United States. The CRTC (Canadian Radio, Television & Telecommunications Commission), a regulatory board responsible for granting licenses to radio and television stations, had ruled in favor of a new Canadian television video network that would broadcast a country video channel (NCN), but through an obscure bureaucratic entanglement this decision would also dictate that CMT would lose their Canadian license. The CCMA convention that September kicked off with a get-acquainted party hosted by TNN and CMT. The two were there in Calgary to mount a protest about CMT being kicked out of Canada by the CRTC. By this time,

QUARTETTE

TRACEY BROWN

MICHELLE WRIGHT

**PATRICIA
CONROY**

**LISA
BROKOP**

FARMER'S DAUGHTER

STEPHANIE BEAUMONT

a backlash had already begun to be mounted in the United States. Wasn't it almost *communist* to have a state decision remove them after nearly ten years of successful operation? Hadn't CMT and TNN been playing a whole lot of Canadian country music videos for all of their audiences in the U.S., Canada, and Europe from day one? What the hell did 'Free Trade' mean, anyway?

Surely, someone would have to pay some retribution for this. I feared it would be singers like Michelle Wright, Joan Kennedy, and Patricia Conroy. Michelle did host the TNN/*Music City Awards*, but soon after that an official statement had been issued to the press stating that Canadian independents would no longer be aired on CMT in the United States. Michelle's new Arista album THE REASONS WHY, which had been released in Canada, was never released in the U.S. I heard through the grapevine that, "Arista doesn't hear hit songs on the package . . ." Of course, record executives can make mistakes. A few years down the line, when Martina McBride covered Michelle's *Safe In The Arms Of Love*, Martina's release went all the way to number 4 on the *Billboard* country chart.

It was really too bad that the singers had paid for the political shenanigans. *Take It Like A Man* had been the perfect vehicle to launch a major career in the U.S. Steven Goldmann has said that it was a breakthrough video production that changed the approach to filming country videos, forever. "It didn't look like any other video," he told *Country Weekly* writer Catherine S. Rambeau. "It was about photography and glamor. I used a film stock and a camera speed no one else was using. And I focused on Michelle's face, eyes, and mouth as she looks at the portraits of men. One of the other directors told me it 'upped the ante', made them want to get better, made them go, 'Wow!' We don't have to just do front porches and pickup trucks . . ."

NCN the *New Country Network* was bought out by CMT, but through further bureaucratic entanglements it was partitioned as CMT Canada. Canadian country videos, although in heavy rotation domestically, are no longer seen in the U.S. on the *real* CMT.

I had the opportunity to interview Michelle in 1995 as she embarked upon a 40-city tour of Canada and talked about her career and Canadian country music. "Well, I certainly think that what is kind of cool right now is that the industry here in Canada is growing with myself and Lisa Brokop and Shania Twain and Patricia Conroy and Charlie Major," she noted.

I quipped, "I wondered if you were going to mention a man, Michelle."

"It's kind of funny," she said, "that here in Canada there are all these women and of course in America the market is very dominated by males."

Even though we were doing what we usually did together, which was tape an interview, I felt like I was with an old friend. Michelle has that capacity to make you feel right at home right there on neutral turf in a rented dressing room. Of course, she'd been on the road for a good many of her years on this planet. I thought things were getting altogether too schmaltzy, but I said, "Personally, I like some of the nostalgic stuff, like *The Old Song And Dance*, there's a lot of variety on this album."

Michelle thought about that before she answered. "I'm quite enjoying being a woman and getting older. It gets better with age. I find that I feel better as I get a little bit older and a little bit more settled. And maybe not so uptight or concerned or worried about things. . . . And the traditions will go on and on forever. Children will be born and they will grow up and go off on dates and mom and dad will be scared to death about what's going on and how they are doing. I just felt that that song celebrates the traditions that go on and will always go on. It's a real, real song! I love the part where mom and dad stayed together."

Eight months later in Hamilton during Country Music Week 1995, Michelle was no longer the leading lady of Canadian country music. Shania Twain had already lapped Wright's accomplishments several times with THE WOMAN IN ME, a release that had already in a few short months sold more records than Michelle Wright had in her entire eight-year recording career. Of course, Anne Murray and Michelle Wright had been the women who had first pried those doors open for Shania. That night Shania Twain took home most of the hardware, but Michelle Wright was once again named the Bud Country Fans Choice Entertainer of the Year. Handed her trophy by Canadian novelist Grahame Green, Michelle put it in a nutshell when she said, "It's kinda been a girl's night out, eh!"

PATRICIA CONROY

Born in Montreal, Patricia Conroy surfaced in Vancouver during the late 1980s, first coming to public attention due to stand-out performances with her Patricia Conroy Band, which was so good Patricia won $10,000 worth of recording time from Ron Barkwell, owner of Boone County Cabaret and Gabby's Cabaret, beating out One Horse Blue on the final night of a talent competition. As her touring horizons widened to include festivals from Vancouver Island to Craven, Saskatchewan and the big Texas-style Alberta clubs like Ranchmans in Calgary and Cook County Saloon in Edmonton, she built a loyal fan base, continually improving her performances, changing her show-closing production number from a hugely popular cover of *Suspicious Minds* to an emotionally charged delivery of *Desperado* that had audiences begging for more.

Some said that Patricia sounded like Emmylou, but through a personal involvement with the singer at Bullfrog Studios, where she eventually signed a working agreement with Rana Records, I saw that it was her originality and her sense of fashion, both in her stage costumes and her music, that was the key to her popularity. She soon became a national star, signing to Warner Brothers Canada on the basis of only three independent singles: *My Heart's On Fire* and *Baby, Come On Back*, released as vinyl 45s, then *A Thousand Trails*, released on the Rana Records CD compilation WEST COAST COUNTRY VOLUME ONE. She issued three CDs on Warner Canada. The first was BLUE ANGEL produced in Ontario by longtime CCMA Producer of the Year, Randall Prescott. Her second Warner album, BAD DAY FOR TRAINS, was one of Randall's truly brilliant productions, and the title track, co-written by Conroy and Ralph Murphy, hit big in Canada, with the video receiving heavy airplay on CMT in both North America and Europe. Gretchen Peters' *My Baby Loves Me (Just The Way That I Am)* was a huge hit in Canada for Conroy. Bob Funk and Bruce Miller's *What Do You Care* and Patricia's own *Blank Pages* both became Cancountry number ones. I was very happy to see Patricia at the 1994 CCMAs in Calgary where she proudly handed me a pre-release copy of her third Warner Music CD YOU CAN'T RESIST. Recording at Morin Heights, Quebec, in what used to be called Le Studio, she had fashioned tracks that were almost dance-track grooves, yet were country to the core. Lyle Lovett's *You Can't Resist It* with Kenny Aronoff's driving drums was relentless. The lead single, *Somebody's Leaving*, written by Kostas and Matraca Berg, was a smouldering production. Tom Kimmel and Jim Pittman's *The Bridge* had these Motown underpinnings. The cut that did the most for Patricia Conroy, however, was a cookin' track she called *Keep Me Rockin'*. Produced by Mike Wanchic and engineer Justin Niebank, this was first class product, and different, too. It was Patricia Conroy music. If the Warner label in Nashville had released this CD and promoted it as thoroughly as Mercury Nashville did Shania Twain's THE WOMAN IN ME, history might have turned out a whole lot differently.

Patricia had her sights set on the international country market, but she was being held back in the U.S. by her Canadian record deal. That I was involved with her publicity and introduced her to key musicians like Billy Cowsill prior to recordings sessions is something of which I can be proud, though if I had not been there doing it, someone would have. I was on Patricia Conroy's tour bus in the artist's compound behind the main stage at the Merritt Mountain Music Festival when Patricia relayed the glowing news that her CD YOU CAN'T RESIST had begun to sell very well in the United States on the Intersound label, some 40,000 copies in less than two months, where Warner Canada had only managed to flog a mere 35,000 in two full years. Not long after that, a few months, perhaps, I learned through the grapevine that Patricia had not renewed her option with Warner.

On Monday, April 7, 1997, Patricia made the front page of a Vancouver daily, the *Province*, but the news was bad: she had been viciously attacked by a dog while she had been walking on a beach in Gaeta, Italy. Bob Funk had saved the singer's life, but she was in critical condition, recovering from multiple bites and lacerations to her head, back and arms. Patricia had been treated at a local hospital before being transferred to a U.S. Naval hospital in Italy. The first post-attack photo I saw of Patricia Conroy was published in *Country Music News* a few months later. Paul Kennedy, a regular columnist for the publication reported that he had spoken with Patricia who had been on Prince Edward Island for a concert. There was a short interview between Paul Kennedy and the recovering singer. "What was the most difficult part of the recovery period?" Kennedy asked. I winced as I read: "The recurring nightmares were bad! I just never in my life felt that someone or something hated me enough to want to kill me! I never felt that before. I've been lucky to be well-loved and to have a lot of friends. It just kind of scared me to think that anybody in this world would want to do me that much harm. I love dogs. So, it was especially difficult to accept that one tried to kill me."

"Could the situation have been even worse?" asked Paul.

"Absolutely, it could have been a defenceless child instead of me. I don't know why things like that happen, but I think there was an angel watching over me. I was taken and held by the hand and told what to do with this situation and I think I did well."

Was she ever concerned about disfigurement, Kennedy asked, in his own less-disturbing words. "For some strange reason," Patricia said, "as soon as my head wounds got stitched up, I just assessed my wounds and said to myself, it could have been worse. Now, you just heal! I really looked positively at the situation. I really didn't expect to handle it as well as I did, so, maybe, I'm a stronger person than I thought I was."

When Paul turned to less disturbing questions, I began to put the paper down, but his next one had caught my eye. "What was it like to have your *I Wanna Be The One* video go number one on CMT Europe?" I hadn't realized. My old pal, Patricia Conroy was doing pretty well ... and she was alive.

When I learned that Patricia had released her new album WILD AS THE WIND, I breathed another sigh of relief. A few months later, I found myself in the Calgary audience for her first CMT special and heard the new songs. *Direction Of Love* and *Ain't Nobody Like You* were particularly strong. If she'd lost anything at all in her voice, looks or enthusiasm *I* couldn't tell.

A nother singer from British Columbia, Lisa Brokop, was born in Surrey on June 6, 1973. By the time Lisa was 12, she was climbing **LISA BROKOP** up onto stages and singing with the country artists who were making hit records in nearby Vancouver. As a reporter covering that scene for *Country Music News*, I remember Brokop as a gangly teenager with a voice you had to hear to believe. In 1992, when her first Nashville album, EVERY LITTLE GIRL'S DREAM, was released on Patriot Records, Lisa remembered her early years. "Mostly, at that age, I just wanted to have fun. But, ever since about age eight or nine, when I heard about this word *Nashville*, this place, I had no idea where it was, but I knew that was where the country music people went ... and that's where I wanted to go. So, from then on, that was my goal. And somehow I ended up sitting in with bands like Bootleg and all sorts of other people, and just hoping that someday I would get to where I am now. And, that's where I am."

Bootleg, one of the top Canadian country bands of the era, was fronted by singers Ron Irving and Gerry King, one of many West Coast recording acts during those years. For a few short years, nearly 25 percent of the Canadian cuts on the Canadian country charts were recorded in Vancouver studios; even K.D. Lang moved to Vancouver and recorded her 1989 *Torch & Twang* album at a local studio. In 1987 Country Music Week came to Vancouver for the first time in its 20-year history. Lisa was 14 and thrilled just to be seated in the Centennial Theatre audience for the national television live broadcast of the annual event. In a few short years, she would be up there in the lights and seen from coast to coast delivering a show-stopping performance of Tammy Wynette's *Stand By Your Man*.

Of course, for every girl who has that Nashville dream there are thousands who never even get to Nashville to take in a show at the Opry, let alone to record with producers like Jerry Crutchfield. For years, I have wondered what the special ingredient was that made the difference between a Lisa Brokop and the rest of the pack. Lisa has an answer. "I think many of the successful people are born with it. I can never ever remember not wanting to be in this business and not wanting to be successful. It's in your blood."

Ron Irving's song, *Daddy Sing To Me*, the sparkling acoustic arrangement worked out by producer Larry Wayne Clark, and Lisa's inspired vocals were the ideal combination for launching her career on Clark's indie label, Brainchild Records. This single was one of the last 45 rpm vinyl records to be pressed in Canada. The debut release climbed confidently toward the top of the charts and hung around for a record-setting 24 weeks. Lisa Brokop was next paired with award-winning songwriter and producer Hagood Hardy. She co-starred with Jim Byrnes and Kim Coates in the Canadian feature film *Harmony Cats* and collaborated with Peter McCann on seven tracks to fill out her first CD, MY LOVE, which was released in Canada on her own indie label, Libre Records.

Brokop's collaboration with Peter McCann originally came about when Nashville-based songwriters McCann, Ralph Murphy, Pat Alger, Bobby Wood, and Richard Leigh came to Vancouver as part of a radio station promotion. CKWX's Ted Farr had put together a five-year deal whereby winners of a local songwriting contest would co-write with one of the 'Nashville Five'. Lisa won a section of the contest and her co-write turned out to be a radio hit. McCann had already seen his songs recorded by Reba McEntire, K.T. Oslin, Crystal Gayle, and many others.

At the 1990 BCCMA awards show, Lisa Brokop won her first two awards: the Ray McAuley Memorial Horizon Award as best new artist and the Gospel Award for her recording of *Amazing Grace*, the flip side of *Daddy Sing To Me*. In 1992, Lisa made her first music video to support the release of *Time To Come Back Home*. Her film role in *Harmony Cats* served as a preparation to working with producer Jerry Crutchfield, but it was the footage from another performance that won the veteran producer over. Lisa remembers the incident vividly. "Just before the Christmas of 1992 I went down to Nashville to do a showcase, and we invited as many industry people as we could. We knew that Liberty Records had some interest. The main focus was for them. We did the showcase and found out that no one had come. I thought, oh great, it's just going to take that much longer, you know how things go. But it turned out that one of their A&R people *had* come to the showcase and was impressed. The next day I did the *Nashville Now* show on TNN with Ralph Emery and we had the footage sent over to Jerry Crutchfield at Liberty. He was very impressed with that. And, he basically got me the deal."

Crutchfield, himself, heaped praise on the Surrey singer, telling journalist LuAnn Reid in an October 1994 cover story printed in *Country Wave* magazine that, "Lisa is the most impressive new female singer I've heard in a long time."

News of Lisa's major label deal was the talk of the town in Vancouver and everyone who had heard the singer looked forward to hearing EVERY LITTLE GIRL'S DREAM. When Lisa Brokop's first single *Give Me A Ring Sometime* was released and her first major label CD was in the stores, her fans believed she was going to be the next superstar. When Lisa's bus pulled into the entertainment capital of the world to play Boulder Station, she saw her name and a video clip flashing at the tourists on a huge Vegas video screen. She toured constantly, often opening for stars like George Strait and Alan Jackson. "With Alan Jackson it was really quite a thrill," she told me. "You really can't get used to something like that! You get out there and there's thousands of people. . . . We were in Auburn Hills, Michigan, which is just outside of Detroit, and I guess at that point *Take That* was the number one request on the radio station there. When we started the song, the place just went wild. It was really exciting."

Lisa Brokop seemed to be on her way to genuine stardom as a Nashville country singer, with her CDs selling as far away as Tokyo, where on one chart she even out-sold Garth Brooks for one reporting period. Three years, two CDs, and seven singles after Lisa's U.S. debut on Patriot Records, she no longer had a record deal. In the Vancouver *Province* writer John P. McLaughlin reported that "she fired her long-time manager, Paul Mascioli, and then dissolved her relationship with the label. The reason? In spite of continued solid success in Canada, she just wasn't breaking through in the big American market." As Brokop told McLaughlin, "It did freak me out a little bit. . . . There was part of me saying, well, you might not get a second shot. And then there was the bigger part of me saying, this can't be it." The plucky singer did get on track, signing a new management deal with Bill

Carter in 1997, and shortly after that, Sony Nashville vice-president Paul Worley signed Lisa to a deal with Columbia Records.

In 1998, right on the heels of the release of her first Columbia CD, she was nominated by the CCMA, along with Shania Twain, Terri Clark, Michelle Wright, and Tracey Brown, for Best Female Vocalist award. On the 1998 CCMA Awards show, Lisa sang *How Do I Let Go* the initial Canadian release from WHEN YOU GET TO BE ME.

STEPHANIE BEAUMONT

Stephanie Beaumont is one of the bubbliest people I have ever met. She quit a very attractive job in the corporate advertising world to seek out a career in country music. The combination of her effervescent personality and a string of hit singles and videos from her 1996 indie debut LOVE AND DREAMS has catapulted her into the spotlight of the Canadian country scene in three short years. When she was featured on the November 1996 cover of *Country Music News* she told Larry Delaney, "I was in corporate marketing. Essentially, I was an account director. My tasks went all the way from Fed Ex-ing out packages to sitting in front of presidents of international corporations and presenting them with corporate identities. It was exciting and challenging. A lot of 80-hour work-weeks and we dealt with everything from broadcast television to print advertising, brand identities, product launches . . . you name it, we did it. But I really loved to sing. One of my clients was the CN Tower in Toronto, and at an event there I slipped a tape to one of the local radio personalities. He introduced me to Randall Prescott. I met Randall on a Friday. On the following Saturday, I was in his studio in the Ottawa Valley cutting the title track for my first CD." In 1996 she was nominated for the CCMA Vista Rising Star award, which Terri Clark would win.

During my interview with Stephanie at Country Music Week in 1998, Stephanie's image was all over the place, not the least important of these locations being the cover of *The Record*, the Canadian equivalent of *Billboard* magazine. Stephanie explained her marketing approach: "One of the biggest principles in marketing is a consistent message. We have one central visual image which we have used in the marketing of the second album, WAY OVER MY HEART. It is the CD cover and we've used it everywhere. It is the same image that appeared on the cover of *The Record* magazine on their latest issue. If you are building up a recognition factor, people need to see a TV commercial, or any image, about six or seven times, so that they will retain it."

Stephanie's first album on the Iron Music label was an indie. With her second album WAY OVER MY HEART she chose to remain independent but to cut a distribution deal with BMG Canada, leaving herself open to cut a future major label deal with any of the U.S. labels. Beaumont is the prototypical urban country female, wise beyond her years as a result of her corporate background, and totally at home when she finds herself in front of a camera. Stephanie was now saying, "This cover and this album, WAY OVER MY HEART, is definitely 'Beaumont.' It's part of the lead single, *Already In Way Over My Heart*. Our primary focus for the album launch is Canada. The next will probably be Europe. We have a U.K. distributor and also one in Australia. I'm not going to kid myself. America is a real tough market to break, if you don't have the support of a major label down there. We have just so many dollars. We could put product out, but you can't just put product out. You have to get radio play. You have to have advertising. Otherwise, no one will know it is in the stores."

At the 1998 CCMA conference in Calgary, she filmed her own CMT Special backstage during the Awards show, an idea Beaumont had conceived of herself and pitched successfully to CMT, another iteration of her image. While she is totally in control of her own career, it would be wrong to form the impression that her career is all business.

"For me," she says, "it's only been three years since I started. I know I have a sense of business, but I'm real emotional, too, when it comes to the music. I am writing, now. I did have a co-write on the first album: *I'm Tearing At The Heart Of Me*. I wrote that with Stewart Harris. I had always written poetry, but that was my first song. . . . On this new album, WAY OVER MY HEART, I co-wrote *You And Me And Love* with Jeffrey Steele. He's the former lead singer of the band Boy Howdy and one of my producers. I originally had it so . . . perfect. When I sat down with Jeffrey, he said, 'You know, there really needs to be some conflict.' So, we changed it around a little. I co-wrote two other songs with Lynn and Kerry Chater. One of them is too country for me, it would be perfect for someone like Julian Austin. The song title, *Should Have Pulled The Chute By Now*, came from something we used to say in corporate marketing. I love country music, but what I do is 'new country', and I really wanted a consistent package, an emotional thread that goes through the whole album, and a 'consistent creative promise' which is totally a marketing term. For me 'new country' is a term that works. I came into the business when the boundaries were totally expanding. Totally.

Three years earlier, and I might have had a really hard time at country radio, but then, again, I don't know. There were some songs that we left on the cutting room floor, so to speak, one of them someone like Deana Carter could do to a tee. But I am on the lite end of the 'new country', definitely, and you're hearing more and more of that on the radio today." In her songs and her videos, Stephanie Beaumont's message is simple: Hey, buy this music, look how happy it makes me when I sing it, dance to it . . . you could be this happy, too. At the end of the year, Stephanie was invited by CMT to co-host their Top 98 videos of 1998 program filmed at Banff, Alberta.

FARMER'S DAUGHTER The trio Farmer's Daughter features Angela Kelman, Shauna Rae Samograd, and Jake Leiske, a 'new country' act who are closer to the Pointer Sisters singing country than they are to the Dixie Chicks. In the five years since this West Coast group was first heard on the radio, they have shot to the top of the rankings with major awards, a television special, and an overseas tour performing to Canadian peacekeeping troops. The trio surfaced in Vancouver during early 1994 when they released their debut indie CD GIRLS WILL BE GIRLS. Their manager, Gerry Leiske, Jake's dad, had already tasted success in both the United States and Canada with a touring and recording act known as The Heritage Family Singers, a gospel group with ten albums released on the Word label, before he formed Farmer's Daughter with Angela, Shauna Rae, and Jake. To build the myth, though, the jovial Leiske would often tell journalists he was just an old sod farmer from the prairie regions.

Early Farmer's Daughter releases to Canadian country radio caught the immediate attention of music directors and singles like Bruce Miller's *I Want To Hold You*, a remake of the Dusty Springfield hit *Son Of A Preacher Man*, and the title track *Girls Will Be Girls*, with a boisterous spirit, were heavily playlisted.

> There's a hand-me-down lesson
> My mama taught to me
> 'Goes back as far as
> The dawn of history
>
> There was this thing about an apple
> And a snake up in a tree

And Adam said what in the world
Am I goin' do about Eve

A voice said: 'Girls will be girls
It's out of our hands
You can control
What you can't understand . . .

(written by Montans / Reeves / Allison)

Supporting videos were even more popular. A controversial video release of *Borderline Angel*, a song written by Tony Rudner and LuAnn Reid, featured Angela singing lyrics about a single mom turned hooker who sold her body on the sordid meat-market of the Granville Street Mall in Vancouver in order to make ends meet and feed her baby. At first stone-walled by dubious programmers at several video networks, the *Borderline Angel* video eventually saw the light of day and was listed at number 88 on the June 1998 chart of CMT Canada's Top 100 Videos of all Time.

In 1995, the group was nominated for a Juno award and won their first CCMA trophy as winners of the Vista Rising Star Award. A second CD, MAKIN' HAY, was produced at a Vancouver studio by Nashville cat Marcus Hummon and yielded radio hits like *Cornfields Or Cadillacs* and *Inclemency*. By the time the group's third CD THIS IS THE LIFE was released in September 1998, they were signed to a distribution deal with MCA Records in Canada and had won both a Juno and a CCMA award as top country group in Canada.

In Calgary during the 1998 Country Music Week gathering, I taped a short interview with Shauna Rae, Jake and Angela at the Palliser Hotel. For a journalist, an interview with the daughters can prove to be both fun, when doing the taping, and a nightmare to translate later due to the trio's penchant for speaking as one unit with one of the three finishing another's sentence. I began the taping on a serious note, suggesting that the male infrastructure of the country music industry had been for years been preaching, "Women buy the records . . . so, that's why we've got to have lots of male recording artists." Angela said, "What a myth." Jake added, "Women buy fashion magazines. Are their fashion magazines filled with men? No. Women want to know other women." And Angela finished the thought off, "They are proud to see other women excel, especially in a field which is predominantly male."

I asked if the trio had experienced harassment while spending all those days and nights on the road as they did. A twinkle came into Angela's eyes. "I think that *our* males in our team feel that they exist in an all-Farmer's-Daughter world. I'm not just being cheeky, saying that. Our bus is *our* bus and the boys know it's girl world, the boys in the band know that." "And they've all accepted it very well," said Shauna Rae. "We don't have a big stash of male-oriented movies on our bus. We have a big stash of *Absolutely Fabulous* on our bus."

Angela said, "They've all let us talk them into having their hair cut short and do groovy things with us. They let us style them." And Shauna Rae finished the thought. "We've been with Revlon all the time. And we are affiliated with Le Chateau as you know and the boys are all involved with our look onstage. That's a female-oriented thing."

"We've just hired a new guitar player," said Jake, "and the first thing he asked me was, 'When do I get to go to Le Chateau with you girls and get new clothes?' He's not asking about guitars or tapes. He's asking when does he get to go shopping with us!" A chorus of laughter at this, then Angela: "There's a sense and spirit about the three of us that is very, very female that we insist in pulling people into. We never get pulled into the male-dominated side of this industry. We're very aware of the business of this industry and we've been involved with the business from day one. We've made all of our decisions with our manager, Gerry. We've made all of the decisions together."

Jake continued to steer the interview in a more serious direction: "I think right at the very beginning, when we started on a stint in the bar circuit, which we had to do at the start, that we may have run up against some obstacles at that time because people didn't think that a three-chick-trio could handle the atmosphere of a bar. But that myth was dispelled quite quickly. But that situation, right at the beginning, is the biggest wall that we've had to . . ."

"What," said Angela, "you mean when they were screaming, 'Shower?'" Jake, as if now being interviewed by Angela, answered, "No. We've had a few humdingers, though. And we've played some serious skanky rooms, man."

Shauna Rae had been composing her thoughts and now she *was* serious when she said, "The three of us and Gerry started Farmer's Daughter as a partnership, as a unit. And we've built our company up around that. Gerry's the only *guy* in the office. Our controller is female. Our publicist is female. There's the three of us. Our office manager is female. Gerry's sort of an island . . ."

"Gerry's one hundred per cent male," Jake interjected, "but he's been forced to contact that part of his psyche and his degree in psychology has helped him to deal with this whole situation ..."

"How many times," quipped Angela, "have we told him, 'Don't question it. Just do as we're saying?'" And when the laughter died away, again, Shauna Rae continued: "The three of us hired a female lawyer to give us some legal advice ..."

"But that was not a conscious decision," put in Angela. "All of those people were just the best people for the job. Which, to me, says that you can create your own reality."

Now, we were honing in the nitty-gritty, as Jake followed up with, "I think it's been a survival tool for us ... to create our own reality. Because everyone knows that there are huge walls and huge frustrations for artists. We have always been about the music. We are not a cut-and-paste act. It's always been about the music and what we are creating and what we love to sing and how we act on stage. There's never been people coming in to say, 'Okay, you act this way, and you act this way, and you do your hair this way.' This band has never been about that. I think, in an industry that seems to be led and directed that way, especially these days, we had to create everything around us, just to keep from going ... wacko."

It was an unlikely sounding bottom line for three such wackos, but I knew it to be the truth. The first release from THIS IS THE LIFE was to be the really really Pointer Sisters-go-country cut *Freeway*. Later that same night, the daughters' live version of the tune kicked off a special showcase sponsored by TNN at Cowboys nightclub a few blocks from the convention center. The club was packed for Farmer's Daughters' performance and it was truly urban cowgirl stuff right from the get-go with songs like *Cornfields Or Cadillacs* and *Lonely Gypsy Wind* being some of the very best contemporary country you could hope to hear live.

The scheduled second release, *Blue Horizon*, from the new CD is far more traditional than *Freeway*, while a sleeper hiding down near the end of the 12-track CD is Randy Bachman's *Let It Ride*, the number the daughters used to open a recent Pacific Coliseum show in Vancouver. With Bachman guesting on the guitar solo and the daughter's harmony riding a familiar rock & roll classic, it is the track I'd test-market in the United States. And, if I was a betting man, I'd put more than a few markers on Farmer's Daughter.

EIGHTIES LADIES & SINGER-SONGWRITERS

☆ ☆ ☆

While the 1980s country music scene was dominated by the superstar career of Dolly Parton, there were many other women artists who provided country music fans with some of the most wonderful music ever created within the idiom. The Mandrell Sisters brought a sense of show business to their nationally-televised weekly show, and Reba McEntire emerged as Dolly's eventual successor to the newly created title of "Country Music Superstar." Running counter-current to the glitz and glory were a number of female country singers who slugged it out in the trenches, so to speak, carving out rights for country women who were not exactly super but were intent upon changing the working conditions in the country music business for once and for all. Gail Davies, Lacy J. Dalton, Juice Newton, Janie Fricke, and Becky Hobbs were not willing to settle for the ground gained by women who were resigned to singing 'answer songs,' duets, and backing vocals. But it was K.T. Oslin, the most unlikely country star of all time, who laid it all on the line when she dropped all pretense of inferiority and second-class citizenship in her song-writing and declared that women could be sexual predators, too. They could feel good about expressing their sexuality and they could hold their heads high while doing it.

As the decade progressed, more and more women came forward with songs written from a female point of view. Spurred on by the acceptance of K.T. Oslin as both a songwriter *and* a recording artist, they stepped forward from the confines of the jingle singing sessions and backing vocal sessions that had become accepted niches for women working in the country music business to astound the world in the 1990s. Singer songwriters like Matraca Berg, Kim Richey, Jess Leary, Gretchen Peters, Nanci Griffith, and Lucinda Williams composed lyrics and music for some of the greatest songs performed in this era.

A child prodigy who was proficient at several stringed instruments, Barbara Mandrell was born in Houston, Texas on Christmas Day, 1948. Raised in California, she gained notoriety as a 12-year-old demonstrating steel guitar at a national convention and playing in Vegas with Joe Maphis. When she was 14, Barbara toured with George Jones and Patsy Cline, bunking with Cline for most of that tour. Her parents, Irby and Mary Mandrell, formed a family band, and Barbara played saxophone, guitar, banjo and bass for the group. The Mandrells toured as far away from their Oceanside, California home as U.S. Armed Forces bases in Vietnam. Members of the Pentecostal faith who celebrated their belief in Jesus through music, the Mandrells created country music that was laced with gospel and rhythm & blues.

BARBARA MANDRELL

When Barbara began a career as a solo artist, she excelled on releases like *Do Right Woman — Do Right Man* and *Treat Him Right*, an answer to Roy Head's *Treat Her Right*. Barbara's cover of Tammy Wynette's *Woman To Woman* was also well-received, but she first hit the number one spot on the *Billboard* country chart with *Sleeping Single In A Double Bed*, the first of half a dozen chart-toppers she would log in her career.

Contradictions abound in Barbara Mandrell's career, not the least of which is the fact that — even though her smooth Vegas-style approach to country was hardly traditional — she became a member of the Opry in 1972. Barbara's best known release is the Kye Fleming-Dennis Morgan penned *I Was Country When Country Wasn't Cool* with a guest vocal contributed by George Jones. During the early 1980s, Barbara Mandrell set new standards for staging country shows when she applied dance choreography and comedy routines — honed during productions of the popular network television show *Barbara Mandrell and the Mandrell Sisters* — to the touring stage. In 1979 and 1980 Barbara won the CMA award as Best Female Vocalist. In 1980 and 1981 she was the CMA's Entertainer of the Year.

At the height of her career in 1984, Barbara Mandrell was severely injured in a motor vehicle accident. It took the support of many friends and family and a whole lot of courage for the singer to recover and return to the stage. However, Barbara did recover and go on to entertain for many years with her Do-Rites band. Although her dance numbers with partner Vince Peterson were as Hollywood as anything Olivia Newton-John and her partner, John Travolta, ever performed, and her music was as facile, to say the least, as Newton-John's, Barbara Mandrell has remained one of the most beloved country entertainers of all time, the eighth most successful woman on country radio and listed by Joel Whitburn as the number 44 country artist of the modern era of country music (1944-1996) in the *New Billboard Book of Top 40 Country Hits*. Barbara's sister, Louise Mandrell, also forged a successful solo career during the 1980s with more than a dozen Top 40 hits. Where Barbara has gone on to an acting career, Louise regularly hosts her own country music shows in her Pigeon Forge theater.

REBA McENTIRE Reba McEntire was slow out of the gate, taking nearly six years after her major label debut until she had her first number one hit with *Can't Even Get The Blues* in 1982. In 1984, Reba won her first CMA award as Best Female Vocalist. After that, the former barrel-racing champion never looked back. Cutting away the dead wood of an early marriage and stuck-in-the-mud management, she took control of her destiny and formed her own management company, Starstruck Entertainment with Narvel Blackstock, her former road manager.

Born on a ranch in Chockie, Oklahoma on March 28, 1954, a teenaged Reba sang with her brother Pake and sister Suzie as the Singing McEntires. When she sang the national anthem at the 1974 National Finals Rodeo in Oklahoma City, Reba was discovered by Red Steagall and signed to Mercury Records. Her first single to chart in the Top 40 was *I Don't Want To Be A One Night Stand* in 1976. During the late 1970s and early 1980s, Reba became hugely popular with the rodeo crowd and gradually carved out a fan base who responded to her simple approach to country.

When she began winning awards and hitting the top of the charts regularly in the mid-1980s, Reba came out of her shell and turned to glitz, creating a stage show renowned for costume changes and a good deal of pomp and circumstance. As feisty as they come, Reba has confronted the Nashville establishment on more than one occasion, but the time she was thwarted from landing a helicopter on a pad at her office building on

Music Row so that she could shave a few minutes off her commute has become a popular story told to the new visitor being shown the sights in Nashville.

In her biography *Reba: My Story*, McEntire credits her mother with talking her out of returning back home during an early trip to Nashville to record her first album. A reluctant beginner as a recording artist, Reba was also a reluctant bride. She describes the poverty years of her liaison with the man who wouldn't take no for an answer, Charlie Battles, as challenging. She would be out on tour with her band, a star in her fans' eyes, but would return home to a life of near-poverty in a small ranch house and an indifferent and uninterested husband. When a few dollars began to accrue, she began to acquire some personal possessions, but found that her hubbie had a penchant to trade away most anything on their property due to what was almost an addiction to swapping stuff. When Charlie traded her prized favorite horse, he was history. Ending the relationship was costly, however, as Reba learned that every penny she had made had been placed in a bank account in her husband's name. She was forced to resign herself to a costly divorce.

Of course, once Reba wrestled control of her career away from those who had controled her, she and her new associates began to address issues as alarming as the fact that for years she hadn't received regular royalty checks from her record label. A switch from Mercury to MCA, where she first worked with Jimmy Bowen in 1984, has continued to the present day. Bowen supported Reba when she complained about production on her albums, and she began to co-produce her sessions. And her 1989 marriage to Narvel Blackstock brought what her first marriage did not bring when Reba became a mother for the first time.

When it became clear that Reba McEntire had succeeded Dolly Parton as country music's female superstar, it also seemed evident that she had inherited a status that seemed to come under fire every which way she turned. Often compared to Dolly, Reba has made very different choices when it came to film roles. Her part in *Tremors*, a horror film that had many in the audience laughing rather than screaming, was scarcely the endearing kind of role that Dolly had portrayed in *9 To 5*, although, *Tremors* and a role as Annie Oakley in *Buffalo Girls*, has led Reba to a hobby. She loves to go out to the skeet-shooting range with the likes of Barbara Mandrell and Linda Davis, shotgun in hand, to blast away at clay pigeons.

Although Reba has sold in excess of 20 million albums, she has also come under criticism for heavy-handedness. She has been cited by her critics for building a monolith office building for Starstruck Entertainment that dwarfs many of the major label head office structures on Music Row. She was accused of distancing herself from her fans when she stopped signing autographs after her shows, stopped attending Fan Fair, and just seemed to be above everybody. When she returned to Fan Fair, but sat on a raised dais and then left many fans standing out in the rain, merely walking away after a few hours of signing, she was raked over the coals by journalists.

At first, Reba had become identified as a woman singing about women's hardships and was often likened to the new traditionalists as being responsible for keeping country music 'country'. In 1988, however, a flirtation with pop material that had come and gone throughout her career went a whole lot further with the release of her self-titled album REBA. A cover of Jo Stafford's 1947 pop hit *Sunday Kind Of Love* drew criticism from traditionalists when it was released as a single. The release of REBA also coincided with the end of McEntire's four-year stint as CMA Female Vocalist of the Year, although follow-up releases of *I Know How He Feels, New Fool At An Old Game*, and a cover of the Everly's *Cathy's Clown* were all number one hits on the *Billboard* country chart. When called to account for abandoning traditional country for pop, Reba, never one to phrase her statements to the press in sugar-coated aphorisms, began to sound just a little bit arrogant. Where Dolly had said, "I'm takin' country with me," Reba answered *her* critics, "I can sing any kind of song, but whatever I sing, it'll come out country."

To give her credit, Reba has remained distinctively Reba throughout the years. She was one of the first to realize the potential of making a music video when she took control of the reins and supervised the making of a video for her single release *Whoever's In New England*. It was her idea, she maintains in her biography, to make the video. It was a timely decision as well as a topnotch production, and the added exposure resulted in Reba's first Grammy win for Best Vocal Performance by A Female in 1986. In 1987, *Whoever's In New England* was named video of the year at the TNN/*Music City News* awards.

On March 16, 1991, tragedy hit the Starstruck organization when seven members of Reba's touring band were fatally injured in a plane crash near the San Diego airport. Reba became the brunt of further criticism when she didn't spend a whole lot of time dressed in black mourning the loss of her employees. A rumor that still circulates to this day has one of her employees on the phone that same night hiring new bandmembers. More eyebrows were raised when she capitalized on the tragedy by granting a cover story interview to a writer from *People* magazine, then proceeded along to the Academy Awards show less than two full weeks after the disaster. A year later, when Reba survived a forced landing of one of her own flights, she recorded FROM MY BROKEN HEART, an album that did well at the cash registers of the music marts but drew criticism from writers in the mainstream press who saw the move as merely further capitalization on the earlier tragedy.

Her loyal fans might ignore and push these harsh realities from their thoughts, but journalists did not. And what had at one time been an open willing-to-praise attitude on the part of the press became hardened into a stance of waiting in ambush for opportunities to slag her latest extravagant exhibition of behavior. By the time Reba came to speak with celebrated CBC-TV interviewer Pamela Wallin in 1998, she, at first, seemed ultra-careful before answering even the most straight-forward of queries. Perhaps, I wondered, while viewing the early footage from the interview, Reba *was* a bit self-conscious that she had might have actually become a greedy, aloof star with little regard for the poverty-stricken people she'd left behind in her dust. She hadn't helped raise funds at the Farm Aid concerts, had she? And she'd been noticeably absent from the CBS *Women of Country* special. Perhaps, she was now concerned that even her female fans might be watching this show with a more critical eye than ever before.

Still, there was something you had to like and admire about Reba as she thoughtfully responded to Wallin's probings. A wily businesswoman, she was one of the richest to ever record country music, wasn't she? She was successful. And she had a quality family life now, sandwiched between flights to stadium shows where she had her own dresser, her own hairdresser, and her own legion of bodyguards. But unlike Anne Murray who had taken a whole lot of time off to spend with her children and many of the other superstar singers who have done the same, Reba just didn't seem to know when enough was enough. By 1996 she had become the third most played female in the history of country radio and was said at that time to have sold some 40 million records, more records than any country female singer, unless of course, you believed the press releases issuing from

Dolly Parton's camp that declared (on the back cover of her best-selling biography) that Dolly had sold more than 50 million records world-wide, a figure that no one at Starstruck was boasting in their press releases.

But had country music become merely a contest measured by the number of records an artist could boast to have sold? It was certainly something that seemed to be driving Garth in the late 1990s. Garth was out in San Diego generating press each time he struck out at the San Diego Padres spring training games. When Garth rolled a grounder through the infield and finally reached first base, it was big news. Was that what country music was all about? You could bet that there were not many rookie pitchers willing to let the 37-year-old Brooks hit their best pitches. In fact, he'd been dusted off and nicked by fastballs more than a few times. In some ways, it was not that different than what was happening with Reba.

Of course, Pamela Wallin was no rookie, and she was serving up big, fat, slow-pitch lobs. Pamela wanted to see her guest become more comfortable, to hit some drives into the outfield, at the very least. When they got past why Reba turned down a role in *Titanic* to questions about *Tremors* and then to the singer's love of skeet shooting, Wallin hit something McEntire felt comfortable about. The two eased through the question of why Reba cut her hair, even though Pamela used that "big hair" phrase. "I feel more frisky, more mischievous," said Reba. "Did her fans object?" Pamela asked. "No, no, they were ready for a change," answered Reba. Looking to the camera audience, she added, "I only got *one* boo at one of my concerts."

When they moved on to rodeoing, Reba had lost her initial wariness and the two women skipped merrily through the gory details of the times Reba had assisted her father when he castrated bulls. "You did actually . . . with your father and other farmhands . . . you would help castrate bulls? And you just did that?" asked Wallin. "Daddy actually did the castration," Reba responded. "He would hand 'em to us and we would put 'em in the bucket. About 30 minutes before we were through, he would say, 'All right girls take 'em to the house.' And we would go clean 'em and take 'em into the house to momma and she would fry 'em up and that's what we had for dinner."

"And that was considered a treat?" Wallin probed.

"No," smiled Reba, "that was what we ate at that time. It was just . . .

our meals. Daddy had a lot of bulls comin' in at that time from Florida and Mississippi and sometimes old Mexico. They came in as bulls and left as steers."

"I'm assuming that this is now not part of your weekly activities," prompted Wallin.

"No, not any more. But, you know, it is a way of life that I look back on with fondness. It was hard work. It really was."

Pamela asked about Reba's dad. "He was tough? A bit of a taskmaster?"

"He was worked hard as a kid and was shouldered with the responsibility of an adult at a very early age and that's the way he raised us kids."

"And so you worked like that . . . were involved in what I consider to be pretty tough chores," said Pamela. "I don't know, you seem to be smiling as you talk about it."

"It was. It was rough. I mean gettin' up at daylight and havin' to go out and catch a bunch of horses out in a 40 acre pasture and then get 'em saddled and its cold and you get 'em cinched up and they roll over and step on your foot which was frozen and you are pushin' tryin' get 'em to try and roll off. Yep, it was tough. That's why I'm singin'."

The two women shared laughter as the network went to a commercial. I was enjoying the interview, too. Pamela Wallin wasn't taking the role of a confrontive questioner. She was on Reba's side, and Reba had opened up with the colorful stuff. Those controversial harder-to-answer questions about her current career were a million miles away. But I wondered, would Pamela Wallin eventually get around to asking any of them? Or would this continue to be a slow-pitch game. As it was, the audience was getting to know Reba, getting to know her past, at any rate, even if they might wonder themselves how she had gotten to be the ivory-tower Reba.

But when they came back, Pamela and Reba continued on to discuss non-confrontive issues. They talked about the price of fame. The divorce. The responsibility that comes from having fans. Reba's new marriage. Her son, Shelby. What it meant to be a working mother.It was quite different stuff than you would learn about if you read one of those exposés of country music that had mostly been written by male journalists. I wondered if I'd been too severely influenced by reading those books. Perhaps, Reba McEntire was not living in an ivory tower, after all. Perhaps she was just doing the best she could to cope with the many alienating factors that being a country music superstar imposed on you when you became one.

Early in 1999, Reba's *Wrong Night*, a spirited electrified hillbilly romp, hit into the Top 10 amid the young country releases. Reba was not prepared to "fade away," merely because country radio had banished many of the women her age.

**K.T.
OSLIN**

K.T. Oslin scarcely qualified as a candidate to become a Top 40 country singer when at the age of forty-something she put out the critically-acclaimed and massively popular album 80'S LADIES. If country radio programmers in 1987 had been total slaves to demographics compiled by consultants, the "Eighties Lady" might never have gotten her songs to the people. Born Kay Toinette Oslin on May 15, 1941 in Crossitt, Arkansas and raised in Alabama, the singer-songwriter had 'been there and done that' as far as kicking around in the music business was concerned. While attending college, she'd worked with famed songwriter Guy Clark in a folk trio in Houston. She had studied art and toured with Carol Channing in a road version of *Hello Dolly*, before hitting the Broadway musical scene.

It was not until she'd appeared in several Broadway productions and then become a jingle singer that K.T. Oslin began writing songs. When she turned to recording, she brought a dramatic flair to her performances of songs like her first Elektra single, *Younger Men (Are Starting To Catch My Eye)*, that she'd written from a woman's point of view. Needless to say, *80's Ladies* became both an anthem and a rallying point for women late in the decade during which singers like Gail Davies, Juice Newton, Becky Hobbs, and Lacy J. Dalton had been furthering the role of the female country vocalist.

We were girls of the '50s
Stone rock & rollers in the '60s
And more than our names got changed
As the '70s slipped on by
Now we're '80s ladies
There ain't much these ladies ain't tried

We've been educated, we got liberated
And that's complicated matters with men

174

Oh we've said I do and we've signed I don't
And we've sworn we'll never do that again
And we've burned our bras and we've burned our dinners
And we've burned our candles at both ends
And we've got some children who look just like
The way we did back then ...

(written by K.T. Olsin)

When *80's Ladies* was released as a single in 1987, it only went as high as the number 7 position on the *Billboard* country chart, but *Do Ya', I'll Always Come Back*, and *Hold Me* all topped the chart and *Hey Bobby* peaked at number 2. In addition to suggesting an attitude adjustment in her lyrics, the hip production of Oslin's tracks foreshadowed the 'new country' pop edge of the early 1990s. The unabashedly forward character that Oslin portrayed in both her videos and her personal appearances set the record straight for once and for all: it was alright for a single woman to come on to a man. Genuinely provocative and sexy in her music, K.T. Oslin continued that assertion in the title of her 1993 RCA release GREATEST HITS: SONGS FROM AN AGING SEX BOMB. A survivor of a triple-bypass operation in 1995, K.T. returned to recording to romp through the tracks on her 1996 release MY ROOTS ARE SHOWING, although by this point in time the exponents of young country had nudged the older stars from the airwaves. K.T. Oslin's most significant contribution to the progress of women in country music was her assertion of character in a market that was already suffering from the imposition of image and package over substance. Liner notes for MY ROOTS ARE SHOWING proudly announce that K.T. Oslin was significantly involved in the production of her own tracks. It was an issue that had dogged country women for decades.

In 1987 the Academy of Country Music named K.T. Oslin its Best New Female Vocalist and awarded her a second ACM win for the video of *80's Ladies*, the first-ever ACM win for a video featuring a country female. The following year the Academy named her its Best Female Vocalist and THIS WOMAN was named top album. Winner of the CMA Female Vocalist of the Year award in 1988, K.T. Oslin was also winner of the 1988 CMA Song of the Year award for *80's Ladies*, the first time the association had awarded *that* honor to a woman songwriter. That same year Oslin was awarded a best song Grammy for *Hold Me*, as well as a Grammy for Best

Vocal Performance by a Female. More than any other single country singer, K.T. Oslin rallied the female forces who were poised to make their assault on sales and airplay in the 1990s.

GAIL DAVIES

Hassles over production on her albums and opposition as to the direction she wanted to take country music were to result in singer-songwriter Gail Davies being literally shunted off into the wings in the 1980s shuffle of careers where males still ruled the charts and producing records was regarded as a male vocation. Born in Oklahoma and raised in California, Gail Davies first turned to songwriting when she lost her voice in the late 1970s. She hit right away with *Bucket To The South*, a Top 20 hit for Ava Barber, and returned to recording herself, scoring minor hits on the Lifesong label, before signing with Warner Brothers. Top 10 hits like *Blue Heartache* (1979), *I'll Be There (If You Ever Want Me)*, *It's A Lovely, Lovely World* (1980), *Grandma's Song,* and K.T. Oslin's *'Round The Clock Lovin'* (1981) proved to the world that a woman could write, arrange, and produce her own albums.

Gail Davies' accomplishments also opened doors for many other women in the music business. Gail further experimented with an even hipper country-rock approach when recording songs by writers like John Hiatt for an album and band she called WILD CHOIR in 1986, but was stonewalled at radio. Gail eventually settled for a position as an in-house producer for Liberty Records, where she stayed until the mid-1990s when she issued the provocative production ECLECTIC on her own Little Chickadee Records label.

LACY J. DALTON

Lacy J. Dalton, like K.T. Oslin, had kicked around considerably before she put out her first Nashville records. Born Jill Byrem on October 13, 1946 in Bloomsburg, Pennsylvania, she attended Brigham Young University only briefly before casting her fate to the wind and drifting through the 1960s. She eventually settled in the Santa Cruz, California area, where she found initial success fronting the psychedelic rock band Office. When her husband, John Croston, the band's manager, was severely injured in a 1971 diving accident, she retired to a cabin in the nearby mountains to nurse both a new baby and an ailing husband. In this rural setting, she began to write country songs. A widow and a single-mom in 1974, Jill Croston waitressed to keep the wolf from the door while recording an album of her original material in a garage. When CBS Records producer Billy Sherrill heard her efforts, he envisioned the potential for creation of a progressive country sound melding the diverse blues, country, and rock influences Jill Croston had sent along on her homespun production.

It was Sherrill who demanded creation of a stage name, but Jill Croston who came up with Lacy J. Dalton. LACY J. DALTON was also the title of her Columbia Records debut and the lead single *Crazy Blue Eyes* was to become her signature song, although it only made it to the number 17 position on the country charts. Dalton only hit into the Top 40 a total of 20 times during the 1980s, and *16th Avenue* at number 7 in 1982 was her top chart achievement. But the smoky-voiced singer was hugely popular as a live entertainer and written up in major publications like *Time* magazine as a woman in country music to whom women all over the country looked as a symbol of the emerging independent roles available for women in the 1980s.

A 1989 comeback album for Dalton was SURVIVOR, and the self-written *Hard Luck Ace*, although not a huge chart success, became another of the songs to which women related more than the male disc jockeys and radio programmers of the day. Lacy J. Dalton, who had early-on been compared to Janis Joplin, continues to tour despite the fact that she's been cut from radio playlists.

Another accomplished equestrienne who sang country that crossed over hugely into the pop market, Juice Newton was born **JUICE NEWTON** Judy Kay Newton on February 18, 1952 in New Jersey and raised in Virginia Beach. She surfaced in the mid-1970s in the Los Angeles area with a band called Silver Spur that recorded for RCA. When she went solo and signed with Capitol Records in the early 1980s, Juice hit big with *Angel Of The Morning* and *Queen Of Hearts*. Regarded as a country artist, these early smashes sold well and also charted in the Top 10 on the pop charts. Her Capitol Records album debut, JUICE, sold a million copies and the follow-up, QUIET LIES, half a million. Number one country releases of *The Sweetest Thing I've Ever Known* (1981), *Break It To Me Gently* (1982), *You Want Me To Make You Mine* (1985), and a duet with Eddie Rabbitt in 1986, *Both To*

Each Other (Friends And Lovers), consolidated Newton's reputation as a country performer, although by 1990 she was no longer heavily playlisted by country radio.

BECKY HOBBS

Becky Hobbs' rambunctious piano-driven recordings and exuberant vocals endeared her to country fans when they discovered *Are There Any More Like You (Where You Came From)* and *Jones On The Jukebox* on her 1988 MTM album ALL KEYED UP. Born Rebecca Ann Hobbs in Oklahoma in 1950, Becky is one of many country women who formed an all-girl band as a teenager. She first began to record in the 1970s on the Tattoo label and then on Mercury Records. In 1983, she hit the number 10 spot on the *Billboard* country chart with *Let's Get Over Them Together*, a duet with Moe Bandy. Along with K.T. Oslin, Hobbs hit a harmonic that appealed to self-assertive women in the late 1980s. Cuts like *Hottest "Ex" In Texas* and *Mama Was a Working Man* created interest in her as another woman songwriter who had something unique to offer.

> It seems to me every day, I hear somebody say
> How a working man today has got it bad
> And then my memory will take me back to the one who raised me
> And I think of all the troubles that she had
> Back in '58 after daddy went away
> Mama took a job a-workin' at the plant
> And she put in her time on that old assembly line
> And she held her own with any union man
>
> Mama was a workin' man
> Mama was a workin' man
> And she raised me
> To be proud of who I am . . .

(written by Rebecca Ann Hobbs/Don London/Mike Darwin)

Author of Conway Twitty's number 2 hit *I Want To Know You Before We Make Love,* as well as songs recorded by George Jones, Loretta Lynn, Glen Campbell, Emmylou Harris, Alabama, and Helen Reddy, there have been few singer-songwriters to exhibit as much energy as a recording artist as Becky Hobbs. However, a life-threatening automobile accident led Hobbs to write more than to perform during the early 1990s, and her song *Angels Among Us*, co-written with Don Goodman, was a Top 40 hit for Alabama in 1994. Becky's experience was also the inspiration of a book bearing the same title.

Becky Hobbs has performed her piano-pounding country music in 35 countries on five continents and entertained troops in Bosnia as well as performing for AIDS victims in Rawanda. In 1994, the irrepressible Hobbs, known to her many fans as "the Beckaroo," was named Top Indie Artist by Cash Box magazine for her Intersound album THE BOOTS I CAME TO TOWN IN. Becky's 1997 CD FROM OKLAHOMA WITH LOVE was released on her own Beckaroo Records and produced by her new husband, ex-Glenn Frey band guitarist, Duane Sciaqua. Named one of the top albums of 1998 by Tulsa critic John Woolsey, her new music inspired reviewer Ralph Novak to proclaim it "country music with brains and bounce."

J anie Fricke was born on December 19, 1947 in South Whitney, Indiana. Her parents were both musicians. While attending **JANIE FRICKE** Indiana University, Janie began singing jingles for the Pepper-Tanner Agency in Memphis, where she met Judy Rodman and Karen Taylor-Good and performed with them for a short period of time as Phase II. Moving to Nashville, Janie became a first-call studio singer but gained notoriety when some answer lines she had recorded on Johnny Duncan's Top 10 hit *Jo And The Cowboy* and her harmony vocal on his 1976 number one release *Thinkin' Of A Rendezvous* had people asking, "Who *is* that girl singer?"

"I had no intention of recording on my own," Janie remembers. "I was happy with that. I was making a very good living doing that. And they kept saying, 'Don't you want to start recording on your own?' I said, 'No, I just want to keep on singing backup.' But they kept pursuing me, so I eventually decided to go ahead and go for it. I went around and got advice from various people. I didn't know anything about that end of the business . . . the touring, band, bus, part of it. I was used to the studio. It was a big gamble to give all of that up."

The gamble paid off big time for Janie Fricke when she signed with Columbia Records and began to work with producer Billy Sherrill. Janie remembers, "I was doin' duets with Charlie Rich and Moe Bandy and Vern

Gosdin and I was still doing my studio backup. When I did my first record, SINGER OF SONGS, I got a bus and a band and got right on the road. My first single was *What're You Doing Tonight* in 1977 and it got nominated for a Grammy award."

A 1977 duet with Johnny Duncan, a remake of Jay & the Americans' 1964 pop hit *Come A Little Bit Closer*, hit the number 4 spot on the *Billboard* country chart. *On My Knees* a duet with Charlie Rich topped the chart in 1978. Janie hit the Number 2 spot in 1980 with *Down To My Last Broken Heart* and the top spot in 1982 with both *Don't Worry 'Bout Me Baby* and *It Ain't Easy Bein' Easy*. When the CMA named Janie Fricke its Female Vocalist Of The Year for 1982, Lynn Anderson sent Fricke a present. "I had toured a little bit with Lynn Anderson and sang backup for her," Janie remembered. "She sent a quarter horse down to me here in Texas from her ranch in Tennessee as a present when I won my first CMA award. The horse's name is Circus and I still have her here with me, today."

Janie had five number ones in 1983 and 1984, including her signature tune *He's A Heartache (Looking For A Place To Happen)* and was again named Best Female Vocalist of the Year by the CMA. The Academy of Country Music and both *Billboard* and *Cashbox* magazines showered awards on her during this period. In 1984, Janie hit the top of the charts with *A Place To Fall Apart*, a duet with Merle Haggard. By 1985, Fricke was making music videos for releases like *The First Word In Memory Is Me* and *She's Single Again*, both Top 10 hits in 1985, and for her ninth number one *Always Have Always Will* in 1986.

Janie remembers the times she sang for Presidents Ronald Reagan and George Bush as special highlights. "I sang for President Reagan and attended a State Dinner at the White House. We sang at Camp David by the swimming pool. The President was entertaining the President of Mexico, Lopez Portio, and we were the entertainment. George Bush liked country music a lot, too. I sang at a show at the Ford Theater and he was sittin' in the front row and I was very nervous."

The Indiana-born singer — who had started as a backup singer for Elvis, Loretta, Dolly, Ronnie Milsap, Barbara Mandrell and Lynn Anderson, recording on more than 20 Top 10 hits for other artists before she made her own records — had certainly had an exciting ten years as one of the top country performers of the 1980s. Although her releases were no longer hitting the Top 40 by the end of the decade, she has continued to tour and to

REBA McENTIRE

**BARBARA
MANDRELL**

**K.T.
OSLIN**

**BECKY
HOBBS**

**JUICE
NEWTON**

**JANIE
FRICKE**

**MATRACA
BERG**

**KIM
RICHEY**

**KAREN
TAYLOR-GOOD**

**NANCI
GRIFFITH**

**JESS
LEARY**

**LUCINDA
WILLIAMS**

release records like her greatest hits package NOW AND THEN.

Janie became her own producer for the 1992 Intersound release CROSS-ROADS and created a unique country-gospel CD that featured cuts like Eric Clapton's *Tears From Heaven* and Curtis Mayfield's *People Get Ready*. In 1999, Janie took another brave step when she decided to take the fully independent route. "My new album is BOUNCIN' BACK," she says. "I just decided to go in and record my own album and form my own record label, JMS Records. We're doing it on our own. We're going to market it ourselves out of our office and our web page and at our concerts and through our fan club. There's a clip of it on the web page (www.janiefricke.com) where people can listen to it."

Janie Fricke's many accomplishments guarantee her a continued national television presence. "*Bouncin' Back* is the single we're going to take from it. I sang it on *Crook & Chase* back in November and a couple of weeks ago, I sang it on the *Grand Ole Opry* during the TV segment, so a lot of people got to hear it then." She was also featured singing on the 1999 ACM Awards show. Nearly 30 years after she began recording and 20 years after she began issuing her own records, Janie Fricke had authored only one of the songs she had sung. On her first Indie record on her JMS Records label, she has written another. "I just have written one on BOUNCIN' BACK and that one is called *Love Forever More*. I don't have that gift of comin' up with poetry and makin' things rhyme. That's a talent you have to be born with. It's very hard to be a good songwriter. You can't just sit down and write a great song. You have to have the know-how, the talent, the feel for it, and it has to flow out of your mind, and I can't do that at all. I have never been able to just sit down and write a song."

The 1980s were distinguished by a growing number of country women singer-songwriters, more so than any previous decade in country music history. Women were now taking charge of the lyrics, appealing to other women and countering the male language of traditional country music.

SONG-WRITERS

Ralph Murphy is a producer and songwriter whose productions of bands like April Wine, as well as his many excursions to music conventions around the world where he speaks about the significance of the 'song' in country music, have moved the Nashville office of ASCAP to make Ralph their ambassador at large. Murphy has run his own publishing company, Pic-a-lic, in Nashville and written many hit songs, but *Seeds* recorded by Kathy Mattea and performed by her at the White House is one of the ones he is most likely to be remembered for. In 1998 Ralph extended his continuing monologue on songwriting to a column in the Nashville Songwriter's Association newsletter that he calls *Murphy's Law*.

One of Ralph Murphy's closest friends is Harlan Howard, the dean of Nashville songwriters and author of such memorable tunes as *Heartaches By The Number* and *I Fall To Pieces*. Ralph often quotes Harlan when speaking about songwriting. "One time," Ralph remembers, "Harlan told me that: 'I only write songs for women. I think about what a woman thinks about. For instance, if you've got a line in a song that goes: We need some time apart . . . a woman hears that and says: You're seein' someone else. Or, you're gone.' Harlan believes that what a man says and what a woman hears are quantum leaps apart. They're just totally different. So, Harlan says, 'When I've finished writing out my man's song, I sit back for a minute and look at what I'm saying in there and I say: What is a woman going to hear in there?'"

In addition to being an explicator of Harlan Howard's songwriting methods, Ralph Murphy is a huge Harlan Howard fan. "I can't even begin to tell you how many hits Harlan has had, hundreds of them, and he only ever writes for women. A woman is always right in his songs. If she's a hooker, she's a hooker with a heart of gold because some man dumped on her. Harlan writes for women because they're going to listen to the song, not necessarily for women singers. It takes a brave woman to sing some of his stuff. Harlan also says, and this is his way of looking at it, that women buy 50 per cent of all records . . . and they make men buy the other 50 per cent. In country, that is true. The only genre where that is not true is in that testosterone-laden 14 to 22-year-old area of pop music where women become objects or things of frustration, where they're definitely not people."

I asked Ralph Murphy why women were now buying so many records by women. "Well, women generally feel that only women can only speak to women's issues and there are a lot more women's issues going around. Now, there are women in the work place. They are being faced with all of the same issues but they approach them as women, not as men. Men are more confrontational. The laws to protect women, harassment laws, are on the books, now. Women are totally responsible for bringing them in."

I wondered if Ralph had written songs that he had felt were more likely to be pitched successfully to women artists? Had he crafted songs specifically for women to sing? "Well, there are some things that a man simply would not say. Men are more reluctant to shed tears over something. If the song is very sensitive, very deep emotionally, you tend to write in the feminine gender. It comes out of the material. A true songwriter never writes a song *for* someone. Songs that are written *for* an artist usually sound very contrived. There's not a natural flow in them. In most cases you'll write in the third person and you realize that a song is basically a script for someone to stand on the stage and be loved, worshipped, and adored while they sing. So, the pronoun needs to be changed to the first person. When a beautiful woman stands on the stage and sings: 'I love *him*,' I don't give a damn. When she leans over the footlights and sings, 'I love *you*,' then ... she's got me.

"But see, most writers will write in the third person. A good friend of mine, a psychiatrist, said a few years ago: 'Because, by their natures, most writers are dysfunctional, they tend to distance themselves.' And the easiest way to distance yourself from a relationship, as a writer, is to write in the third person. So you can say, 'he said,' and 'they said,' when in actual fact the protagonists are you and I."

I wondered about *Seeds*. How had the song been pitched to Kathy Mattea? To the audience, now that she's recorded it, it seems to us to be a woman's song. I knew Ralph had written it with Pat Alger, but it seemed so much more fragile and meaningful to me when a woman sang it. Ralph smiled at that comment. "It was a total act of God. Pat Alger and I demoed it at Allen Reynolds' studio where Allen was producing Kathy *and* Garth Brooks. At the time we demoed it, Garth Brooks stopped by the studio. When we were running through the song, Garth said, 'Wow! That's great. That's a wonderful song.'

"He went on about it, so, I said, 'Look, Garth, do you want to sing the demo?' He said, 'No, no, Pat's doing a good job.' So, I said, 'Do you want a copy of the tape?' And Garth said, 'Man, I know it already.' In the meanwhile, Allen Reynolds heard the tape and he said, 'Look, I've just finished Garth's album, but I'm working on Kathy's ...'" So, it had been Pat Alger's demo of the song he and Ralph had written that Garth Brooks liked and Allen Reynolds had pitched to Kathy Mattea that would become known to the public as a 'woman's song'.

"Kathy and Garth are both good friends of mine," Ralph continued. "As a publisher I've placed *Eighteen Wheels And A Dozen Roses*, *Burnin' Old Memories*, and *I Have You* with Kathy. So, that's the way it happened. Serendipity. It was just because we demoed it in Allen's studio. That was an easy one."

"At the White House," Ralph remembers, "Kathy was going to sing *Eighteen Wheels And A Dozen Roses* and President Clinton requested *Seeds*. It was his favorite song. My mom called me when she heard about that. It raised a lot of money for March of Dimes and it also raised a million and a half dollars for a group in Michigan working with learning disabilities. The song has really done a lot of good for a lot of people. It's sung in churches."

I had one more question for Ralph Murphy. What I wanted to know was, what was the factor that was most responsible for changing the songs that we were now hearing on country radio from the songs we used to hear? Ralph didn't have to think about it at all before answering. "What is changing is vocabulary. There are words being used that 20 years ago wouldn't have been used. In *This Kiss*, which was put out by Faith Hill and written by Beth Nielsen Chapman and Los Angeles writers Robin Lerner and Annie Reboff, there are some words used that 20 years ago some country folk would have maybe not gotten. It is a reflection of the country audience who read a lot more, who are more worldly. They just put a country perspective on a more worldly world. A lot of country is the cadence of the language, the inclusion of the extra syllable. Well is we-ell. There's two syllables in every mono-syllabic. Therefore it makes it more musical. It was the hardest thing for me to learn when I moved to Nashville, learning the language. And I do it by writing with people who know the language."

During the time that I was in Nashville researching this book, I had lunch with Ralph Murphy and Harlan Howard. We met at Sammi's Place on Music Row, a cafe and bar that caters to the songwriting community who were out in force that afternoon. Many songwriters stopped off at our table to visit with Harlan and Ralph. When Harlan learned that I was a hockey fan, he invited me to come along to the Nashville Predators hockey game that night. When I arrived at the arena, Harlan and Ralph were seated in balcony seats with Pat Alger and Susan Bowman. Not long after I arrived, Pam Tillis dropped by for a chat. The songwriters seemed to have their own little section at the Predators games. As a fellow writer, yet not a songwriter, I was moved that they had accepted me into their circle.

When you get to know songwriters, you gain a special insight into the essence of country music. These days, there are more and more women who have become successful at pitching their songs to top recording artists and their songs are not necessarily sung by female vocalists. For example, Jess Leary wrote Tim McGraw's recent hit *Where The Green Grass Grows* with Craig Wiseman. Jess recorded it for her independent CD SONGWRITER and it works for her. It also works very well for Tim McGraw.

JESS LEARY

Whether songwriters are women or men, both genders seem to share an equal amount of slugging it out in the trenches before they get that first big hit. Jess Leary had a successful career as an entertainer in the Boston area singing in coffeehouses and clubs six nights a week, but she didn't want to go on just doing that "until she was 50." Leary considered New York and L.A. but first made an exploratory trip to Nashville. "I loved it there," she told me. "I went back home and packed up my van and took my dog and rolled on into town. I started waitressing and I had my own little business cleaning houses. It was hard to come up with the little bit of money I did have. You can't make a nickel in the clubs in Nashville. You can't make parking money. I thought that was *so* strange."

Of course, there were plenty of songwriter showcases to attend and soon Jess Leary was one of the people showcasing her songs. "I started getting my name and face and songs out there as much as I could. And I started getting some calls back. Reba was starting a publishing company and Leigh Reynolds — who was putting it together for Starstruck Entertainment — was in the audience when I was singing one night. I was one of the first writers that Leigh presented to Starstruck. I started at the top. My first paying-gig in Nashville was with Reba. My first song to get recorded was a number one. I was a ten-year overnight success."

Before that first number one, Leary toured with Reba as a backup singer and guitar player. She also toured with Garth Brooks in his early band Stillwater and worked with Faith Hill. When *Mi Vida Loca (My Crazy Life)*, a song Jess had written with Pam Tillis, hit the top of the chart, Jess had been on the road for four years.

If you're coming with me you need nerves of steel
'Cause I take corners on two wheels
It's a never ending circus ride
The faint of heart need not apply

Mi vida loca over and over
Destiny turns on a dime
I go where the wind blows
You can't tame a wild rose
Welcome to my crazy life

(written by Jess Leary and Pam Tillis)

It was time to quit the 'crazy life' of touring. "It all switched over," she remembers, "and completely did a somersault. I'm very happy with the way things are going, now. I'm plugged in to the writing community. I had a good run with it and now I play around town at the writer's nights."

KAREN TAYLOR-GOOD Karen Taylor-Good got her start singing jingles in the 1970s. "I moved to Memphis and started singing in a jingle mill," she recalls. "Janie Fricke had just left there and gone to Nashville to become a session singer. Judy Rodman was there. I used to work with Judy, sometimes. That was just a great training ground to learn to work in the studio and work with a microphone." When Karen began to get calls from Nashville, she first worked with Lucille Ball at the Opry, then moved to Music City, herself. "Once again, I slipped right into Janie's spot. She had just started doing her artist thing, so I slipped right into her spot. Oh man, I had some great sessions. I worked with George Jones on his albums. I worked with Willie. I got to sing on the soundtrack of *Best Little Whorehouse in Texas* with Dolly. I was a first-call studio singer. I think I picked up a lot on country songwriting there . . . I got to sing so many great country songs."

When Karen was offered the opportunity to once again follow in Janie Fricke's footsteps and step into the spotlight as a recording artist herself, Karen was reluctant to leave the security of session work. But record she did and by 1984 found herself nominated for an ACM award as best new female vocalist. "When I didn't win the ACM award," she explains, "I got really depressed and out of that depression I discovered that I was a song-writer. As an artist, I had been singing other people's songs. I was singing whatever other people thought country radio wanted. I was not paying attention to who I was or what I wanted to do. It was not a healthy situation. I was young and foolish." It would be a few more years down the line before Karen Taylor-Good hit big in 1994 with *How Can I Help You Say Goodbye*, a number 3 hit for Patty Loveless that Karen had written with Burton Collins.

> I sat on our bed, he packed his suitcase
> I held a picture of our wedding day
> His hands were trembling, we both were crying
> He kissed me gently, and then he quickly walked away
> I called up Mama, she said, time will ease your pain
> Life's about changing, nothing ever stays the same
> And she said, how can I help you say goodbye
> It's okay to hurt, and it's okay to cry....

(written by Karen Good-Taylor and Burton Collins)

A year later, Collin Raye's recording of Karen's *Not That Different* hit the number 3 spot again. "I haven't had that many," she confesses, "but I got a whole bunch comin' up, I believe." With two of her songs on Collin Raye's first album and four on hold for his coming up one, she appeared on Gary Chapman's *Music City Tonight* show on TNN with Collin a few nights after we spoke.

Karen also has a few songs on hold by other artists, including two on hold for Reba, but writing Top 10 hits has not meant that she now lives in a mansion. "It certainly helps," she admits. "It improved my lifestyle tremendously." And Karen is still active as a recording artist. "I couldn't ever give it up. I make my own CDs. And I'm at the Kerrville Festival at the end of March . . . the women of Kerrville tour in Texas with Katie Wallace and four other women. You can check out my CD at *www.songs.com/ktg*."

Rona Goodman hasn't quit her day-job as director of publicity for the Merritt Mountain Music Festival, yet. But she saves her **RONA GOODMAN** dollars from that job and is able to spend nearly six months of the year living in the songwriting capital of the world. Rona is a songwriter with hopes as huge as Karen Taylor-Good and Jess Leary, she just hasn't struck pay dirt, although she's giving it her best shot. Of course, working for Mountainfest from March until July, Rona has a fair amount of contact with the stars she one day hopes will record her songs, especially when she wanders back to their green-room trailer or their tour bus and walks them to the media tent for their meet-the-press session prior to their show. It is an opportunity Goodman has not been willing to over-exploit, but someday soon she knows that she will get one of her tapes into the right hands.

In Nashville, Rona has gotten into the thick of things and the demo tapes she played for me sounded promising. A near-miss with a song a few years ago had proven inspiring rather than discouraging for Goodman. "I have been going back and forth between Nashville and Vancouver since 1995 when I got a wonderful call from Kathy Mattea. I met Kathy at the Merritt festival and got a tape to her. I got this message on my phone machine stating that she had listened to my tape and thought that it was a great song. She thought she might want to record it. We did correspond quite a few times through the year and she had the song on hold, then it didn't make the cut for the album . . . but it opened the doors between me and Kathy and I met with her down there. She actually called me to let me know that they did pass on the song. It was so inspirational for the artist to call a songwriter, even though they passed on the song."

Rona Goodman not only hasn't given up in believing that her songs are good enough to one day be a hit for the right artist, she has literally fallen in love with the Music City lifestyle. "Nashville," she says, "really truly is the home for songwriters. You live and you breathe writing songs. It is an incredibly creative community, but it can also be brutal. You have to believe in yourself. You also have to be open to hearing critical feedback. Getting positive feedback is important, too. And other writers are very supportive. You never know who will hear your song when you sing at the Bluebird Cafe. Mostly, it is a way to get heard by other writers. But you never know. Nashville is a co-writing town and that is huge."

When a local band back in Vancouver recorded several of Rona's songs for their CD, she was further encouraged. In Nashville, she began to delve deeper into the infrastructure. "There are other venues. If you join the Nashville Songwriters Association, they have pitch-a-thons once a month. ASCAP puts things on. Ralph Murphy is a great help. He has helped me get hooked up with some publishers and other writers. Everybody knows Ralph in Nashville. And there are other events. There is this guy, Mike Williams, who has these parties once a month. He has this big house and he invites all these people to his house to sing songs. One time, there was this one woman who began singing a sort of gospel song a cappella, just by herself, and then someone picked up a guitar and someone picked up a fiddle and then an accordion and then the bass . . . after a while the whole room was filled with the music of these people playing behind this single voice and the people started clapping and getting into it. It was magical. That is the heart and soul of music."

For Rona Goodman, it is moments like these that keep her going. "Being down there in Nashville," she says, "is being in an incredible melting pot of talent and you can do demos for a really reasonable cost. Right now in Nashville they are going through some major changes. Yes, everything does sound the same. The same cookie-cutter bands. We do need a change."

A Dixie Chicks concert Goodman attended in Vancouver also pushed some buttons. "Not only can the Dixie Chicks sing and play their instruments, they are so talented that I was inspired to go out and learn the fiddle. The Dixie Chicks are trendsetting. Going to the millennium, these girls are something to watch for — as role models they are positive! It was definitely the wow effect watching them. They were at the Rage club, the crowd was standing at the front, it was almost like a mosh pit. Seeing the Dixie Chicks live was great. Natalie Maines is a great singer!"

What people among her fellow songwriters, I wondered, were the ones to whom Rona looked for personal inspiration? "Matraca Berg is an incredible writer. She's one of my idols. She wrote Deana Carter's *Strawberry Wine* and that was massive! *Strawberry Wine* is a great song! It's the true heart and soul of a song. A great song has got to grab you and touch your heart. It's gotta last. It's got to have substance. You can dress up, you know, you can have the package, but if there's no substance, it's not going to last."

N ashville-born Matraca Berg has put out albums, charted a couple of times as high as number 36 on the *Billboard* country chart, and then had album projects stall at the drawing board stage. As it turns out, the singers who have covered her material have put a whole lot

MATRACA BERG

of dollars in her bank account. Matraca Berg has released only two albums, LYING TO THE MOON and THE SPEED OF GRACE. Her third project never got off the cutting room floor, but Trisha Yearwood cut one of the tracks *XXX's and OOO's (An American Girl)*, a Berg co-write with Alice Randall that went number one for Trisha. Martina McBride cut *Wild Angels*, the song that had been planned as Matraca's third album title but ended up being Martina's first number one single as well as the title of her second album. When Matraca's personal hero, Linda Ronstadt, cut *Walk On*, it just about made Berg's entire year. "Ronstadt was one of the earlier females that I identified with," Berg told David Simmons for an article in the June 1996 issue of *New Country* magazine. "It's cool to have a seasoned veteran who's been there and done that, heard it all, do your song."

Matraca was born and raised on country music. Daughter of respected Nashville songwriter, Icee Berg, Matraca also found time enough to listen to a whole lot of music from every genre. Her mom sang backup and Matraca tried that out, too, recording harmony vocals for Neil Young's OLD WAYS and singing backup on Neil's tour to promote the album's release. You will hear traces of songwriters like Carole King and Chrissie Hynde in Matraca's material, along with the indelible experiences Berg has experienced first-hand in her own life. "I write from existence," she told Simmons when speaking of Pam Tillis' recording of her own *Calico Plains*, "and that's a very autobiographical tune. It was more of an observation of relatives of mine. It's probably my favorite tune. Because I am a female, I guess it will often lean towards the female point of view, but just about everything I write about, I've been there."

By the time that Deana Carter recorded Matraca's *Strawberry Wine*, Berg had also seen Trisha's early success with a number one on *The Wrong Side Of Memphis*, seen Patty Loveless take her *I'm That Kind Of Girl* and *You Can Feel Bad* to the top of the charts, and Reba sing the living daylights out of her *The Last One To Know*, another number one. So what if the radio consultants and the record execs didn't 'hear a hit' when they listened to her recordings, other women did. Matraca Berg has resigned herself to being raided. Some of the women who have come song-hunting have sung her songs really, really well. And you can't ignore the fattening of the bank account as well as the pride you might feel. "Women writing powerful songs is not a new phenomenon," Berg told *Country Weekly* writer Robbie Woliver for a June, 1998 story. "Hey, Loretta had records banned! Women are such a mystery to so many men . . . there's a certain earthiness . . . rawness about them. I just try to give a realistic viewpoint." *I'm That Kind of Girl* is just that kind of song.

> There's a man in a Stetson hat, howling' like an alley cat
> Outside my window tonight
> Sayin', 'Baby put on something hot, meet me in the parking lot
> About a quarter to nine.'
> I get this feeling he's never read *Romeo and Juliet*
> I'm getting tired of all these one night stands
> But if you want real romance
> I'm that kind of girl, I'm that kind of girl
> I ain't the woman in red, I ain't the girl next door
> But if somewhere in the middle is what you're lookin' for
> I'm that kind of girl, yes I'm that kind of girl . . .

(written by Matraca Berg/Ronni Samoset)

A distant relative of Patsy Cline, Berg has learned how to express a woman's point of view, Hoss, you better believe it! Married to Dirt Band singer Jeff Hanna, she's been in the thick of things in Nashville since she was born. No wonder that she relates to Deana Carter and no wonder at all that her lyrics about her own coming-of-age experiences became a hit for Deana. "I am so happy that Deana recorded that song," Matraca told Woliver. "I'd known her for about three years, and she's always been so unique. I was sad to let the song go, but she's just the coolest girl."

If you think that cutting loose your ego and setting your creations free to just start 'blowing in the wind' is easy, consider that Matraca also confessed to Woliver that, when her own album project was rejected, "I was so angry, so disgusted, I called my publisher and said, 'Sell everything . . . even *Strawberry Wine*,' which I wanted to record very badly." Writing songs is a whole lot like giving birth. Matraca Berg just thought, just hoped, that she might nurse her own tunes along a little bit further. Of course, nearly every one of those number ones and top forties had been co-written with one of the guys, so, maybe she didn't *own* them after all. Maybe her creations were just part of creation itself.

Gretchen Peters is not only one of the more significant female country songwriters for female recording artists during the decade in which women have surged to the forefront of the genre, she has also written hits like *Traveller's Prayer* for George Jones, *High Lonesome* for Randy Travis, and *Chill Of An Early Fall* for George Strait. Peters wrote *My Baby Loves Me (Just The Way That I Am)*, a Canadian hit for Patricia Conroy, but a career awakening number 2 smash for Martina McBride in 1992, before McBride's recording of Gretchen's *Independence Day*, which tackles the taboo subject of abuse, ignited Martina's career in 1994 and was named the 1995 CMA Song of the Year.

Well, word gets around in a small, small town
They said he was a dangerous man
But Mama was proud and stood her ground
She knew she was on the losing end
Some folks whispered, some folks talked
And when time ran out, there was no one about
On Independence Day

Let freedom ring, let the white dove sing
Let the whole world know that today is a day of reckoning
Let the weak be strong, let the right be wrong,
Roll that stone away, let the guilty pay
It's Independence Day . . .

(written by Gretchen Peters)

Born in Brooklyn, New York, Gretchen Peters violates all of the rules when it comes to large poverty-stricken families and whatnot that have characterized past generations of country writers and singers. She surfaced in Boulder, Colorado, singing in clubs, and migrated to Nashville in 1988 where she has left an indelible mark.

When Gretchen Peters visited Vancouver as one of five Nashville writers to participate in a local songwriting competition, she sang at a songwriters showcase at Richard's on Richards. I was impressed by her performance *and* her songs. As a recording artist, Gretchen continues to entertain her audience with the same enigmatic sets that gained her notoriety in Colorado, presenting her own songs gathered in a bouquet that includes her stylistic version of Steve Earle's *I Ain't Never Satisfied*. SECRET OF LIFE, a 1996 CD on the Imprint label that has yet to be discovered by the masses, is a must for the curious as well as the diligent student of the the songwriting process.

KIM RICHEY

Kim Richey is that rare breed of songwriter who really enjoys touring. She's better than a lot of the solo artists at singing and entertaining and she's shown an ability to transcend genres and win over audiences wherever she goes. Kim has also fed some key songs to Trisha Yearwood and Radney Foster, watching Trisha have mega success with *Believe Me Baby (I Lied)* and Radney hit the cherished number one spot on the country chart with *Nobody Wins*. For a performing artist with recording projects of her own, it could be frustrating. Not for Kim. She told Robert Oermann for a March 8th, 1997 story in *The Tennessean* that she's not unhappy at all when that happens. "People ask me, 'Well now that you've seen your song go number one by somebody else, aren't you bummed out?' I'm like, 'Oh yeah, I can't tell you how sad I am, getting a big check in the mailbox and a Grammy nomination. I couldn't be sadder.'"

While Top 40 country radio hasn't played her much, Kim's 1997 Mercury album BITTER SWEET has caught the ear of some of the more progressive formats. There's a very good reason for that. BITTER SWEET is one of the best albums, ever, by a female vocalist out of Nashville. It's not boom-chuck traditional country or honkabilly or cowpunk, though. In fact, as hard as journalists sweat over their processors to define Kim Richey's sound, her niche, she just plain makes good music. Music as good as Rosanne Cash's KING'S RECORD SHOP, as good as Linda Ronstadt's HEART LIKE A WHEEL, but not necessarily music that sounds like either artist or either of those albums. Produced by guitarist Angelo Petraglia, BITTER SWEET has better songs and better grooves than Kim's self-titled 1995 Mercury release. Angelo and Kim used their road band in the studio, and the wisdom of doing so is present in the easy-going naturalness of the grooves Petraglia and his band mates lay down. Songs like *Lonesome Side Of Town* work a special alchemy where you find yourself swaying to the music and moved to cry and smile at the same time. BITTER SWEET could be a veritable garden of ripe radio hits for Top 40 artists in the near future when the song-raiding begins. But few vocalists from any genre will surpass Kim Richey's distinctive heartfelt vocals, the rich layered harmony arrangements, or the relaxed ambience of what is basically one of those albums you can stick on auto-reverse and let it roll. Kim is not doing anything that different than Deana Carter. She's heard the Beatles and The Band, too. Kim is just a little more relaxed, a little more laid-back, she's having fun while she sings ... that's for sure. And there's not a formula-generated song on BITTER SWEET. Her music is the best reflection of the other side of Nashville, the side where good music is put before package, image, and 'show business'. Kim Richey is more intent on nurturing that delicate quotient of creativity, especially in her live performances, intent on keeping the relationship between the singer and the listener alive, at all times.

NANCI GRIFFITH Nanci Griffith is another singer-songwriter who has placed quality of presentation over willingness to sell out and go for the quick buck solution to success. Griffith has, like Kim Richey, had relationships with labels who have welcomed her aboard, knowing what they were getting into, but willing to endorse such a talent even though the bottom line may not be the corporate equation of ever ballooning sales. Perhaps best known as the writer of Kathy Mattea's *Love At The Five And Dime*, Nanci Griffith comes from a long line of Texas-based creators of music that has seldom been understood or endorsed by the Nashville-created Top 40 radio audience. However, Texas is a nation unto itself, large enough to claim its own country music capital, Austin, and populated sufficiently that centers like Dallas and Houston provide venues where Texas-based acts can survive without Nashville endorsement. In Texas, jazz and blues have always existed side by side with country music in the music of famed Texan performers like Bob Wills and current day practitioner Lyle Lovett. During the honky-tonk era, Ernest Tubb, the 'Texas Troubador', was a national star. When Texas spawned rockabilly singers, it gave the world Buddy Holly & The Crickets and Steve Earle. When Texas melded hispanic and hillbilly, it gave the world San Benito Valley singer Freddy Fender and rockabilly filly Rosie Flores. When Willie Nelson had had his fill of the paint by numbers approach on Music Row, he headed home to the wide open spaces of his home state where he got back in touch with his roots. Willie, Waylon, Tompall Glaser, and Jessi Colter would become known to national audiences as 'outlaws', a Nashvillism for 'outsider' spawned by the RCA concept album WANTED: THE OUTLAWS, but they never robbed any banks or trains, they just stole the focus of country music from Music Row conservatives for a few years. Texas is the birth place of George Strait who celebrated his home state in the quintessential new traditionalist western swing recording *All My Ex's Live In Texas*. Texas has produced its share of songwriters, too. Writers like Cindy Walker, Guy Clark, Jimmy Dale Gilmore, and Billy Joe Shaver, whose songs like *Old Five And Dimers Like Me* were celebrated on Waylon's HONKY-TONK HEROES. Then there was the whole Armadillo Headquarters thing in Austin with Jerry Jeff and the Lost Gonzo Band. Texas country has always been the real deal.

Folkabilly is the nomenclature that Austin, Texas-born Nanci Griffith came up with when backed into corners to define what she did. A graduate of the University of Texas with a major in Education, Nanci created several minor gems before she ever made the trek to Nashville. The best of these albums is LAST OF THE TRUE BELIEVERS, a 1986 Rounder Records release that included Nanci's *Love At The Five And Dime* and Pat Alger's *Goin' Gone*. LONESTAR STATE OF MIND was a great title for an album and a great song by Pat Alger, but Griffith's collaborations with producer Tony Brown proved uncomfortable, especially when the promotion department at MCA began jamming her feet into sequin-studded pink cowgirl boots. People will tell you that Nanci Griffith is a singer-songwriter, but her finest hour came when she recorded *Other Voices, Other Rooms*, a tribute to her heroes and heroines like Kate Wolf, Woodie Guthrie, and John Prine. In the 1990s, she has found a niche with VH1-style productions.

A singer-songwriter with attitude, Lucinda Williams has seen her albums raided by the likes of Mary Chapin Carpenter **LUCINDA WILLIAMS** (*Passionate Kisses*), Patty Loveless (*The Night's Too Long*), and Tom Petty (*Changed The Locks*). The Louisiana-born Williams has not raised a fuss over any of that, but she had been feisty when dealing with record label people, even before the recent breakthrough success of her fifth album, CAR WHEELS ON A GRAVEL ROAD. It was an album she'd planned to put out on American Recordings, a minor label, and then go out and tour and do her thing, an approach she'd been successful enough with that there were no immediate wolves at her door. But Polygram execs caught wind of just how good her cuts were and she got signed up to the corporate-plan way of life. When she wouldn't let the label shorten her songs to get them on the radio, the 'suits' were sweating bullets. *Rolling Stone* and *Spin* were running stories, she had the top critically-acclaimed release of the year ... and she was out on the road in some ... venue, somewhere, singing and selling CDs. It was her way. "It all comes down to what you want," Williams told *Georgia Straight* writer Mike Usinger. "If you want to sell two million records, you make a video. I don't feel that I have to sell two million records. ... Everyone else wants me to, but I'm not everyone else. Because of where I come from, I prefer the grassroots approach. ... You make a good record, and then you go out on the road."

Williams put up a stonewall when it came to editing her music. "If they want to play the songs the way they are on the record then, great. If they want to edit them down, that's not going to happen." It was a horror show for the suits. No video. No shortened 'radio versions' of the album cuts. What they had was a tiger by the tail, a cult figure, a self-made artist who knew who she was, and that she was ... who she was ... because she had never done it any other way. CAR WHEELS ON A GRAVEL ROAD was never made for airplay formats. The music runs a full gamut from hard-country to gutsy, vulnerable and very real folk. The music runs long. Six minutes a cut and more. But this was the music that had the fans excited. Why in hell would you want to fix it if it ain't broke?

This clash between individual and corporation, Lucinda and Goliath, so to speak, is the basic equation of the contemporary dilemma. It is a situation that is not confined merely to the music business. The modern novel is said to be a book in which an individual's relationship within society is discussed. The post-modern novel and the alternative music movement often discuss the looming confrontation between the individual and the corporation. Will little Lucinda prevail over big bad corporate Goliath? It's not quite that simple. By February 1999, Lucinda had sold 30,000 units in Canada and 345,000 in the United States. She had certainly paid her way. But what bugged her the most was that as soon as she began to sell big, everybody seemed to want a piece of her. The suits wanted her to sell more, when she'd already eclipsed her previous efforts.

Austin-based Jimmy Dale Gilmore had this to say to Mike Usinger on the subject: "'Some people say that she's sort of a classic temperamental artist. That could be said, but the thing is she's very sensitive — at times to the point where it's almost painful. At the same time, she's extremely true to her own vision, and I admire that immensely. On the one hand, she seems so fragile and scared, and on the other, she's a rock. She has a really strange mix of wanting to be accepted and approved of, but she *will not* alter herself for the sake of boosting her record sales. Lucinda Williams is a beautiful paradox, and I love her for that." The suits, to give them credit, had played a part, too. Steve Cranwell, a Polygram VP, told Usinger in a phone interview from Toronto, "We put it on our priority list. When this record first came out, we had tiny orders. That's when I took over and started sabre-rattling from the office here. I told our people to get to the record stores, sit down with the buyers and make them listen. I had stickers made up which we stuck on the albums — they were five star reviews calling it a masterpiece. We also made sure that we had heavy in-store play for the record, because it all comes down to letting people hear the music."

By this time, the suits and their temperamental artist both knew that something extraordinary was going on. Williams had been told that a really varied list of artists liked her music, including K.D. Lang. She told Usinger, "I've seen a lot of genre-spanning. The people who like it run the gamut from Joey Ramone to David Byrne to Bernie Taupin. A while ago I got a really sweet letter from Captain Beefheart ... I thought that was so cool." What she didn't like was that along with the accolades from her peers there seemed to be an endless demand on her for interviews. She told Usinger, "That's what bugs me most about all this — the bigger-than-life, put-people-on-a-pedestal way that people approach you with. It's got me thinking that too much fame isn't healthy. I've been inundated with all these interviews and stuff, and, quite frankly, it's been draining."

Lucinda Williams, along with Shania, Madonna, Alanis, Lauryn Hill, Sheryl Crow, and Celine Dion won a Grammy in 1998. But Lucinda won for best roots recording. Her roots were what had kept her grounded through her worst nightmare ... a successful album that people all over the world really ... liked. In this instance, Goliath was more like a big old teddy bear Godzilla who just wanted to pick her up and put her on top of the Empire State building. When she didn't want that, her suits went to bat for her, anyway. No one tied her up and filmed a video. No one surreptitiously chopped minutes off her album tracks and put them out to radio. A manager *could* have fielded those interview requests and put up a safe zone.

What I couldn't understand was, why was she protesting so loudly? I didn't make it to Lucinda's Vancouver concert, but I did learn that her performance had been so loud that she'd knocked plaster off the ceiling of the venue and pissed a few of the people who'd bought tickets right off. No one had promised it was going to be easy to listen to Lucinda Williams, though, so what *was* the problem?

NEW
COUNTRY

☆☆☆

'New country' began as a new traditionalist movement that caught fire when Ricky Skaggs left Emmylou's Hot Band to pursue a solo career. Skaggs revived feelings every country music fan had for the roots of the music by pickin' and singin' in that old bluegrass style on his early Epic releases. His heartfelt approach led to a string of number one hits that included *Heartbroke, Honey Open That Door,* and *Country Boy.* Ricky sang gospel music, too, and when he won awards he thanked the Lord for his success.

At least as important as divine intervention in the new traditionalist recordings that brought country radio back to life during the 1980s were improved studio equipment and techniques for recording acoustic instruments. The Nashville penchant for doubling standard six-string guitars with 'high-strung' guitars to create a wash of strummed instrument upon which the dobro stings, mandolin frills, and fiddle licks sparkled, had never sounded better than on recordings by Ricky Skaggs, Randy Travis, and the O'Kanes. When broadcast by the new high-powered FM band country stations that were popping up all over the place, dobros and mandolins had never sounded fatter . . . richer, and yet they sparkled as bright as morning sunshine gleaming off your favorite trout stream. Some of the best of this vital new music was made by Kathy Mattea, the Judds, the Sweethearts of the Rodeo, Patty Loveless, Tanya Tucker, Paulette Carlson, and Pam Tillis, women who championed both the return to country's roots and a new attitude in the lyrics they sang.

When Kathy Mattea came along, she added a folk sensibility to country radio that had been missing for a few years. Mattea **KATHY MATTEA** was born on June 21, 1959 in Cross Lane, West Virginia. While attending West Virginia University, she joined the bluegrass group Pennsboro. When she moved to Nashville, she become known as the tour guide at the Country Music Hall of Fame who made it in country music. Beginning in 1983, Mattea began to record for Mercury Records with producer Allen Reynolds at the helm. Reynolds was eager to fuse country with folk. "I hooked up with Allen Reynolds," Mattea remembered in a bio posted at country.com. "The Urban-Cowboy-style music happening all around us at that time disturbed him greatly, and he had even contemplated a return to songwriting." It took the Reynolds-Mattea team a bit of time to refine their approach, but in 1986 Kathy Mattea hit it big with Nanci Griffith's *Love At The Five And Dime*. When she hit the number one spot on the country charts with Pat Alger's *Eighteen Wheels And A Dozen Roses*, the CMA's Single of the Year in 1988, Kathy was the uncrowned queen of the new traditionalist movement.

Further recognition for her music came after she released *Come From The Heart* and *Burnin' Old Memories*, both number ones with a beat. *Where've You Been*, a heart-wrenching story ballad that Kathy sang with compassion, established her as a vocalist possessed of a rare talent. Kathy Mattea was named Best Female Vocalist by the CMA in both 1989 and 1990. In 1991, a Grammy for her vocal performance on *Where've You Been* went to Kathy and a second Grammy went to her husband John Vezner who had co-written the song with Don Henry. In 1993, she was again awarded a Grammy for her bluegrass flavored gospel album GOOD NEWS. Kathy Mattea released a string of Top 40 hits in the 1990s that include *She Came From Forth Worth*, *Lonesome Standard Time*, and *Walking Away A Winner*. In 1997, Kathy's video of *455 Rocket*, directed by Steven Goldmann, was the CMA Music Video of the Year.

A survivor of vocal chord surgery, Kathy Mattea is as emotional a singer as you are likely to encounter and one of the true talents of the new traditionalist movement. Moreover, Kathy's music is people music. *Where've You Been* had shown insight into the lonely years that seniors experience when sickness strikes a lifelong love-inspired marriage. Her gospel song *Mary Did You Know* inspired others who were healing from the loss of loved-ones as is testified by the posting of the tear-stained internet story of Walter Moodie who, along with his wife Marlis, was beside himself with grief over the death of his 16-year-old son, Joshua ... until he discovered the healing quality of Kathy's *Mary Did You Know*. Not a country fan when he first heard the song on the radio, Walter joined Mattea's fan club and wrote her a letter. Sometime later, he and his wife heard Kathy sing at a concert in Tulsa and met with the singer who thoughtfully recalled, "You're the Walter who sent me the letter about your son, aren't you?" Moodie credits the song and a hug he received from Kathy Mattea as being the ingredients that healed his sorrow-stricken heart.

Although the father-daughter duo of Royce and Jeannie Kendall had carved out a successful career singing cheatin' songs during the late 1970s and early 1980s, no one on the planet was prepared for the mother-daughter combination of Naomi and Wynonna Judd, whose names soon became household words as they first hit the top of the *Billboard* country chart in 1984 with their second single *Mama, He's Crazy*, and followed up with a steady stream of ten consecutive number one hits, broken only by their cover of Elvis Presley's *Don't Be Cruel*, which peaked at number 10 in 1986. Musically, the production on the Judds' records was a breath of fresh air, a minimalist blend of acoustic guitars spiced with pedal steel, dobro, and electric piano riffs on hip arrangements put together by producer Brent Maher. Working with guitarist Don Potter, Maher melded bluegrass and rhythm & blues in a soulful accompaniment for the honeyed harmonies fashioned by lead vocalist Wynonna and backup vocalist Naomi. Together, the two had massive appeal for female country fans who responded to the 1995 release *Girls Night Out* as if it were an anthem.

THE JUDDS

> Friday finally came around
> This girl's ready to paint the town
> Tonight ain't nothin' gonna slow me down
> I did my time workin' all week
> I wanna hear a band with a country sound . . .
>
> Well, it's a girl's night out
> Honey, there ain't no doubt
> I'm gonna dance every dance 'til the boys go home . . .
>
> (written by Brent Maher / Jeffrey Bullock)

In addition to their radio hits, Judds' album cuts like Mark Knopfler's *Water Of Love*, the rockabilly-flavored *Not My Baby*, and the emotional

209

River Of Love written by Naomi and John Jarvis allowed fans to put their cassettes on auto-reverse and just let them roll. Soon, everybody you talked to seemed familiar with the soap opera lifestyle of the two singers, who had changed their names from Diana and Christina when they took to the stage, yet carried on more like a mom and daughter-in-law during sometimes feisty interviews. Naomi Judd had been to Hollywood with her daughters Wynonna and Ashley. She'd tried her hand at acting as a speaking extra in *More American Graffiti*, and she'd learned the appeal that their Kentucky hills heritage had out West. When she and her daughters moved back to Tennessee, Naomi put that knowledge to work. By the time that Wynonna had developed the passion for music Naomi already had in her heart, Naomi had achieved what could be described as groupie status in nearly every Music Row office. She could walk through most of the doors. And, although she regularly overdressed for her appointments, she had developed a resolve to use the attraction men felt toward her rather than to be flattered by their attentions. She had a vision, which very few performers had, and people like Chet Atkins saw promise in the mother-daughter act. Number-crunchers like Joe Galante had succeeded Chet's chosen successor, Jerry Bradley, as head honcho at RCA, however, and Chet was no longer a powerbroker in 1982. Eventually, the Judds' records would be issued on RCA, but not before their publicist Woody Bowles had brokered their music through Dick Whitehouse at Curb Records. Ricky Skaggs also dug the Judds early tapes, and it was Ricky who introduced them to Woody Bowles. Ricky's success on the radio, when his bluegrass-inspired records hit the top of the charts, created a receptive environment for the heartfelt acoustic-based gospel, rhythm & blues, and country blend that became known as Judds music.

Some people, especially the wives of some of the execs, saw Naomi as a hair-brained predator, a threat. Others like Jon Schulenberger gave Naomi and Wynonna a serious shot, but felt that the talent was Wynonna and merely tolerated Naomi's self-promotions. As Bob Millard puts it when describing the elder Judd, "Wynonna has called her 'the neurotic, dramatic Naomi of the universe,' referring both to her driving ambitions and her behavioral style." By the time Naomi and Wynonna finally met producer Brent Maher, the two women knew well the ingredients that created their sound. They'd linked up with songwriter Kenny O'Dell who had listened to their harmonizing and had crafted the remarkable *Mama He's*

Crazy specifically for them to sing. As Wynonna told biographer Bob Millard, "We became fascinated with some unusual variations that you can get from four-part harmonies. So, we went out and bought these two 30-dollar blue-light special tape recorders from K-Mart. We'd sing our duets into one tape recorder, then play it back and sing harmonies against ourselves into the other recorder."

A final tension-creating ingredient came from the fact that although Wynonna had graduated high school before the act hit the big time, mother and daughter seemed to exist in a constant state of bickering. "Life got crazy," Millard wrote, "for the responsible people around them. Rehearsing new songs or working on demo tapes with Potter and Maher seemed to be the only place where they could suspend their animosity and cooperate."

"Coming as it did right after high school," Wynonna told Millard, "I didn't have a chance to move out of the house, become responsible, and make mistakes. I had to make them in front of her." Naomi said, "And of course a mother sees any mistakes the child makes as a reflection on her parenting. So, I was under a lot of pressure." Added to the highly emotional nature of both women, and the fact that as Wynonna sought her identity she was experiencing the initial inspiration of young love with her first boyfriend, the Maher-Judds recording sessions captured a maximum of emotion. The mutually competitive relationship between Naomi and Wynonna continued into the public eye as their records became hits and they confronted the public in interviews, but it was toned back and they came across as this marvelous mother-daughter duo who loved each other so much they could afford to disagree on things. People couldn't help but love them both, especially when they put aside their differences and began to sing.

Judds radio hits like *Grandpa (Tell Me About The Good Old Days)* and *Why Not Me*, the 1994 CMA Single of the Year, sold plenty of records. However, it was not until the 1990s, when Naomi was forced off the road by continuing poor health, that Wynonna's first solo album sold into the millions. Wynonna, a lot of people had been noticing, was ready to rock, but seemed held back by her mother's country sensibilities. Although smouldering vocals on *Young Love* and *One Man Woman* had pointed to a real break with the easy-going Judds' approach, Wynonna's first solo number one was the heartfelt story-ballad *She Is His Only Need*.

Wynonna and producer Tony Brown seemed to have found a nearly perfect balance between country and pop on cuts like *I Saw The Light* and *No One Else On Earth* on that first solo outing, balancing the tough and rough with the lyrical and emotional material like *My Strongest Weakness*. Wynonna's debut has sold four million copies since it was released in 1992. Subsequent releases have not done as well in the market place, although Wynonna's recording of Mary Chapin Carpenter's *Girls With Guitars* echoed the appeal of *Girls Night Out* when released to radio in 1996.

One of the most awarded groups in the history of country music, the Judds have won six Grammies, nine CMA awards, eight Academy of Country Music awards, an American Music Award, and numerous TNN/*Music City News* acknowledgements as top achievers during the 1980s and early 1990s. The Judds' final concert on December 4, 1991 was an emotional moment for both the performers and their fans. Captured on film for the full-length video release *The Judds (Their Final Concert)*, Naomi and Wynonna, despite the fact they were recovering from a flu bug, turn in classic performances. Intimate camera work and editing provides the home video viewer with plenty of facial expression from both singers and lends insight to their huge appeal as a performing act. Where Naomi shines her eyes wider and brighter than the headlights on a brand-new Cadillac as she beams at her audience between her lines, a sultry Wynonna, backed by the Jordanaires on *Don't Be Cruel*, curls her lip in an eerie recreation of Elvis Presley's trademark vocal style that parents inevitably mistook for a cheeky sneer in the 1950s. Carl Perkins stops by to recreate his efforts on *Let Me Tell You About Love*, and Naomi manages to wring every drop of emotion out of the occasion, introducing band leader Don Potter and just about everyone else on stage during the proceedings. Her almost whispered confidential confessions are played to an audience packed with celebrities like Reba McEntire, who turned out for the event and appeared to be as moved as Naomi herself with each ladeling on of the shtick. Heck, I had a tear or two in my eye myself the first time I viewed the farewell footage.

Of course, I was also laying bets with my friends as to just how long it would be before we were to sit down again to view the Judds' reunion concert. Call me a cynic, call me whatever you will, but before this book went to press, that very reunion has been announced for the end of the millennium, that's correct, the very last night of 1999. A friend called, when he heard the news, and quipped, "As if we needed more complications ..."

"What?" I said, "the Y2K thing?"

"More like the why two Judds? . . . thing," he smart-assed.

After he hung up, I thought about that for a while. Apparently, there was to be an album of new recordings, as well, which had nothing to do with the uncertainty looming on the horizon concerning computer switching systems that might or might not continue to work after midnight on December 31, 1999. And, without electricity, you wouldn't even be able to hear the music on a CD unless you had put aside a stash of Duracell batteries in preparation for the predicted doomsday. Perhaps, I speculated, this was what we should all do, gather together and celebrate the moment with music.

Born Patricia Ramey on January 4, 1957 in Pikeville, Kentucky, Patty was the sixth of seven children, the daughter of coal miner John Ramey and his wife Naomi, and a distant cousin of Loretta Lynn. When her father's coal dust-damaged lungs and an ailing heart needed more medical attention than could be gotten in Butcher Holler or nearby Pikeville, the family moved to Louisville. There, Patty performed bluegrass and country in high school with her brother, Roger. When Patty was 14, she and Roger began knocking on doors on Music Row. Roger found enthusiasm when Porter Wagoner liked one of Patty's early songs. Dolly Parton, Wagoner's singing partner, took Patty under her wing for a while. Then Patty got a foothold in the music business when she replaced Loretta Lynn on the Wilburn Brothers tours, singing with the Wilburns on weekends while she was still in high school. However, Doyle Wilburn imposed a patriarchal control on her, forbidding her to carry on with the band's drummer, Terry Lovelace. Doyle's way was to have her work menial jobs in his many cafes and offices. He controled her publishing. A girl singer in those days had little say, but Patty left the Wilburns and married Terry. The marriage was not a happy one, and playing in nowhere Top 40 cover bands with no future of getting anywhere nearly ended her passion to sing country music. Playing in those wateringholes, alcoholism is a ready made occupational hazard, and Patty let the bottle get her down.

However, she got herself back together and began working with her brother, Roger, once again. Roger managed to get Tony Brown at MCA to listen to a tape. And Tony convinced his label boss, Jimmy Bowen, to let him sign Patty. Bowen wasn't fond of traditional country singers — he'd

PATTY LOVELESS

spent much of his career as a corporate executive smoothing things out into more contemporary equations — but Tony persisted and Patty was signed to MCA. Tony Brown and Emory Gordy Jr. had played together in Emmylou's Hot Band. They were co-producing in Nashville and they collaborated on Patty's early albums. When the albums produced turn-table hits but few sales, Tony took over.

Divorced from Terry Lovelace, Patty kept the in-joke name she'd used on her love letters written to Terry. As a name for a performer, "Patty Lovelace" was a might close to blue movie actress Linda Lovelace, thank you very much. Besides, "Loveless" provided a kind of mysterious side that matched the throbbing ache in her vocals. However, she was not free from the influence of Terry Loveless who spilled his guts to the tabloids for a few quick bucks, and Patty, who had had an abortion at one time during the couple's futureless career together, had to face the humiliation of reading about herself in stories that bore headlines like "Patty Loveless Killed Our Baby." She was getting used to living in the male-dominated South by this time, getting used to the treatment men often meted out, but it hurt all the same. "I wish that he could just get on," Loveless told Mark Bego for his book *Country Gals: The Superstars of Today's Country Music*. "I hope that people will understand and that I'll be forgiven. I told my mother before the story came out. She said I'd done the right thing. Imagine how hard that was for her to say. Her daddy was a Baptist preacher, she grew up in a house where it was considered sinful to even dance . . ."

Patty recorded five albums for MCA. She first hit into the Top 10 with *If My Heart Had Windows*, *A Little Bit Of Love*, and *Blue Side Of Town*. In 1989, she hit the number one spot for the first time with *Timber, I'm Falling In Love* and again in 1990 with *Chains*. There were more readjustments to be made, however, and like Loretta and Dolly, Patty had to take over the reins of her situation from her relatives, in her case, her brother, Roger. With new management from Larry Fitzgerald, she addressed the final issue that was keeping her from a full measure of success. She seemed to be fourth on the MCA female vocalist totem pole. Releases by Wynonna, Reba, and Trisha seemed to get priority when it came to promotion. A move to Epic Records in 1992 rectified the situation. Her husband, Emory Gordy Jr., moved on over with her from MCA to produce her records at Epic. But there was still one obstacle in her path. This time it was no male impresario or ex-husband, it was her own vocal chords, and in the midst of recording her first Epic album, she went under the knife.

Surgery is a terrifying proposition for any singer. However, female vocalists have proven more prone to nodes and growths and scar tissue on their vocal chords than male singers, and it has to be done or careers will end. Patty got support from Larry Fitzgerald who went with her to her appointment with Dr Robert Osoff. The medical specialist told her she had to quit singing and get treatment right away. Her last performance before the operation was the taping of the CBS Special *The Women Of Country Music*.

Patty's husband, Emory, helped out during the time following surgery when she couldn't speak or sing. People like Pam Tillis, Barbara Mandrell, and Emmylou Harris sent flowers. Naomi Judd and Kathy Mattea lent personal support. Hundreds of fans wrote supporting letters. Surprisingly, it cured her head problems, the psychological wounds she'd suffered while being passed around like a piece of meat by the men in her early life...and the available guilt that women in the South often felt, blaming themselves rather than facing up to the patriarchy. Self-esteem is such an elusive quality in life that she'd found it difficult to see herself in a positive light. The crisis had threatened her career, but the support she got helped immensely to heal all wounds. "At the end of November," she told Bego, "I was able to start whispering. I had voice therapy and slowly began to sing scales." She went back into the studio on her 36th birthday, January 4, 1993, but she had to start over from square one. "I had to go back and re-sing all the material. It was scary for me." Fortunately, it turned out that her voice was stronger than ever and it wasn't long before she had her confidence back.

Patty Loveless appeals to the traditionalist who also yearns for a touch of country-rock in the mix. By the time she came to record for Epic she had become the quintessential 'new country' artist. Her performances were a straightforward, matter-of-fact delivery of country songs and seldom veered toward the world of entertainment where shtick often made up for lack of talent and raw appeal. But she was also known for being from the *Blue Side Of Town*. Her last MCA single to chart had been *Hurt Me Bad In A Real Good Way*. It was a typical twisted Nashville cliche, but it was also part of her personal dilemma, her inability to feel self-esteem. At Epic, working with her husband, things changed. It was a song that Epic A&R guy Doug Johnson brought to the sessions that put her over the top into her own identity. *How Can I Help You Say Goodbye* had been written by Karen Taylor-Good and Burton Collins but it was so emotionally wrenching that, at first, Patty didn't seem to be able to get through the verses and chorus. Both Collins and Johnson lent their support. Collins wrote a letter to Patty that revealed the emotional turmoil *he'd* gone through coming to terms with the death of his grandmother in the song lyric. "The song was hitting me so hard," Patty told Bego, "that I was crying to the point that I couldn't get it out. I was so emotional with it because I've been through all these situations — of moving away from friends to a bigger city; I've been through divorce and I have lost a parent."

Patty's first public singing appearance after her surgery was at the Opry on January 16th. By the time that ONLY WHAT I FEEL was released in April, Patty was back on the tour circuit and the lead single was headed toward the top of the chart. *Blame It On Your Heart* went number one for two weeks that summer. A year later, when *How Can I Help You Say Goodbye* was the fourth single from the album to be released, it hit the number 3 spot. Through inspired song selection and innovative recordings, Patty Loveless has continued to carve out a place for herself despite the changing tableau of country radio in the 1990s. Recordings like *I Try To Think About Elvis, You Can Feel Bad,* and Gretchen Peters *You Don't Even Know Who I Am* have kept Loveless near the top of the charts and in the spotlight, a singer much-loved by her fans and a popular performer wherever she appears.

The move to Epic brought four million-selling albums and awards galore. Winner of a CMA award for her vocal collaboration with George Jones and others on Jones' *I Don't Need Your Rockin' Chair* in 1993, Patty won the 1995 CMA Album of the Year for WHEN FALLEN ANGELS FLY. In 1996 both the CMA and ACM voted Patty Loveless their Female Vocalist of the Year. In 1998, George Jones contributed a special guest appearance on Patty's *You Don't Seem To Miss Me* and the two were awarded a Grammy. By 1999, Patty seemed surrounded by poppy country divas and would-be divas, one of few traditional country singers still heard regularly on the radio, yet she hit into heavy rotation with her hard-country rocker *Can't Get Enough.*

The first time I heard Pam Tillis sing was when she appeared as a member of Women in the Round at a Vancouver club. She was a singer-songwriter in those days, daughter of famed country songwriter-entertainer Mel Tillis, a personality and talent who seemed, to me, to shine just a little bit brighter as a performer than her fellow songwriters, Ashley Cleveland, Tricia Walker, and Karen Staley, all of whom had enviable publishing deals of their own and hits out with respectable recording artists in the 1980s. Basically, Tillis and company were not a group at all but four songwriters who were brash enough to take the Nashville guitar-pull and tour it as far away from Music City as they could.

PAM TILLIS

The second time I heard Pam Tillis sing, she had already distinguished herself as one of the leading recording artists of the 'new country' era with such memorable releases as the number 3 hits *Maybe It Was Memphis* and *Shake The Sugar Tree*, and was about to release *Let That Pony Run* and the 'new' hurtin' song, *Cleopatra, Queen Of Denial*.

Well I said he had a lot of potential
He was only misunderstood
You know he didn't really mean to treat me so bad
And I swore one day I would tame him
Even though he loved to run hog wild
Just call me Cleopatra everybody
'Cause I'm the Queen of Denial . . . .

(written by Pam Tillis/ Bob DiPiero/ Jan Buckingham)

These were all singles that contributed to Pam Tillis being named the 1994 CMA Female Vocalist of the Year.

On the stage of Vancouver's Orpheum Theatre, a former Opera House with excellent acoustics, Pam Tillis really got in our faces courtesy of the innovative use of online monitors or 'earphone monitors' that she and her band utilized, freeing themselves from the cumbersome use of those chubby black speaker boxes that used to stud the lip of all performance stages. As her well-choreographed show unfolded, the immediate effect was that she had erased the barriers between herself and her audience. We felt as if we were in the same 'space' as she was. In addition to the forward-looking technology, Pam Tillis utilized age-old techniques that had done so well for generations of entertainers who had preceded her. I will never forget her recollection of the times when her father had taken her along to his scheduled songwriting sessions on Music Row when she was knee-high-to-a-grasshopper and propped her up in his guitar case while he picked and sang and created. It was a vivid picture to which her audience could relate. Country music was in this woman's blood, we all felt.

Born in Nashville on July 24, 1957, Pam Tillis' Opry stage debut came when she was a mere eight years old. She was raised on country, but she studied classical piano, worked as a session-singer, attended the University of Tennessee, played jazz in a San Francisco fusion band, and recorded a pop album for Warner Bros before she began to record her own country records. Of course, she'd already sung on very good records like her dad's 1980 Top 10 country hit *Your Body Is An Outlaw*. And she'd already had her songs recorded by artists as varied as Conway Twitty, Juice Newton, and Chaka Khan. Pam knew that if she was going to be successful as a country recording artist she had to connect with her audience, and to do that she needed to record very good songs. "If a song is a hit, if it has any impact at all," she told Kimmy Wix during an interview for *country.com*, "it gets incorporated into the fabric of people's lives. . . . When we launch into *Maybe It Was Memphis*, you can feel the emotion go across the room. That's the power of a great song."

Pam also realized, right from her 1991 debut single *Don't Tell Me What To Do*, that making distinctive music videos would be important in putting a face to that song. By the time that CMT viewers had seen her innovative videos for *Maybe It Was Memphis* and *Shake The Sugar Tree* in heavy rotation, they felt they knew her when they turned out to her concerts. The unashamedly Liz Tayloresque production for the *Cleopatra, Queen Of Denial* video was so powerful that it was easy for viewers to imagine that the singer was already a major star. Men found her video performance provocative. Women felt they were hearing and seeing a message directed to them, as well.

Pam was displaying the same kind of intellect, talent, and creativity that K.D. Lang had introduced to the country equation a few years earlier. Pam had 'attitude', too. But where Kathy Lang had met opposition in the late 1980s, Pam was doing her thing in the 1990s and was named CMT's Top Video Artist in 1995. She was a *Homeward Looking Angel*, although at times it seemed to some observers that her career was change-driven. "I just get bored easily," Pam told *country.com* writer Kimmy Wix for the June

1998 internet article, "so, I like to keep it new. I never like to repeat myself and I always want to be breaking new ground."

Pam had been the first female country artist of the 1990s to solo produce her own album when she took full control of production on ALL OF THIS LOVE in 1995. The following year, Pam racked up a little bit more country music history when she and fellow second generation country stars Lorrie Morgan and Carlene Carter set out on an all-female tour. Of course, Pam Tillis was a willing fundraiser for the "Nashville CARES" benefit AIDS concert, which she headlined with Kathy Mattea, Clint Black, Mandy Barnett, and K.T. Oslin. By 1998, Pam was performing with her dad at Mel's Branson Missouri Theater shows where they spiced their sets with comedy routines.

One of the few things that Pam hadn't changed over the years was her record label. She'd been with Arista, right from her first Top 40 country hit. Many of her albums had gone gold. HOMEWARD LOOKING ANGEL was certified triple platinum. But the dissolution of her marriage to Bob DiPiero and a longtime management deal had her reeling. "At first I thought I couldn't do the album," she told Jim Bessman for a May 23, 1998 *Billboard* magazine article, "but I just rolled up my sleeves and went into the studio every day and surrounded myself with people I felt comfortable with — and it felt a lot like when I first started out in the business." When her next album EVERYTIME was released, *I Said A Prayer* shot up the charts. Pam still had what it takes to be a country star in 1998, but she continued to look for new horizons. Television parts on *L.A. Law*, *Diagnosis Murder*, and *Promised Land* led her to the Broadway stage. On March 16, 1999 she was in New York City for a three week stint as a member of the cast of the musical theater production, *Smokey Joe's Cafe: The Songs of Leiber and Stoller*. After that, with new management in place, she would hit the tour circuit with her band. She was just letting that pony run.

TANYA TUCKER

Tanya Tucker may have been goaded into being fully prepared for stardom by a bull-headed daddy, Beau Tucker . . . but Beau just might have known what he was up to when he disciplined Tanya, sending her outside in the dark to sulk when she didn't get things right as far as her home-made music lessons were going. This mutually confrontive relationship has held together throughout her long and successful career, although she did try out some flaky L.A. music biz types for a short time.

From the times that she defiantly sang Hank Williams and Elvis numbers to her parents, Juanita and Beau, and anybody who would listen to her, declaring that she was going to be a star, just like Presley ... to the time she and Beau arrived in Nashville in a big old Caddy that they subsequently hid down the street from the Music Row office doors they beat their knuckles against ... Tanya Tucker was destined to become ... Tanya Tucker, the fifth most played female country singer on radio, ever, and a champion of children's rights in country music before people cottoned to the fact that children had rights. In her adult years, Tanya has become known as an outspoken believer in the assertion that women could do just about anything that men could do, they just hadn't had the chance to do it, yet.

Even after the legendary linkup with Billy Sherrill and the remarkable *Delta Dawn* debut, Tanya insisted on telling folks that she wanted to be just like Elvis. She sometimes wore an Elvis costume with a high-neck collar, and a posed photo of Tanya, reproduced in her biography *Nickel Dreams*, has her looking very much the convincing Elvis impersonator, although still a teen. Of course, right from the start, she irritated a whole lot of people and caused a whole lot of controversy when she sang supposedly adult lyrics to songs like *Would You Lay With Me (In A Field Of Stone)* and *I Don't Believe My Heart Can Stand Another You*. As soon as she reached legal age, Tanya rebelled against Beau's generationally-limited vision of who she really was. Heading west to L.A., she recorded the sizzling TNT, a country-rock album that was only exceeded in its boldness by the 'hot' posed photo of Tanya that emblazoned its cover.

Tanya had an eager appetite for life and soon found herself acting in Hollywood films like *Amateur Night At The Dixie Bar*, *Hard Country*, and *Georgia Peaches*. Tanya made new friends, too, with people like Beverly Hills, who became a close companion, Jan Michael Vincent, and Bette Midler's backup singers Katy Seagal and Linda Hart. And she loved to party, carrying on with the likes of Cher, Don Johnson, Candy Clarke, Clint Eastwood and Katy and Linda. When she hooked up with Glen Campbell and the two became an item, fun times soon turned sour. During this period of time, her recording sessions were not what they had been, and by 1983 nobody was playing her records on the radio.

If that had been all she wrote, the angels in country music heaven would still have held a place of honor for Tanya until she finally arrived. But in 1986, Tanya Tucker came back strongly with the album GIRLS LIKE ME, a 'new country' trendsetter, and followed up with the excellent LOVE ME LIKE YOU USED TO in 1987. Fourteen years after she'd been discovered by Sherrill, Tanya was back with Jerry Crutchfield at the helm and creating the best music of her career on cuts like *One Love At A Time, Just Another Love, Love Me Like You Used To,* and the show-stopping vocal collaboration *I Won't Take Less Than Your Love* with Paul Overstreet and Paul Davis. A relentless assault on the top spot of the *Billboard* country chart continued with the number one hits *If It Don't Come Easy, Strong Enough To Bend,* and the playful good-times song, *Highway Robbery.* Tanya seemed like she just wanted to have fun.

> Okay officer, I admit it, I was speedin'
> But before you write me up, let me tell you the reason . . .
> I was cruisin' along when he pulled up out of nowhere
> He was hotter than the Jag he drove and just one lane over
> He aimed those angel eyes at me
> And smiled like we were meant to be
> Oh, he stole my heart, from a movin' car
> It was highway robbery . . .

> (written by Michael Garvin / Bucky Jones / Tom Shapiro)

Tanya was right at home in the music video medium, a strumpet in leather who knew how to turn the men on. For her 1990 video of *Walkin' Shoes,* Tanya simply went shopping on camera and won over any of the women in the audience who had not been sure exactly what she was all about. At the Orpheum Theatre in Vancouver for an early 1990s concert, she strutted about the stage in a new leather outfit she told her audience she'd purchased while shopping with her mom at one of Robson Street's exclusive boutiques. "So, what do y'all think, do you like it?" she asked before her band launched into the rollicking *Walkin' Shoes,* the rockin' *It Won't Be Me,* the smouldering *Some Kind Of Trouble,* and the trembling ambience of *Two Sparrows In A Hurricane.*

Tanya's biography, *Nickel Dreams,* is just about the most intelligent and no-holds-barred country biography ever written. What comes out of a read of the book is the fact that even when her parents and friends installed her in the Betty Ford Clinic, and she was almost driven nuts by her fellow patients, Tanya kept her wits about her, as well as her sense of humor. She knew she could kick her substance abuse. But she knew that what she'd been up against all these years, that had maybe even caused some of her rebellious actions, was patriarchy. It was men who imposed a male world upon women and it was high time things changed. It had just about broken her heart. *Tell Me About It* she sang in a duet with Delbert McClinton. Through her talent, and her stubborn confrontations with an even more stubborn daddy, she was able to put food on the table and pay the rent for her family before she was old enough to operate a motor vehicle.

In the 1990s, Tanya Tucker has emerged as one of the most intelligent spokespersons of the women's movement in music, although, as had been the case for Tammy Wynette, for Tanya, there would also be some downsides. Like the time during September 1991 that she was laid up in a hospital bed about to give birth and the CMA deigned to, finally, after all the years of ripping her heart and lungs open onstage for country music, award Tanya with her very first CMA Award as Best Female Vocalist.

PAULETTE CARLSON AND HIGHWAY 101   Paulette Carlson was born October 11, 1953 in Northfield, Minnesota. In 1978, she arrived in Nashville where she secured employment as a staff writer for the Oakridge Boys publishing company. It was Dirt Band manager Chuck Morris' idea to put Paulette together with a band, and guitarist Jack Daniels, bassist Curtis Stone, and drummer Cactus Moser seemed to fit the bill. The group formed in Los Angeles and took their name from the coast highway, a ruggedly scene route.

Highway 101, along with Chris Hillman's Desert Rose Band and Southern Pacific, cranked out some of the best country-rock of the decade. All three bands had a West Coast flavor, but it was Paulette Carlson who brought Highway 101 a decided edge. Paulette was a slender wisp of a woman with big wide open eyes and a voice you had to hear to believe. The group's 1987 debut single, *The Bed You Made For Me*, was an intelligent variation of the hurtin' songs of yesteryear and peaked at number 4 on the *Billboard* country chart. With distinctive guitar-styling from Jack Daniels and group harmonies that would become trademark for the band, Highway 101 was on the map. The follow-up single, *Whiskey, If You Were A Woman*, continued the hip lyric trend and peaked at number 2. The

KATHY MATTEA

TANYA TUCKER

**PATTY
LOVELESS**

**SWEETHEARTS
OF THE
RODEO**

**PAM
TILLIS**

band's third single of 1987, Harlan Howard's *Somewhere Tonight*, hit the number one spot in early 1988. Further releases consistently hit the Top 10 until *Who's Lonely Now* became the band's last number one. A final Top 10, the strident *Walkin', Talkin', Barely Beatin' Broken Heart* epitomized what Highway 101 could be at their best. It was a joy-pain thing, really. They were happy, especially when they sang their music live with Cactus Moser's drum-kit pushed to the front line beside everyone else, but they sang about sorrow. Of course, their music warmed a whole lot of cold, cold hearts and both the CMA and the ACM twice named Highway 101 top country group.

When the good songs no longer turned up and airplay for Highway 101 began to diminish, Paulette Carlson left the group to try out singing on her own. She was not successful. Neither were the boys, Jack, Curtis, and Cactus, when they tried out a replacement, Nikki Nelson, in the studio. Nikki's rendition of *Bing, Bam, Boom* just didn't have the same oomph that Paulette's smokey vocals did. A 1995 reunion failed to re-ignite the original magic. But Paulette Carlson's remarkable vocals survive on the original recordings that Highway 101 made when the initial excitement was there.

California born and raised sisters Janis and Kristine Oliver took **SWEETHEARTS** their duo name from the classic 1968 Byrds-do-country album **OF THE RODEO** SWEETHEART OF THE RODEO. Hanging out on Manhattan Beach in Southern California during the 1970s was pretty cool for Janis and Kristine. The teenagers loved those surf dudes, but when it came to making music, they were folkies. "Emmylou Harris had made her first record PIECES OF THE SKY and it took us by storm," says Janis. "There was a real cool underground of folk and country-rock in southern California at that time. They had bluegrass festivals and Linda Ronstadt would jump up stage and sing. They had these cool people that you could listen to that were not mainstream rock and they were not traditional country. My sister and I were led in that direction." Even in those days, Janis and Kristine knew that they had something unique when they performed together. "Kristine and I sing very well together," says Janis. "We have a buzz that happens with our vocals when we sing harmonies."

When Janis married budding singer-songwriter Vince Gill and Vince got a record deal in Nashville, the couple moved to Tennessee. It was a rush being in Music City, and Janis and Vince quickly got to know people like Tony Brown, who was working at RCA, and Joe Galante, who headed the label. Their friends Rodney Crowell and Rosanne Cash were there, too. Things were happening and Janis knew she had to get her sister into the mix. "We rushed Kristine out here and we went into the studio together and cut some demos, and I said, 'You know what? There are no female duos!'"

There was interest from the people at Sony, but by the time Janis and Kristine were in the studio, the Judds first release hit the airwaves. "It is incredible what they have done," Janis acknowledges. "But it's kind of funny. Before that, we were the ones who were saying, 'If we get a record deal, *we'll* be the first ones. The Judds were there first and they were wonderful. We signed with Sony. They were ready to go the distance. I'm sure they were plotting to have us go against the Judds. That's what you do when you want to have hit records."

Janis and Kristine's debut Columbia album SWEETHEARTS OF THE RODEO hit the stores in 1986 and their cover of The Clovers' 1956 Top 10 r&b hit *Hey Doll Baby* got played on country radio. The follow-up, *Since I Found You*, a song that had been written for the act by Radney Foster and Bill Lloyd, hit into the Top 10. Their third release *Midnight Girl/Sunset Town* peaked at number 4. Success brought interviews where, suddenly, they were asked to define their music. The fans loved them, but the reporters wanted to know what it was that they were doing that was so different. "We were young," Janis remembers, "we just wanted to fit in. We used to try to define it and say, 'we're rockabilly' or 'we're this and that.' But when I look back on it, you know, you just pick the right song, the right feel, and if that's what we are, then that's what we are. I don't try to label it any more." Janis recalls that it was an exciting time to be cutting records for radio. "I think it's amazing that we had the hits that we had. When you look at country radio as a whole . . . what a short amount of time that was when music like ours was accessible. . . . We had Steve Earle and Lyle Lovett for a while. What a wonderful space in time that was!"

Chains Of Gold hit the number 4 spot in early 1987 and by and large the two sisters were able to meet the challenge. Of course, in addition to touring, there was pressure to produce more hits. "Back then we were making records specifically as singles," Janis explains. "You'd pick the best ten songs and record those and the best of those would be your releases. But in those days there was considerably less pressure than there is today with numbers and product sold."

Gotta Get Away was the last track from their debut album to chart when it reached number 10 late in 1987. They had done pretty darned well with their mix of bluegrass and rockin' country. In 1988, singles from the duo's second album, ONE TIME ONE NIGHT, did even better at radio. *Satisfy You* and *Blue To The Bone* both hit the number 5 spot that year. In 1989, the Sweethearts' country version of the Beatles *I Feel Fine* made it to number 9. "Some of the best memories I have are of those days," Janis admits. "And I'm grateful to have had some success with hit singles. My sister and I have some friends who are trying to go back and recapture that again and have singles. Maybe we will, too. But at this point, getting on the radio is not a priority for us."

When the critically acclaimed BUFFALO ZONE was recorded in 1990, a thorny issue was put on the table for discussion. "If you want to sell records, you have to tour," Janis and Kristine were told. "We had conversations with our manager Chuck Flood at that time and our label. They said, 'You're going to have to make a decision here. You're going to have to put your families on hold, leave your kids at home and your husbands or forget it.'" It was a tough call. But when they thought about it for about two seconds, not that tough at all. "Kristine and I looked at each other. What is more important? Back of a tour bus or babies in arms? Back of a tour bus or being home and cooking meals for our husbands? We just looked at our manager and said, 'Family comes first.' We didn't just walk away from it, but we put family first. And we are proud of what we've done as independents with Sugar Hill Records."

The move to the smaller more eclectic label was a compromise, but it was rewarding, too. Janis and Kristine opened a fashion boutique. They spent time with their families. And there was plenty of time for music. "I had aspirations that go beyond being an artist," Gill says. "It went beyond just hearing yourself on the radio. When I would put on one of our Sugar Hill records, I would say, 'You know, *I* produced that.' Our public diminished, but the creative highs went beyond that. We picked these songs. We did these arrangements!"

Their Sugar Hill albums RODEO WALTZ and BEAUTIFUL LIES were well-received by their fans and have gotten good reviews. They were no longer in the Top 40, but Janis and Kristine felt that they had made the right decision. Their indie records represented them more clearly as what they were. Sometimes in the past, they had made other compromises, just to get to the radio market. "As much as I pretended that that was not the case at the time," Janis admits, "it was true. You look back on decisions that you made and how you dressed and how you presented yourself and records that you made . . . back then you were saying, 'I am my own woman. I am calling the shots . . .' But we weren't calling the shots. Sometimes we cut songs that I didn't want to cut. But I didn't want to rock the boat. I wanted to be a team player."

After a few years, her thoughts on the subject clarified themselves. "As women," she says, "there's just a different approach that is called for in doing business. Just because men and women are different. There is not anything anybody can do or say to change that. And the respect we show for each other and the way we deal with each other is very important. It is important the way men treat women, but it is also important the way women treat men. I wanted to earn respect because my idea really *was* the best. Not because I stood up on the table and said, 'Dammit, I'm walkin' out of here.' I wanted to prove myself."

Having seen the two women perform on several occasions, I could remember how they'd had a sort of unique thing going on between them. They weren't exactly sweet all the time but their fans had loved that carrying on. "My sister and I carried our relationship as sisters on stage with us," Janis explains. "We bickered. We would play tricks on each other. If something embarrassing happened to my sister during the day . . . darn it, I'd get up on stage and when she was least expecting it, I'd pull it on her. I'd tell everybody about it. The women in the audience, they have sisters, they have mothers, they have cousins and they have women they interact with . . . and they saw that we were just silly, bickering, funny . . . sisters. Kristine would kid me about changing my hair color every week, you know, 'When was it going to fall out?' and I'd tease her about being flat-chested. I think people, especially women, found it funny."

Now that she is a single woman and her independent-minded daughter Jenny Gill, who also spends some quality time with Vince, has almost come of age . . . what does Janis Gill see herself doing next? Will she produce other artists? Will she put out her very first solo record? It *was* something she'd thought about. "Several years ago Vince suggested that a solo career might be very interesting for me. We talked about a project, but it just never got off the ground. The Sweethearts thing was still going strong."

"Hey," I suggested. "Vince would help you. He's helped everybody else . . ."

Janis had to smile at that. "He's the man to do it. Boy, if he believes in an artist and they need a helping hand, he's there! Before we got started, he was supportive of me and my sister. I actually have some tracks already recorded as a solo artist. It's not very country. It's rootsy. It's very Americana. It's more like the kind of music I grew up on. The Band. Early Tom Petty. Early Mellencamp."

When Jenny Gill took one of the demo CDs that had four of Janis' new tracks on it upstairs to her room, Janis was surprised. Jenny was up there in her room with her friends and they were playing her mom's CD, listening to *I Know Who You Are*, a song that Janis had written. "I tiptoed upstairs and I could see that they had all these CDs lying around. Alanis Morissette, Jewel. They were listening to *I Know Who You Are* and I overheard one of Jenny's friends say, 'You can hear the pain, can't you!' I thought, well, that really means something to me as a writer."

Now that Janis Gill's new music has opened some unexplored doors to communication, Jenny wants to collaborate with Janis. As it is, they listen to the same records. "I was totally blown away by Alanis Morissette's performance on the Grammies," gushes Janis. "I was mesmerized. And Sheryl Crow. It's so funny, I just turned 45 the other day and my daughter is 16. But we have such a connection!"

I said the obvious. "You could be the next Judds."

Janis' eyes opened real wide before she said, "Well, we sound real good together."

It would be ironic if that were to happen, and Janis and I shared a moment of genuine laughter. Janis had already told me that she is a huge Judds' fan, adding, "They have been so good to my daughter and I . . ." But there was a gleam in her eye. The way Janis saw it, Jenny just could be the ultimate songwriting partner. She was totally capable of saying, "You're so uncool, mom." Between the two of them, they just might come up with something hot!

CONTEMPORARY COUNTRY

☆☆☆

The contemporary country era began when Garth Brooks ascended to the throne as the new 'King', the first claimant to the title vacated when Elvis Presley faded away during the 1970s. For a while following Presley's tragic overdose death, no one wanted the crown. Of course, Garth's declaration that he was going to sell a 100 million records in one decade set him up as taking Elvis and the Beatles on in hand to hand combat, so to speak, and if Nashville is the modern Olympus . . . and many deem it so . . . then Garth could be seen as the new King. Certainly, he has been the savior of country music. Garth's immaculate onstage companion has been Trisha Yearwood, but Yearwood, as good as she is at singing, has not been a charismatic leader for women.

That charismatic leader would not arrive on the scene until 1993, and it would not be until her second Nashville album, THE WOMAN IN ME, that Shania Twain would step fully into the national and international spotlight. Once Shania bared her navel in the videos made to support THE WOMAN IN ME, she became the most imitated singer on the planet. If imitation is an acknowledgement of greatness, as it surely is with Garth who spawned a whole generation of hat acts, then Shania Twain is the leader of contemporary country women singers. With her third album, Shania set the record straight with bold reversals of age-old cliches like "Honey, I'm Home" and saucy taunts like "You're Brad Pitt? *That Don't Impress Me Much.*" Before Twain's arrival, Pam Tillis, Lorrie Morgan, Martina McBride, Mary Chapin Carpenter, Faith Hill, and Trisha Yearwood led the way toward full emancipation of country women in music, but none of these artists made the commercial breakthrough and accomplished the mega record sales that Shania did. Since 1995, Shania clones have appeared as frequently as Barbie gets a new outfit.

When LeAnn Rimes appeared on the national scene and began to sell millions upon millions of CDs, she became a prototype that encouraged corporate executives to go after a very young market. They set about cloning LeAnn. Few of these clones have shown the resilience and talent that Rimes has demonstrated. And, if being chosen to sing with Elton John, the queen of pop, is the ultimate compliment for a singer . . . then Shania and LeAnn are the chosen ones.

The final emancipation of the female country singer came when Dixie Chicks came to Nashville to record their remarkable album WIDE OPEN SPACES. Where Trio was a studio group, Dixie Chicks were a genuine version of pop music's Spice Girls, although making reference to the shallow Spicers got many a country journalist in deep doo doo with the Chicks, who not only championed being politically incorrect, but also knew with certainty that they were the real deal that Music Row had always been searching for but could never fabricate artificially. The more than six million units sold of WIDE OPEN SPACES testifies to their authenticity.

Trisha Yearwood's story is among the best known among women artists in the 1990s. Her longtime friendship with the number one recording artist of the era, Garth Brooks, has helped her career in many **TRISHA YEARWOOD** ways. Trisha has toured and sung duets with the 'Garthmeister' that have put her in front of larger audiences than she might have gained touring on her own. Of course, this has been exposure honestly gained, although Trisha and Garth's relationship has become one of the most speculated upon subjects for gossip columnists and tabloid writers. In an age where paparazzi seem to crouch behind every bush ready to leap out and snap candid flashbulb-popping exposé photos, and interviewers seem to twist the language of interviewees every which way but true . . . Garth and Trisha are suspected of more than friendship simply because it is 'news' to speculate, not because there is fact behind rumors. In the vicious competition for spots on the country Top 40, rumor and speculation nevertheless work as well as fact when it comes to selling records. For corporate strategists in the 1990s, radio airplay, like television videos, has been reduced to little more than an advertisement for sales. At one time, not so long ago, radio and television were forums of entertainment when it came to the music. But Garth and

Trisha will survive this trend because they are, in reality, fine artists with something to offer their fans. They should not be denigrated because both are skilful at marketing themselves.

Born on September 19, 1964 in Monticello, Georgia, Trisha Yearwood began her country career as a session singer in Nashville where she met, among many others, Garth Brooks. When Garth recorded NO FENCES, he asked her to sing backup vocals. She toured with Garth in 1991, and her debut single, *She's In Love With The Boy*, became the first debut by a contemporary country female to top the charts. Hit singles like *We Never Had A Broken Heart*, *The Woman Before Me*, and *The Wrong Side Of Memphis* established her as a major force in contemporary country music. Her first three albums — TRISHA YEARWOOD, HEARTS IN ARMOR, and THE SONG REMEMBERS WHEN — went platinum.

Trisha hit number one in 1994 with *XXX's and 000's (An American Girl)*, written by Matraca Berg and Alice Randall, a portrait of the contemporary country woman.

Phone rings baby cries tv diet guru lies
Good morning honey
Go to work make up try to keep balance up
Between love and money
She used to tie her hair up in ribbons and bows
Sign her letters with X's and O's
Got a picture of her mama in heels and pearls
She's tryin' to make it in her daddy's world
She's an American girl
An American girl . . .
Well, she's got God and she's got good wine
Aretha Franklin and Patsy Cline . . .
She's an American girl

(written by Matraca Berg/Alice Randall)

She hit number one again with *Thinking About You*. By 1997, Trisha was named CMA Female Vocalist of the Year. It was about time. She'd won best new artist from *Billboard*, *R&R*, and the Academy of Country Music, as well as a CMA award for her contribution to The Eagles tribute album, but she'd never won what is considered the most significant acknowledgement in country music for a vocalist short of being named CMA Entertainer of the Year. She was named CMA Female Vocalist of the Year a second time while touring with Garth Brooks in 1998. She'd certainly earned that honor. Since her debut, Trisha has sold nearly 8 million records, scored six number one singles on the *Billboard* chart, and gained a solid reputation from those who know her as a 'singer's singer'. When she sang *I Fall To Pieces* with Aaron Neville for the 1996 RHYTHM, COUNTRY AND BLUES album, the two won a Grammy. She appeared in the film *A Thing Called Love* and performed at President Clinton's inauguration. She sang with symphony orchestras and has seen her career written up by Lisa Gubernick in *Get Hot or Go Home: The Making of a Nashville Star*. In 1995, Trisha married Mavericks' bassist Robert Reynolds. And in 1997, she won a Best Female Country Performance Grammy for *How Do I Live*, a song from the film *Con-Air*, and she and Garth won a Best Country Vocal Collaboration Grammy for *In Another's Eyes*.

Trisha also fenced with journalists who were always bringing up her logical approach, her cool often systematic step-by-step career-building methods. When she began showing up unexpectedly at Garth's shows, Chris Smith, a reporter for *US* magazine, asked, "What's it like singing for his frenzied crowds?" Trisha said, "I'm not an overly emotional person. Music is my outlet. And when I walked out, in San Jose, California, they went nuts. It took my breath away. Garth was loving it, and he stopped the band. I could barely get words out. And then, of course, the crowd went more nuts, because I'm losing it, crying in front of all those people." Smith also asked Yearwood if, now that Ellen Dejeneres had gone public, would Trisha still be willing to appear on *Ellen*? "Sure," replied Yearwood, "I ain't scared. I would probably not want to play her love interest...that would be a stretch."

When Trisha spoke with Pamela Wallin for a CBC Special interview, Wallin was more interested in finding out who Trisha was, letting Yearwood run with her own story, than squeezing out moments of pathos. The picture that emerged was of a very real, sometimes-vulnerable singer who spent a whole lot of time working on her craft and was often dismayed at the attention she was getting, especially the things people fixed upon as news items. It was that very vulnerability and old-style humility, coupled with intense, strutting, pacing performances, a tossing of her blond mane and rocking with the best of them, that put Trisha Yearwood over the top with her fans.

SUZY BOGGUSS

Suzy Bogguss was born on December 30, 1956 in Aledo, Illinois. She graduated from the University of Illinois with a degree in metalsmithery, but instead of settling down to a career as a jewelry designer, she toured around the country in her van for five years before coming to rest briefly in Nashville. There, she made a tape to sell off the stage at Dollywood, and that tape ended up being the item that got her signed to Capitol Records.

Her critically-acclaimed debut album, SOMEWHERE IN BETWEEN, produced by Wendy Waldman, introduced Suzy as an urban cowgirl singer of Patsy Montana's *I Want To Be A Cowboy's Sweetheart*, Hank Williams' *My Sweet Love Ain't Around*, and Merle Haggard's *Somewhere In Between*. A duet with Lee Greenwood on *Hopelessly Yours* and a 'new country' version of Ian Tyson's *Someday Soon* also helped to get her noticed. She won an ACM Best New Female Vocalist award in 1989 and a CMA Horizon award in 1992. Suzy Bogguss has consistently blended her country with folk, rock, and pop to create music that is, in the final analysis, Suzy Bogguss music.

She has done well when singing women songwriters' material, collaborating with Matraca Berg on the Top 5 hit *Hey Cinderella*.

> We believed in fairy tales that day
> I watched your father give you away . . .
> Through the years and the kids and the jobs
> And the dreams that lost their way
> Do you ever stop and wonder
> Do you ever wanna say
> Hey, hey, Cinderella, what's the story all about . . .
> Oh, Oh, Cinderella, maybe you can help us out
> Does the shoe fit you now?

(written by Suzy Bogguss/Matraca Berg/Gary Harrison)

Suzy had another Top 30 hit with *Give Me Some Wheels*, but the best Matraca Berg cut Bogguss has recorded is *Diamonds And Tears*. Nanci Griffith's *Outbound Plane* and Cheryl Wheeler's *Aces* come from the Jimmy Bowen-produced Suzy Bogguss album ACES, which also contains John Hiatt's *Drive South*, a number 2 hit for Suzy in late 1992. Suzy's 1996 GIVE ME SOME WHEELS veers to country-rock on the title track and confronts relationship issues with *Let's Get Real* and *She Said, He Said*.

236

Once Mary Chapin Carpenter hit her stride, she set trends with **MARY CHAPIN** her sparkling drive, hitting the *Billboard* Top 10 with *Never Had* **CARPENTER** *It So Good* and *Quittin' Time* in 1989. Despite the fact that she fitted none of the usual profiles of country singers who had gone before her, she became a 'new country' star with her breakthrough recording of Nanci Griffith's *Down At The Twist And Shout*. Born February 21, 1958 in Princeton, New Jersey, she graduated from Boston University with an Ivy-League degree in American Civilization and kicked around the Washington, D.C. area for several years before she linked up with guitar picking producer John Jennings. As a regional folksinger, she even picked up a few local awards that were known as "Whammies." She had learned that she couldn't punch a nine-to-five time clock, but she couldn't seem to eke out an existence as a performer either. With Jennings, Carpenter would enter the puzzling arena of the commercial music world. She might have been a visionary singer-songwriter, but before she teamed up with manager Tom Carrico and guitarist Jennings, she had played to small club audiences. She got a day-job and cut a demo album with Jennings, and the rest, as they say, is history.

Armed with the demo tape that Carpenter and Jennings had made, Carrico found interest at Columbia Records in Nashville and the demo became her first album release HOMETOWN GIRL. "The first album was a labor of love," Carpenter told reporters. "Then it ended up being bought! I was really very much surprised. . . . It was thrown into this commercial spectrum and was required to do something it wasn't." Her second album, STATE OF THE HEART, was released in 1989 and yielded a string of radio hits. *How Do* broke the *Billboard* country Top 20. *Never Had It So Good* and *Quittin' Time* hit into the Top 10. Reviewers began to heap accolades on her, citing her intelligent approach to songwriting.

The two female country vocalists who had preceded her out of the Washington, D.C. area, Patsy Cline and Emmylou Harris, had both been diamonds in the rough, and they had both pushed the envelope in their careers, but few country artists before Mary Chapin Carpenter had so challenged the male world, offering up a succession of wise-beyond-her-years observations in emotionally delivered songs written from a woman's point of view. Mary Chapin Carpenter is a personal activist intent on shaking up her audience with every song she delivers, a singer-songwriter who can deliver cutting edge tracks that illuminate sexist bigotry, but a woman who

237

ultimately celebrates life more than she would denigrate. "Chapin," as her friends called her, was simply too alive and too brutally honest in her interviews to survive as a Nashville 'star'.

But celebrate she did on the 1991 release SHOOTING STRAIGHT IN THE DARK, especially when teamed with the New Orleans Cajun group Beausoleil on Nanci Griffith's *Down At The Twist And Shout*. Other tracks like *Halley Came To Jackson* and *You Win Again* dealt with the non-traditional country music topics of Halleys Comet and telephone answering machines. There was a depth to "Chapin's" albums, that was for sure. *Down At The Twist And Shout* won Carpenter her first Grammy and sales of the album SHOOTING STRAIGHT IN THE DARK went over the half-million mark.

Where other rising young Nashville personalities would talk about the shtick pablum existences that had been concocted by themselves and their press agents, Carpenter told interviewers of her insecurity, her not being sure she was ready for 'stardom' or for the kind of commercialization of her music that stardom dictated. It was not the wisest approach she could have chosen. Despite the slagging she has often taken for doing so, it revealed a truer world of the singer-songwriter than any other artist on the immediate horizon. When the brilliant album COME ON, COME ON was released in 1992 and yielded seven hit singles, including the distinctive *I Feel Lucky* and an emotional cover of Lucinda Williams' *Passionate Kisses*, "Chapin" was forced to deal with success. While it caused her further anxiety in her personal life, her music videos made her a champion of the emerging feminist country stars.

The video of *I Feel Lucky* made a strong statement when cardboard cut-outs of Lyle Lovett and Dwight Yoakam, named as hunks in the lyrics, are identified as sex objects. But it was her video for *He Thinks He'll Keep Her* with all of the female vocalists from the CBS Special *The Women Of Country* joining joyously in to celebrate the assertive lyrics and heartfelt women's point of view hook — a point of view that was at once a scathing indictment of male hypocrisy and a celebration of the life of a woman who finally walked out on a marriage where she was little more than a household appliance — that really put Carpenter over the top.

> She makes his coffee, she makes his bed
> She does the laundry, she keeps him fed . . .
> When she was 29 she delivered number three

And every Christmas card showed a perfect family
Everything runs right on time, years of practice and design
Spit and polish till it shines, he thinks he'll keep her

When she was 36 she met him at the door
She said, 'I'm sorry, I don't love you anymore.' . . .

(written by Mary-Chapin Carpenter/Don Schlitz)

The Hard Way continued the defiant theme, and Mark Knopfler's *The Bug* was an irresistible groove that reinforced her reputation as a singer of more philosophical than usual lyrics for a Nashville singer.   It was the choice of Knopfler's zen lyrics where the protagonist is both the windshield and the bug, the Louisville slugger *and* the ball . . . a lyric outside of even the "women's issue" songs "Chapin" was becoming known for . . . that established her as being head and shoulders above the other female singers coming out of Nashville and put her fully into the mainstream audience. It was a lyric that assigned no blame.

A rapid rise to become the most awarded female artist followed the release of this album and its video singles. It was an example of what could happen when an intelligent, gifted, and emotional female singer-songwriter met up with the right producer, manager, and record label at the right time and stuck to her original sense of who she was. Five Grammy Awards, including one in 1994 for STONES IN THE ROAD attest to her overwhelming popularity as an artist whose music did more than simply cross over. Mary Chapin Carpenter made statements that were heard in all walks of life. Three million copies sold of COME ON, COME ON, another million of STONES IN THE ROAD. A PLACE IN THE ROAD rocked but it was not as country, and, although good, was not as spectacular as what had gone before.

Mary Chapin Carpenter refused to be bullied into issuing albums on a regular schedule. When she toured, she seldom wrote songs. If there were no songs, she argued, why put out an album? She was an *artist*, not a commodity. In the Spring of 1999, the long awaited next Mary Chapin Carpenter release PARTY DOLL AND OTHER FAVORITES finally hit the record mart shelves. "Every career has its peaks and valleys," she told *Country Song Roundup* magazine, "There are times when you are going to go, 'Gosh, do I have an identity any more in the country music radio format? . . . It's very different from where it was when I was starting to find a niche in country radio. But *different* isn't necessarily bad. I'd still like to think there's a place for me there somewhere." Meanwhile, she'd recorded Don Gibson's *Oh Lonesome Me* for the TRIBUTE TO TRADITION album working with Chet Atkins, and she'd seen her second children's book, *Halley Comes To Jackson*, published by Harper Collins. She wasn't exactly wasting away.

MARTINA McBRIDE The Martina McBride story is a contemporary country legend. Martina was selling t-shirts on a Garth Brooks tour . . . then she got to sing on the show, became the opening act for Brooks and was signed to RCA Nashville. Every country fan knows her story, and the 1992 title of her debut album THE TIME HAS COME has proven prophetic. After a lead single introduced McBride to radio, she hit the number 2 spot on the *Billboard* Hot Country Singles chart with Gretchen Peters' *My Baby Loves Me*.

Born Martina Schifft on July 29, 1966 in Medicine Lodge, Kansas, Martina McBride was raised on a farm near Sharon, Kansas. While the story of her selling t-shirts during Garth's tour is well-known, what is less spoken of is the fact that her husband, John McBride, was the guy who had secured the position of production manager on that tour. John already headed one of the best up-and-coming sound production companies before he got that job and shares in his wife's success, just as he shares in the care of their pre-school age daughter, Delaney.

"I have only been apart from her overnight, once," Martina told Neil Pond for a *Country America* article entitled "I'm Little But I'm Loud." "When she gets school age, I'll probably only tour in the summer and stay home during the school months so she can go to school like a normal kid." When Martina hit the road for a 50-city tour as a member of George Strait's Chevy Trucks tour, it was a family affair for many of the performers with the contemporary country tour buses being converted from bachelor central to include playpens and toddler-friendly areas.

From early releases like *The Time Has Come*, Martina has established herself as a female vocalist determined to stand her ground on lyrics with a strong women's point of view. The video for that hit was the first country music video production to include a closed caption hearing option. The video for *Cheap Whiskey* carried a message. After years and years of lyrics that championed alcoholism, country music heard a singer who sternly indicted the phenomenon. *My Baby Loves Me* extended Martina's fan-base to younger women, and the video featured down-home couples lip-syncing the lyrics and smooching for the cameras. But the video for *Independence Day*, with its controversial domestic violence subject matter, was a breaking point for Martina. Could country fans absorb this real of an issue in a song played on the radio or in a video on CMT? Martina's emotional performance coupled with devastating video production footage put the message across: It was time that people spoke openly about the importance of self-worth and put out a cautionary message to teens about abusive relationships as well as doing something about it in their own lives.

Martina also spoke out strongly about the bubble gum lyrics that seemed to pervade the contemporary charts. "I won't sing some of those lyrics that I hear on the charts. If that's what it takes to be number one, then I don't want to be there." She continued to hit with songs to which women could relate when she released *Safe In The Arms Of Love*, and then hit the number one spot with *Wild Angels*. People have taken to the five-foot-two redhead, and she and her peers have changed the face of country music in interesting ways. Where a few years earlier, country media fed on controversy, adultery, and debauchery, here were these young-marrieds exuding health, happiness, and love for each other in mutually beneficial relationships. They were proud to be photographed caring for their offspring.

There were still journalists who skulked behind the potted plants in hotel lobbies intent on writing stories about how country singers were rich self-destructive 'stars' who ill-deserved their fans' adulation, but their work had become somewhat futile because there were fewer and fewer artists who fit that description. Stardom for country singers meant maturing in the 1990s and much of the effort to make that change come about was due to women sticking to their guns on all issues, not just 'women's issues'.

Martina McBride came of age as an artist with the release of EVOLUTION. She shared a chair at the mixing console with Paul Worley and, as usual, was very involved in the selection of the songs she would sing. The album's title was more than a gratuitous one. "For this album, we threw the mix wide open," she said at the time of the album's release. "We recorded in such a way that I could sing more like I sing live. We experimented a lot; we used more different microphones than I've ever tried before. The result is that the vocals sound real warm. Without bragging, I think it's the best I've ever sounded on a record. I think it's the closest we've ever come to recording the true sound of my voice." The proof that Martina McBride's enthusiasm meant something in the real world would be measured by record sales. On the February 20, 1999, *Billboard* Top Country Albums chart, 76 weeks after its release date, EVOLUTION was sitting in the Top 10, at the number 8 position, with sales in excess of one million.

FAITH HILL

Born on September 21, 1967 in Jackson, Mississippi, Faith Hill was raised in nearby Star, Mississippi. A Reba McEntire fan at an early age, Faith formed her first band at age 17 to play the rodeo circuit. Four years down the road, she moved to Nashville, where she worked as a secretary for a Music Row publishing house until songwriter Gary Burr helped her record a demo tape and pitched it to Warner Bros. Signed to Warner, Faith's 1993 debut album, TAKE ME AS I AM, became a double-platinum release in both Canada and the United States. She has never looked back. Distinctive singles like a remake of Janis Joplin's *Piece Of My Heart* and *Wild One* hit the top of the country charts.

> She's a wild one with an angel's face
> She's a woman-child in a state of grace
> When she was three years old on her daddy's knee
> He said you can be anything you want to be
> She's a wild one runnin' free ...

(written by Jaime Kyle/ Pat Bunch/ Will Rambeaux)

Her early experience fronting her teenage band has been a plus for Faith. With Gary Carter as her bandleader, she has carved out a reputation as one of the top live country performers of the 1990s.

The title track from Faith's sophomore album, IT MATTERS TO ME, hit the number one spot in late 1995. Faith was in the news linked to Tim McGraw, and soon Faith and Tim became the George and Tammy of the 1990s when they released the duet *It's Your Love*, which got the couple nominated for a Grammy and named winner of the 1997 CMA Vocal Event of the Year. Now married with two young daughters, Faith and Tim seem well prepared to make marriage work.

When Faith Hill put out her early records, country fans readily related to Faith's 'message' songs which spoke of the evils men foist on women.

When she tied the knot with Tim, the fans loved her as a wife and mother even more. Where some women in the music business were saying that they found it difficult to juggle a family life and a career, Faith seemed to be doing it with style. Of course, she got a whole lot of support from Tim. They just took their kids with them in the bus. "We added a crib. ... We've covered all of the outlets and tried to baby-proof it as much as possible," Faith told *Country Song Roundup* writer Janete E. Williams. "Gracie travels really well, which makes things a whole lot easier. She's been on the road since she was three-weeks old."

This Kiss, the lead single from the album FAITH, was written for Hill by Robin Lerner, Annie Reboff, and Beth Nielsen Chapman. "We were three girls out at the beach," Chapman explains, "a widow, a divorcee, and a single woman talking about love: the ups and downs of it, how daunting it can be, and how that sometimes all it takes is just one special person to come along and with one kiss 'this kiss' — all resistance melts away."

The composition was an ideal forum for Faith Hill and continued her theme of recording songs written from a woman's point of view. Faith's fans were convinced that she had more than merely survived treatment for ailing vocal chords and had more than returned to the stage after her pregnancy. *This Kiss* was huge! Her fans were also receptive to the positive lyrics and feel of songs like *Love Ain't Like That* and Matraca Berg's *You Give Me Love*. And they loved *My Wild Frontier*, another Robin Lerner song that depicts the plight of a suddenly-widowed single mother. "Her soul mate passes away, but he leaves this child that is a part of him," Faith explains. "Even though he is gone, there is still a bond that is stronger than anything else on earth."

Faith Hill gave single-moms new courage with that song. The birth of Faith and Tim's first daughter, Gracie Katherine, during the time she was recording had seemed like a blessing to both of the singers. "I think FAITH is a mirror reflection of where I am in my life," she says. "Musically, for sure, there's no question about it. I could not have gone deeper to find what this record is. As far as the personal side, there are a lot of positive songs. And that's because I found it hard to sing about something sad and then go home where I was exuding happiness all of the time. I felt I had to sing about things that were about the way I was really feeling."

A few months later, she and Tim hit the road with George Strait's stadium tour, and their albums FAITH and EVERYWHERE hit the number two and number one spots on the *Billboard* Top Country Albums chart. Both releases were still in the Top 10 in early 1999, ten months after Faith's release date. The single *This Kiss* had sold a million copies and FAITH had sold two million.

When Faith performed during the closing ceremonies of the 1996 Summer Olympic Games, she was seen by a television audience numbering 3.5 billion people. It really put Faith's image and music in everyone's face. Faith's videos had all gone number one on CMT, but added exposure on regular network shows like *Late Night With David Letterman, The Tonight Show, The Rosie O'Donnell Show, Good Morning America,* and *Entertainment Tonight* helped to put her across to record buyers in markets she would have never cracked as a traditional country artist. Her music was contemporary and she was a happening commodity. People who never listened to country radio stations or viewed CMT on a regular basis knew her music and who she was. She was the girl who sang *This Kiss.* She also had that video out where she sang that . . . Janis Joplin song.

Cynical critics of the spunky singer have pointed to her recording of *Piece Of My Heart,* deriding Faith's cheerful uptempo country-pop treatment of Janis Joplin's famed soul-shaking give-it-everything-you've-got delivery of the song. However, for people who had never even heard that recording and didn't really know who Janis Joplin had been, it worked in a positive way. It even worked in a healing way for many of those who had heard the original many times and had wanted a better fate for Janis than she had ended up with. Faith Hill, more than any of the emerging female vocalists in the 1990s, is a woman who has come to terms with her world.

KAREN STALEY

When Karen Staley sang backup for Faith Hill, she showed so much promise that she was given a short solo set during Faith's show. Faith helped Karen get signed to Warner Nashville. It was Reba and Linda Davis all over again. Staley, who'd written hits for Tracy Byrd as well as Faith's own *Let's Go To Vegas* and *Take Me As I Am,* was grateful. She had literally hundreds of songs she'd written that no one had recorded. At least she'd get some of them out in plain view where they might get discovered. Once she got into recording her own project, Karen warmed to the challenge. Of course, she was creative, she was a 'renaissance woman', and she didn't want to merely duplicate the usual predictable tracks. "I like bluegrass, I love r&b, I love black gospel and rock & roll," she would say. "I like all this stuff. Why do I have to pick one?" Asking herself questions like that led her to title her album FEARLESS.

Not every one of the new female country vocalists being introduced in the 1990s was going to become a superstar ... there simply weren't enough positions on the charts or hours on the clock for radio programmers to play every female singer and every hat act in heavy rotation. One of the new acts took advantage of the fact that they were women by playing on a politically incorrect designation. They were Natalie Maines, Emily Erwin, and Martie Seidel who they called themselves "Dixie Chicks."

DIXIE CHICKS

Sisters Emily and Martie had been at it for more than five years, slugging it out as an all-female bluegrass group with attitude, a Texas-based version of Ranch Romance, before Natalie joined the group in 1995. Their 1990 indie album THANK HEAVENS FOR DALE EVANS and a 1992 follow-up, LITTLE OL' COWGIRL, received critical acclaim, but various personnel changes they had tried out with the likes of Robin Macy and Laura Lynch in the lineup had not exactly made them country music's answer to the Spice Girls when it came to record sales. When Natalie Maines entered the picture, the group's fortunes began to improve. Natalie's vocals, spiced with Martie's dobro and banjo picking and Emily's championship-level fiddle playing, quickly brought notoriety.

Dixie Chicks were stars in Texas with a fiddle in the band and named Best Country Band for four years by the *Dallas Observer* before they even got to Nashville. When they did arrive on Music Row, tougher journalists would sometimes ignore their abilities and slag their activities because they seemed to be girls who just wanted to be free to take risks, make mistakes, and have fun. This was made clear in the title track to their next album WIDE OPEN SPACES.

> Who doesn't know what I'm talkin' about
> Who's never left home, never struck out
> To find a dream and a life of their own
> A place in the clouds, a foundation of stone
> Many precede and many will follow
> A young girl's dream no longer hollow

It takes the shape of a place out West
But what it holds for her, she hasn't yet guessed
She needs wide open spaces
Room to make her big mistakes . . .

(written by Susan Gibson)

When they got product endorsement deals from companies like Candies, they were criticized. I wondered why. No one was slagging Michael Jordan for being a pitch man for Nike, were they? Ultimately, the male naysaying would not matter one iota. When the three women began a tour to promote their major label debut WIDE OPEN SPACES, they were featured in nearly as many fashion magazine articles as music publication write-ups, which helped to put them over the top. When their recordings began to hit the top of the charts, their videos were in heavy rotation at CMT, and the interviews Emily, Natalie, and Martie gave were often as elusive as Beatles interviews had been during the days when the fab four had won over the entire planet with their zany quips.

If the three young women sensed anyone was really listening, they dropped the idle chatter and leveled with their interviewers. "We were prepared to pay our dues for as long as it took; we were committed to longevity," says Emily. "We know we will always be playing music together, so we wanted to find someone who is just as determined and energetic as we are." Sony Nashville President Allen Butler was the person who came to believe in their music and he signed them to Sony's newly recreated Monument label. "These women are the real deal," Butler would say, long before the Chicks' Monument debut WIDE OPEN SPACES had sold millions of copies and the three women *were* being compared to the Spice Girls. Butler was aware that the group had already taken the Lonestar State by storm when they'd opened for top acts like Garth Brooks and Alan Jackson. He was aware that Ross Perot was a fan, as were Loretta Lynn and Emmylou Harris. Dixie Chicks had played barbecues for Perot and Texas Governor George Bush Jr. They were huge in Texas. So, Allen Butler believed in his newly-signed act. He wasn't about to groom them into something they weren't. "It's important to emphasize the fact that Dixie Chicks are world-class entertainers and that they aren't new to this," Butler would say when speaking about the recording project. "When they brought in songs for the album, they said, 'This is us, this is who we are.'

They put their thumbprint on this album."

"We went from street corners to dance halls, from jeans and boots to tailor-made cowgirl get-ups with rhinestones," Martie explains. "After finding some fashion sense and evolving musically, we finally found Natalie. That was the best thing that ever happened to Emily and me!" When it came time to record, Emily, Martie, and Natalie chose the songs, sang all their own vocals and harmonies, and played the instruments.

Trading in their fringed cowgirl costumes for hipper fashions and honing their rootsy sound to a more contemporary blend has catapulted the act to the forefront of the country scene in one short year. WIDE OPEN SPACES was released in January 1998. Fifty-four weeks later, it was sitting at number one on the *Billboard* Top Country Album chart and boasting a little pyramid icon with the indexed number 4 beside it that informed everyone who bothered to look that WIDE OPEN SPACES had sold more than four million copies. Natalie, Emily, and Martie appeared on national television where they kibitzed with Letterman, jousted with Conan O'Brien, sang for Regis and Kathie Lee, and had a heart to heart with Sally Jesse Raphael. National magazine interviewers and local daily newspaper writers alike ate up quotes like Natalie's, "We want the whole enchilada. I'd give up everything I have today for more." Martie's, "One of the best parts of a record deal is all the free meals you get taken to." And Emily's, "The best part is dispelling the myth about women playing music and being able to turn people around." They were equally nonchalant, yet able to hit the mark with comments like the time Natalie innocently answered one interviewer's query with, "Call me blonde, but I never even thought about the name being sexist . . . I was thinking about a little baby chick."

For the group's set-closing delivery of *I Can Love You Better Than That* during a concert in Albany, Oregon, Natalie urged the 16,000 strong audience to stand up. "If you're hoping that the Spice Girls are about to break up, get on your feet!" she yelled. Albany *Democrat Herald* writer Shannon Tweed noted that this had been Natalie's way of dealing with "criticism from a syndicated writer who had earlier called them the 'Spice Girls of country music.'" Per usual, many of those 16,000 in attendance that night were young women who pushed forward in mosh-pit tradition to celebrate the music along with Natalie, Martie, and Emily.

Of course, there were also some male writers who were *not* into chick-bashing. Neil Pond, senior entertainment editor for *Country America*, enthusiastically endorsed the act with an in-depth story that featured the fab three on the cover of the entertainment tab in the midst of what appears at first glance to be a pillow fight. A closer peek reveals that this is a posed-photo in which Natalie and Emily are seen struggling with an oversized inflated plastic cushion, while Martie sits in the foreground, eyes averted in mock disgust. Pond's "Chick Picks" is a collage of pink, purple, and green guitar picks that bears the caption, "When it comes to hot licks, the Dixie Chicks rule the roost." In a photo accompanying this story, a saucy Martie has her tongue stuck out, a "Chicks Rule" t-shirt-clad Natalie has thrust forward a souvenir button bearing the same slogan, and a mischievous Emily displays a splayed finger Peace Sign that protrudes from behind Natalie's blonde curls like rabbit ears. The quote tagged to the photo says, "We don't want to be too cautious. Be yourself, that's our thing. Tell the truth . . . don't get wrapped up in what's politically correct."

Neil Pond was obviously a fan. He grasped the full picture. There was a whole lot more to Dixie Chicks than the posing, the fashions, and the "Chicks Rule" t-shirts. But they just wanted to have fun. They were . . . chick singers. How could you blame them for being into fashions? But some writers seemed to blame them for everything that was 'wrong" with contemporary country music. The way I saw it, these guys just had their heads stuck back in the 20th century. Dixie Chicks were already living in the next millennium. They were the hottest act on country radio and they were hauling in awards right, left, and center.

SHEDAISY   All of a sudden all-female trios were a hot commodity on Music Row. If Dixie Chicks clucked menacingly when they were likened to the Spice Girls, well, that could be fixed in the mix. You just had to find some singers who were more . . . pliable. The first cloned chick act to hit the market was SHeDaisy, a Lyric Street Records female trio that was actually made up of three sisters. Kristyn, Kelsi and Kassidy Osborn, though, had honed their musical skills singing at retirement homes and country fairs to karaoke tapes in the Salt Lake City area.

When the Osborn sisters headed for Nashville, they knew they had something, they just didn't know what. "We figured there was a void we could fit in," Kassidy offered in a quote provided to journalists. "Of course, when we first came, female wasn't big, groups weren't big and young wasn't big, and the feedback was that Nashville wasn't ready for us." The three sisters slugged it out working in department stores at the Hickory Hollow Mall and kept plugging away. After a while, they lucked out when A&R guy Shelby Kennedy brought Lyric Street exec Doug Howard around to see if the girls could actually sing the music he had heard on a demo tape. In no time flat, an album titled THE WHOLE SHEBANG was recorded.

As I read through the printed promo material, I wondered if the girls had come up with that, or if record label people, intent on cashing in on the success Dixie Chicks were having, had made up "she-bang." It sounded suspiciously like a male kind of "bang." I stuck the CD sampler on and began to listen to their music. *Little Good Byes* was decent stuff. Produced by Dann Huff, the track had a kind of British Invasion flavor with a snappy 60s-ish backbeat and catchy slide guitar and harmonica riffs. Best of all was the vocal arrangement. I remembered that I'd just read in their bio that the girl's mom had taught them harmony singing to eight-track tapes on their way to the family's annual Disneyland vacation. When I read on to learn that Lyric Street was owned by the parent corporation, Disney, and that the group was to be marketed by the use of a little Hollywood glitz, a 13-minute film, it all seemed to make some giant-sized media conglomerate sense. Instead of merely putting this documentary and performance footage on a VHS tape and mailing it out, Lyric Street's promotion team would travel to various radio markets and screen the mini-movie in genuine movie theaters. While this sounded a mite automatic and the three sisters seemed a bit, um, inexperienced, I wished them well. If not too many more chick vocal groups showed up in the next year, they might do reasonably well. Of course, it is one thing to pay your dues busking for change and honing your skills in clubs while undergoing enough hard knocks and ups-and-downs in life that your attitude songs are to be believed, it is another ball of wax altogether when you co-write women's issues songs with a couple of write-by-appointment male songwriters who punch a nine-to-five clock for a Music Row publishing company.

Lari White is another singer with a record out on the Lyric Street label. She was back for a second kick at the can in 1999, after three albums on RCA a few years earlier had not sold well enough to persuade the label to renew her contract. Born in Dunedin, Florida on May 13,

LARI WHITE

1965, Lari had entertained with The White Family Singers while studying music engineering and voice at the University of Miami. She first gained notoriety in 1988 when she won TNN's *You Can Be A Star* contest, although the prize she received, a recording deal with Capitol, did not prove fruitful. When Lari toured as an opening act and backup singer for Rodney Crowell, Rodney took a liking to her and produced her RCA debut album. Four singles released to radio from three RCA albums charted in the Top 40 regions of the *Billboard* country chart. *Now I Know* was the best achiever, when it peaked at number 5 in 1994.

"I sold a million albums," Lari White told a reporter who wrote up her comeback attempt in an August 29, 1998 article printed in *The Tennessean*. "Five or 10 years ago acts that were selling 200,000 to 300,000 units were some of the biggest acts around. But numbers have changed and the bottom lines have changed. Now big multi-national corporations own the record labels and they expect 20 percent annual growth. Labels are looking at the numbers; making music isn't always at the top of their list."

Lari White's climb back onto a major label took a few years. She studied music and she had a daughter, M'Kenzy Rayne. She sang on the 1996 Grammy award-winning tribute AMAZING GRACE: A COUNTRY SALUTE TO GOSPEL. She co-wrote *Helping Me Get Over You* with Travis Tritt, and their duet of that song was a radio hit in 1997. When her performance of *Power In The Blood* turned up on the soundtrack of the Robert Duvall movie *The Apostle*, the Disney company called her and she was chosen as the flagship artist for Disney's new Lyric Street label. Even though she'd co-produced some of her tracks at RCA in the past, she was happy to hand over production to Dann Huff, a proven studio achiever who was familiar with the contemporary market place. Lari and her husband Chuck Cannon had written some good songs for the album STEPPING STONE. *Stepping Stone*, the lead single from the album, was written by Lari, Craig Wiseman, and David Kent. *People* magazine reviewer, Ralph Novak, praised the release, writing that it "deftly points out the thin line between stumbling blocks and stepping stones." Lari, herself, admitted that the song had become a mantra she had recited while crafting her comeback and looking after her infant daughter. The track that showed the most promise to crack the tough radio charts was *John Wayne Walking Away*, where hard-hitting lyrics like "Don't show your cards, don't show your pain / Keep tellin' yourself it's either me or your freedom . . ." were juxtaposed with a mesmerizing hook. When *Stepping Stone* peaked at number 12 on the *R&R* chart and at number 16 on *Billboard* there was light at the end of the tunnel for Lari White. I wondered if she was watching those numbers, along with some of the other execs at the media giant's Nashville label offices. I wondered if any of those execs had read what Lari had had to say about the way large corporate labels paid more attention to numbers than they did to the music. I wondered if there was any place at all on any of the charts for artists who stayed at home writing songs and rearing their children. It didn't give the marketing people very much to run with. And there were so many other artists who were willing to tour their faces off, these days, as well as a total — it was said in early 1999 — of 200 unsigned artists looking for a label deal in Nashville.

I remember reading in a newspaper article that Seagrams had bought up a fair amount of music business real estate and wondering at that time just what this move meant for the future of country music. When a Polygram buy-out of the Seagrams group (Universal and MCA Records) was announced in 1998, Larry LeBlanc, Canadian editor of *Billboard* magazine, predicted in a year-end quote in the Vancouver *Province* that "It will have so much bearing on all parts of the business, including country. It's really put a block on any signings this year within Canada, because of speculation over what's going to happen." Leblanc also went on to mention a possible trend — he spoke of a "movement back to traditional country. Certainly Nashville had gotten worried that they'd gone too far into pop." Alan Kates, Nashville-based manager of Keith Stegall, Dan Hill, and Charlie Major, made another prediction in the same year-end article put together by *Province* columnist John P. McLaughlin. "I think the traditional stuff will come back. The cloning is going to have to go away because the market place has been reflecting what all the cloning has done to it. It just doesn't work."

The axe fell in early 1999 when MCA/Universal announced they were downsizing, shutting down Decca Nashville and merging with Mercury/Polygram. Hundreds of lay-offs for Toronto, L.A., and New York employees were announced. The merger and downsizing was one of several corporate-level moves as the world edged ever closer to the prediction made in the film *Rollerball* where nations have become irrelevant and the world is owned by six corporations.

Lari White was on record saying that "labels look at numbers, music is not high on their list." But was that true? Perhaps, some of the people employed by a megalithic corporation might have some ideas about the music, ideas about what it *should* be. It was not a new idea. Shaping the music had come as part of the process of music being turned into a business, and many radio singles seemed to sound a whole lot like radio jingles. Nowadays, you had Alan Jackson going in and recording "Chevy Trucks" commercials over the original "drive a Mercury up and down this road" lyric of a song. It had worked for Alan. He was heard so often on radio and television during his Chevy Trucks Tour that his album sales really amounted to a serious hill of beans. And he was also recording very good authentic country cuts like the western swing zinger *Right On The Money*.

As a result of the corporate downsizing, another 20 or so Nashville artists no longer had major label deals. Dolly Parton no longer had a deal. As popular as country had become in the media and on television, somebody in the corporate pyramid had noticed that record sales for country were way, way down. It didn't ease the pain when you were out in the rain to know that you weren't the only one getting wet. But it had some people wondering what they could do to improve the situation. The people who'd come in at the top couldn't seem to come up with records that country fans wanted to buy, these days. And it wasn't just the artists who were joining the ranks of the unemployed.

SHERRIÉ AUSTIN

Despite these dark days in Nashville, true talent managed to emerge in the late 1990s. Sherrié Austin was yet another hopeful who had managed to get herself from her home stomping grounds in Australia to L.A. and then to Nashville. I had heard that she'd been successful singing country music down under before she decided to pack her bags and make it in the big time United States market place. Even before I peeled the cello wrap off her 1999 Arista Nashville debut CD WORDS, I wondered if maybe she hadn't come just a little bit too late. *Lucky In Love*, the first track, has a kind of street-fighting-man groove that recording acts like Elton John and The Who had once used to good advantage in their heydays. The second track, *An Innocent Man*, has more of a country-rock feel and the chorus says quite a lot: "There's too much wrong in the world tonight / Too much I can't understand / I wanna board

**TRISHA
YEARWOOD**

MARY CHAPIN CARPENTER

SUZY BOGGUSS

**FAITH
HILL**

**MARTINA
MCBRIDE**

255

**MINDY
McCREADY**

**SHERRIÉ
AUSTIN**

**LILA
McCANN**

**LEANN
RIMES**

257

LEE ANN WOMACK

LARA WHITE

DEANA CARTER

DIXIE CHICKS

SARA EVANS

THE LYNNS

**LORRIE
MORGAN**

**TERRI
CLARK**

**SHANIA
TWAIN**

up these windows and turn out these lights / And lie down with an innocent man." Sherrié has a real nice quality to her vocals, especially on the languid *Trouble In Paradise*. Whoever picked these songs must have felt all of the angst being radiated by all those out-of-work recording artists. This is not your usual everything's groovy young country release. Whether Sherrié Austin will pass the number-crunchers questionnaires, though, the test phonecalls to folks selected by those Seattle-based consulting firms, and get the airplay she easily deserves, well, that is a good question. She does look awfully good in her video.

As I was writing the above words Sherrié's CD had progressed on to track six: *I Want To Fall In Love (So Hard It Hurts)*. This cut has real moxie and the band guys sound like they're actually playing together to an actual audience, focusing their driving beat toward the listeners and tearing off guitar riffs and organ stings as if they expect applause when they're done. Not your usual approach when it comes to cut and paste stacked tracks on a 48-track digital mixing console . . . maybe this would work for Sherrié, after all. If she could inspire her musicians like this, maybe when she got out on tour, she would catch on with the record-buyers, too.

Sophomore albums, just like sophomore seasons for professional athletes, are sometimes a hard hurdle to get over. For Deana **DEANA CARTER** Carter, daughter of legendary session guitar player Fred Carter Jr., recording a second CD merely meant that because her first release had been so successful, she was given a little more credit for her own production contributions. Nashville born and raised, Deana had a full musical education in her home situation and then some. As a toddler and a pre-teen she met singers like Bob Dylan, Gordon Lightfoot, Art Garfunkel, and Kris Kristofferson. The singers came to see her dad. And Fred Carter Jr. played on some of the best records they made. Records like Simon & Garfunkel's *The Boxer*. She liked singing, herself, and writing songs. At 17, when she pitched her efforts to Music Row, her first approaches were not met with enthusiasm and she began to consider other alternatives.

"I went to college, got my degree and became a therapist, working with stroke and heart patients," she told *Country Network*'s Kellie Bernell. "I got to be a real person in the real world outside the entertainment industry," she confided to Sandra Coulson for an article in the *London Free*

Press. "So I learned a lot and I think that helped my writing. I had all the jobs. It really helped me form as a person."

When Deana got back into music at age 23 it was to be a demo tape she made, which eventually fell into Willie Nelson's hands, that would change her fortune. Willie liked her tape, and the two got together and swapped songs for a spell. Willie asked Deana if she would sing at his Farm Aid VII concert. Deana was the only woman on that show, and when she delivered the goods, she got noticed. In fact, it wasn't long after that performance that Deana was signed to Capitol Records. Breaking onto the scene when she did, Deana's rookie year as a recording artist featured tough competition from Shania Twain. Where Shania's videos got her notice for her bellybutton displays, Deana's signature trademark came on the performance stage. Peter North, writing in the May 2, 1998 edition of *The Edmonton Journal* saw her as a "90s version of a rockin' Loretta Lynn . . . thanks in part to her spunky, down-to-earth personality and her overall attitude."

Loretta had danced barefoot at times, and Deana became known for her carefree barefoot approach to entertaining her audiences. That came about, she told me, due to wearing those stacked shoes at times and more than once during sound-check tripping up on the wires that the techies had not yet gaff-taped down to the floor of the stage. One time, she just took her shoes off and it felt good. Later that night, she kicked them off again and it became her trademark. Some people felt that she was also her own person because she wrote many of her own songs. I wondered if she'd been successful pitching songs to other artists before she broke out with her own records. "That's how I got into this whole mess," she confessed. "I wanted for other artists to cut my songs. I started initially as a writer and I wanted to get into production rather than as an artist. It just ended up that my demos started getting attention. I had a band that played at writers' nights, and I started getting attention that way and I guess the rest is history. Which I guess is a good problem to have, but I still wish that someone would cut my songs."

Deana had gone to Europe to record and tour and kind of feel things out before committing herself to something as crucial as plunging into the radio sweepstakes and going up against proven stars for album sales. I wondered if she'd been involved in her productions right from the start. It sounded like she had been, although her name had not appeared as a co-producer until her second album. I told Deana that I really liked her arrangements, the color stuff that went on when she fused many styles together, as well as how she sang. I really liked that. But had she been in on the production all the time? I asked. "On the European album that I did with Bowen," she recalled, "Bowen said, 'You're going to do the producing on this record and I'm going to get the credit, just in case it doesn't go over well, you don't get the blame.' Bowen is my mentor, I love him. Seriously, with him and John Guess I had to . . . I wish you could see the notebooks I've got from that, they are filled with a series of production notes . . . and I had to work really hard before anybody in America ever knew that I had any input. On the American album that I did — DID I SHAVE MY LEGS FOR THIS? — I didn't take credit for that because of the way the contracts were done, but I had equal amount input on that. I've always been very involved in production."

Shades of Gail Davies here, I thought. "But it was probably more important to get input than credit on the album?"

"To me," Deana said, "it was a trade-off early on. But now, there is no need for that, to be quite honest. Credibility is my whole MO, that's what I talk about all the time. I want people to know that I'm an artist that's credible on a lot of different levels."

"How," I asked, "was it decided that *Strawberry Wine* would be the lead single?"

"I credit radio for pulling me out of the ashes, if you will. They are the ones that suggested *Strawberry Wine* strongly enough that my record label listened. We were doing these showcases for radio before the album came out, showcases where you go to a town and play and they fly in people and they can check out your show. Conveniently, it's either at the beach or a casino or something, so everybody has fun. And *Strawberry Wine* was the song that really struck a chord with everybody. We had a different single that we were going to release first. Because of radio, their voice was heard, and that's what came first, *Strawberry Wine*. I really credit them for catapulting me out of the pack of what was happening at the time."

We moved on to speak about the 60s influences in her music, British pop band influences, I suggested. Deana readily warmed to the discussion. "I was born in the 60s and raised in the 70s and in my house one of my first albums was Eric Carmen and the Raspberries. The diverse background that I have is what I love. I love The Beatles. I loved Paul Young. A lot of the British thing is what I love. For me, what is melodic is what kills me.

The band Bread kills me. If you put that with Levon Helm and his kinda funky vibe with The Band and throw in a little bit of Zeppelin or Skynyrd ... Bruce Springsteen is one of my favorite artists of all time. He was inducted into the Rock & Roll Hall of Fame last night and I was just sitting on the couch, sobbing. I didn't know if I was crying because I was old enough to see Springsteen inducted into the Hall of Fame or if I was just so happy for him because I have been an avid fan since the age of, like, 12. You just look at all the influences. Musically, I like to incorporate as much of it as I can. To me it's an introspective. I keeps you hooked."

"Discovering Lynyrd Skynyrd rehearsing upstairs before you invited them to come down to where you were recording. Was that a total coincidence?" I asked.

"Totally. I was in rehearsal with this new band I'm putting together and they're, like, in the rehearsal room next to me, again. My ability to work with lots of cool country artists and lots of cool artists from other genres is growing. I hope to feed that, because for me that is what I'm all about. It's like a Southern girl who is very diverse. We all influence each other. My philosophy is that genres hold hands anyway, you know, so why not?"

I said that back in my own home town in the 1950s the one station there played everybody. Marty Robbins and Perry Como, Fats Domino and Patsy Cline ... and I had kind of liked it that way. Deana recalled that "when we were kids, one station we listened to was no format. It was everybody and everybody was considered rock, unless you were Johnny Cash. I'm stuck on the non-genre format. I would love to hear a station that played George Jones and then turned around and played Springsteen and then played Tom Petty and then played ... Heart. And then played Willie. I can feasibly see it happening."

Cool, I thought. It would be my kind of radio.

"I keep sayin'," Deana said, "that I'm going to start a little bitty radio station like on *Northern Exposure*. And just do that ... from seven to nine every night, and take a bottle of wine and some candles in and take my old record collection ... and read poetry for a while, and take callers for a while and then play ... Dizzy Gillespie. Just for a couple of hours."

I said, "I'd tune in to that."

Deana Carter laughed. "It's like I don't already have plenty to do. It would really be fun! Maybe one of these days."

DID I SHAVE MY LEGS FOR THIS? went on to sell over four million copies, resting for two years in the Top 40 of the *Billboard* Country Albums chart, and three of the singles from the debut were number one on the *Billboard* Hot Country Singles chart. The title song from the album added some ironic zest to an odd country theme.

> I bought these new heels, did my nails
> And had my hair done just right
> I thought that this new dress
> Was a sure bet for romance tonight
> But it's perfectly clear, between the tv and beer
> I won't get as much as a kiss
> As I head for the door, I turn around to be sure
> Did I shave my legs for this?

(written by Deana Carter/Rhonda Hart)

Strawberry Wine was named the 1997 CMA Single of the Year. *Newsweek* magazine cited Carter for her "raw honesty" and listed her as one of "100 Americans for the Next Century."

For her second effort, EVERYTHING'S GONNA BE ALRIGHT, Deana would get co-production credits with Chris Farren and the two would keep to their song-driven approach. "That's the most important thing," says Carter. "I'm excited because the stories come from the same place; they're about the kind of life experiences we share in common. Each song becomes a persona. You give birth to it, then let it live and hopefully, flourish." Of course, there was that Deana-meets-Skynyrd-meets-country *Train Song* as well as the marvelous baroque architecture of *Michelangelo Sky*, the sassy *You Still Shake Me*, and the real-deal songwriting of Matraca Berg and Deana Carter's *Ruby Brown* as well as Fred Carter Jr.'s *Everything's Gonna Be Alright*. Good music.

LEE ANN WOMACK

When her disc jockey father took her to work with him, Lee Ann Womack would pick out cuts for him to play from the record archive at the small-town Jacksonville, Texas station. She liked Bob Wills and Ray Price. Glen Campbell was one of her favorites. At home on Saturday nights Lee Ann liked to listen to the Opry broadcast. She made her first trip to Nashville when she was a high-school senior, just to check out Music Row and the TNN studios. While Lee Ann studied music at Texas colleges, she toured with a band throughout the Southwest.

Moving on to Belmont University in Tennessee, she enroled in a Music Business course that had as part of its program a brief internship in a Nashville major label office. Lee Ann interned in the A&R department of MCA Records. By 1990, she was a full-time Nashville resident. Married and a mom, Lee Ann kept after her songwriting and signed a deal with Don Cook at Tree Publishing in 1995. The next year, she signed with Decca Records. At 30-something, Lee Ann Womack was an unlikely candidate to break into a youth-driven market. But break in, she did, and she did it with traditional tracks like *Never Again, Again* and *You've Got To Talk To Me* from her self-titled debut CD.

Lee Ann's sophomore release SOME THINGS I KNOW got good initial reviews and the lead single *I'll Think Of A Reason Later* made steady progress up the airplay charts to the very top. The song immediately caught the ear of country fans when they heard the saucy lipping-off lyrics that Lee Ann sings about her new boyfriend's 'ex'. "I think it's important for every record to have its light moment," she told *Country Weekly* writer Wendy Newcomer. "With this song it's even more important because you're ribbing somebody. I think it's important to show the light side if you're comfortable with it, and I am."

Now that her second daughter, Anna Lise, has been born, Lee Ann is ready to hit the festival circuit again. She gets a whole lot of help with Anna Lise from eight-year-old Aubrie and husband Frank Liddell, and she plans to complete the accounting section of the Music Business course via correspondence course while traveling on her tour bus this summer. Lee Ann Womack is seen by traditionalists as the youngish artist who will turn radio around. Her debut album has sold nearly half a million records and her sophomore effort has already pushed above the 250,000 mark. Her music is selling because it is being enthusiastically endorsed by country music lovers, not because she has been packaged up to be bigger than life itself.

HEATHER MYLES

By the time Heather Myles appeared on the Nashville horizon, riding out of the sunset from Southern Cal into view on the strength of her Rounder debut HIGHWAYS & HONKY-TONKS, which critics were hailing as "stone country" and "real country," people in Nashville were as ready for what they called the 'real deal' as were country fans all over North America. But I wasn't at all sure that the people at country radio were ready for the real deal. They didn't play hard core country on country radio, did they? Not very often, these days, from what I'd been hearing.

The fact that Heather Myles looked, acted, and dressed like a female Dwight Yoakam was beside the point; she was, after all, a genuine cowgirl and had worked as a ranch hand for a few years on her parents' Riverside, California spread where the family raised thoroughbred horses. The storyline got better when it was said that the "lure of the honky-tonks called her away" from that setting. Two albums on HighTone, JUST LIKE OLD TIMES (1992) and UNTAMED (1995) as well as a live recording, SWEET LITTLE DANGEROUS, released on the Demon label in the U.K., were all the evidence needed to prove that this was an artist to be reckoned with.

Chet Flippo flipped over Myles' music in *Billboard*. "Myles has more brass than a hardware store, and she boldly steps out with this big, swaggering assemblage of stone country. She more than holds her own — and shows off her heart-throb voice — in a duet with Merle Haggard on *No One Is Gonna Love You Better*." Alanna Nash, writing in *Stereo Review*, was equally enthusiastic: "Finally, a woman doing country! Real country!" Still, I wasn't convinced that these accolades would translate to airplay.

The urban cowgirls who *were* getting their videos played were Danni Leigh and another positive new female vocalist, Jo Dee Messina, who fit right into the demographic as a cheerful youthful CMT personality. Jo Dee hit big with *Heads Oklahoma, Tails California* and has followed up her debut album ALL I WANT with I'M ALRIGHT, a number 10 *Billboard* charter in April 1999. She's the redhead in the current mix of contemporary country stars.

B ecause of her good-girl-bad-girl image and all of the press she was getting dating Predator hockey players and speaking out about **MINDY McCREADY** women's rights, and how she lived with two men, her brothers, who looked to her as a role model, although she appeared in her promo pictures to be a tart — all this had gained Mindy McCready way more fans than you might think if you merely tallied up her chart numbers. Mindy's debut album TEN THOUSAND ANGELS had peaked in the Top 10 on the *Billboard* Hot Country Singles and Tracks chart and sold more than a million copies.

Her second single, *Guys Do It All The Time*, had hit the top of the chart, and her third, *A Girl's Gotta Do What A Girl's Gotta Do*, had peaked at Number 4. A song written by two men who obviously had learned something from their 'liberated' women counterparts.

> The first thing I did when you said goodbye
> Was sit myself down and had a real good cry
> The next thing I did was put my red boots on
> And go downtown dancing until the break of dawn
> A girl's gotta do what a girl's gotta do ...
>
> (written by Rick Bowles/Robert Byrne)

But Mindy's follow-up album, IF I DON'T STAY THE NIGHT, had not repeated the same radio magic, nor were people forming long lines at the record marts to pick up a copy.

At 21, McCready had been compared to Shania Twain — and not always favorably. She was fond of displaying her bellybutton, true. She was bringing up her brothers, true. She was speaking out about women's rights, true. But her philosophy seemed a bit, um ... one-dimensional. Where Twain's sassy songs hit right at the bone, Mindy seemed a bit pre-occupied with the meat. Sex, wasn't everything, was it? McCready was talking to the media about her teenaged brothers and maintaining that "the subject is always there, constantly surrounding everything in their lives ... sex, girl-friends, boyfriends, who likes who, and why. That's the topic that we discuss, relentlessly. In addition to that, I read my fan mail when I'm out on the road and sex is *the* subject with young girls, too." Stuff like this seemed irrelevant to people who had always viewed country as a mature medium, but it kept Mindy in the media. Nashville columnist Richard Biggs had some suggestions in his *Sticks & Stones* column for *In Review* magazine regarding "Ways Mindy McCready Can Stay In The News." Biggs prefaced his "list" by saying, "For someone who was never known for her musical talents, Mindy McCready sure stays in the news. However, in time Ms. Mindy may run out of ideas for catching the media's eye. We thought we'd suggest a few: Date More Predators, Cover an Aerosmith Song, Become A White House Intern, Die and Get Exhumed, Host *Prime Time Country* ... Marry Mutt Lange, Get into the Whole 'White Rap' Thing, Marry Tommy Mottola, Appear on a Confederate License Plate, Have an affair with Vince

Gill or Amy Grant. . . ." Biggs suggestions got ruder as they went on to finally land on: "Cut a record worth hearing."

So, Mindy McCready did pretty well — at least, at first she did. People liked Mindy. They dug her in-your-face attitude, plus, she was not the usual pretty face, pretty voice and no personality at all package they saw being marketed here, there, and everywhere. Mindy was packaged, but she had something to say, too. And she thrived on the kind of press that women-bashing journalists like Charles Earle and Richard Biggs dished up to the public. The only hitch had been, she'd sorta signed this archaic contract with an unscrupulous manager on her way to signing with RCA, assigning 25 percent of her royalties to the man for nine years. Mindy got advice and there she was in the midst of a successful career filing for bankruptcy. Go figure. She thought she was doing the right thing, following the trend. She was telling other people to respect women's rights, but she wasn't experienced enough herself that she'd learned to look out for the predators in her own career.

The thing is, though, Mindy's records, like the twangy guitar laden *What If I Do*, are quite good for what they are, aimed apparently at a very young crowd. Does no one at radio wonder just how difficult it might be for a forty-something parent on a potato farm in Idaho or a wheat field in Saskatchewan to relate to either the music or the lyrics? Of course, if radio formats continue to splinter, 'young country' may survive on 'young country stations' and co-exist with all of the other varieties of country music that are being made. There has been no shortage of young female artists in the late 1990s all following trends set by Shania Twain and doing their best to imitate the success of LeAnn Rimes.

L eAnn Rimes has become the focal singer for the 'young country' movement. This emphasis on youth in the 1990s pervades all **LEANN RIMES** forms of music. The corporate strategy here is that if you hook a consumer at 18, you've got them for life. Where generation "X" had rebelled about labeling and being labeled, generation "Y" was more compliant. LeAnn become an overnight success with her recording of *Blue*, but she was far from the first child prodigy to make it big in Nashville through a single record. The first child prodigy wasn't even Brenda Lee. There were many teen and pre-teen singers who climbed up to sing with the touring stars in their home towns, but few who had hit big on the radio by the time Don Grashey arrived in Music City in 1955 with his candidate for the child prodigy sweepstakes in tow, Myrna Lorrie, who was named best new talent by the industry even before there was a CMA to give the award credibility.

Oddly, it was nearly impossible in the late-1990s for an artist who wasn't in their teens to get a record deal. Even the veteran producers and label heads found the situation difficult to get used to. A disillusioned Tony Brown is quoted by Laurence Leamer in *Three Chords And The Truth* as telling 40-something singer-songwriter Linda Hargrove, when Hargrove pitched the idea of a comeback record deal to Tony, "You don't understand, Linda, what it's become. We're looking for kids. Don't you get it? We take these kids. Never sung anywhere, never paid their dues. Run 'em through media training. Turn 'em into something they're not. Throw 'em out on the road. And a couple of years later they're through, outta here. We destroy them, their marriages, their lives. You don't want it. Believe me."

But LeAnn Rimes was the young Patsy that country fans longed to embrace, the third coming after K.D. Lang and the real deal. LeAnn's *Blue* was such a stunning debut, and the claim Bill Mack had written the song for Patsy Cline before Patsy died was such a timely myth, that LeAnn's career had real momentum by the time she hit Nashville and began to make public appearances. Of course, LeAnn had also had parents who had doted on her. Wilbur and Belinda Rimes had put more energy into her life than they had put into their own, so much so, that the day that LeAnn met Brenda Lee at the 1997 CMA Awards, Wilbur and Belinda announced their plans to divorce. They had had enough faith in *their* child prodigy to fly on up to New York from Texas to audition their kid for the Broadway production of *Annie 2*. Of course, LeAnn had only been seven years old at the time, and it might have been rushing things just a little having her compete with 12 and 13-year-olds. But Belinda and Wilbur believed that LeAnn was special. She had very nearly won that early competition. When her marvelous yodel-inflected recording of *Blue* wowed country fans on radio stations all over North America and people began to learn more about the 13-year-old Rimes, they found out that her original heroes weren't Patsy and Loretta or even Elvis Presley. LeAnn had revered Judy Garland and Barbara Striesand. LeAnn had turned to country partly because the family budget couldn't bear traveling to New York or L.A. to audition for big productions or try to beat out all the other young hopefuls on *Star Search*, but she'd kinda got hooked on it along the way. LeAnn's drive to become a singing star had always been her own, she'd just had to make a few compromises along the way.

Jimmy Bowen and Mike Curb both made pitches to sign LeAnn Rimes. LeAnn signed with Curb Records and her albums were put out on Curb/MCA. The fact that Mike Curb hadn't insisted that Wilbur be cast out of the loop — when the new management team that would be needed for an assault on the national charts was formed — has turned out to be a saving grace. Tanya had needed Beau, and LeAnn needed Wilbur, someone she could trust, if she were eventually to take control of her own destiny in the complicated corporate music business world. Wilbur and LeAnn would also choose to keep the western spirit of her music intact, recording in New Mexico and Texas where budgets could be kept to reasonable limits.

When BLUE, her first Curb Records album, came out and sold in the record stores, big time, LeAnn Rimes began to record the wider variety of music she also wanted to sing. And because she'd done so well at the CMA awards shows, exuding both sex and maturity as well as a wholesomeness that was to be believed, country fans went along with LeAnn's wider view of what country music really embraced. It embraced gospel and it embraced pop. Of course, everyone who has sung country and hit big in Nashville has brought their own angle on the dangle to the situation, and LeAnn would change the face of country at least as much as Patsy did or Loretta or Tammy and Dolly when they came along.

When Elton John called LeAnn and asked her to record a song that he'd written for a contemporary version of the opera *Aida*, LeAnn showed no hesitation. *Written In The Stars* was made into a video, too, and it was the most dramatic appearance LeAnn Rimes had made to date. LeAnn was already taking acting lessons and had acted in a made-for-television movie version of a book she'd co-authored. She was being considered for a role in a feature film to be called *Under The Mimosa*. It just seemed like a natural evolution for her. It was what Tanya had done when she'd hit the West Coast. When Dolly got into pop, she got into movies, too. The simple truth of it lay before everyone who commented on the state of country music in the 1990s: country *fans* didn't really mind if their stars went pop, just as long as they were *their* stars, *country* singers with whom they could identify. Thus LeAnn Rimes had a hand in the changing of the music from new traditional to new country to contemporary along with

Shania Twain, Garth Brooks, Mutt Lange, Jimmy Bowen and Tony Brown. And the executives on Music Row who had cloned and packaged up the 'next' Garths and the 'next' Shanias were already busily at work cloning up and packaging up the 'next' LeAnn Rimes.

Of course, from the time LeAnn was singing at Jack High's Opry-style shows as a pre-teen, she had shown that she could sing adult songs and express the hurt and elation of adult country themes, no problem at all. "Dad would explain that it was a sad song," Rimes told Laurence Leamer. "I don't think I have to experience anything to sing it."

When LeAnn made her dramatic coming out at the Opry, she was already a star in Texas. Before her arrival on the national scene, Music Row powerbrokers like Jimmy Bowen and Joe Galante had spent kazillions of dollars developing what were considered, at that time, young singers like Mindy McCready and Mandy Barnett who were usually around the age of 17 when they were signed for the grooming process and nearly 20 years old when their expensive debut albums were hyped to the masses. By this time, of course, the corporate proteges already owed so many hundreds of thousands of dollars, sometimes millions of dollars, that their royalties were tied up for decades unless they hit massively on the radio and toured endlessly to promote the sales of CDs.

Few of the corporate wonderkids were prepared for the ruthless onslaught of autograph seekers, the 18-hour-days that were only followed by another 18-hour-day when you were faced with the task of promoting your record to the fans and to radio. LeAnn Rimes, of course, was cut from different cloth. She had been developed and packaged by Belinda and Wilbur and herself, too, years before she arrived in the national spotlight at only 13 years old. She was ready for the big time; it was not some pie-in-the-sky dream that she had. LeAnn had performed nearly 400 times on Jack High's show alone before she hit nationally with her re-recorded version of *Blue*. And she'd signed autographs after her shows, and, while she was signing, she'd sold quite a few copies of her seven-year-old tape and more than 15,000 copies her 11-year-old album ALL THAT, which had been produced for her by her dad at Norman Petty's recording studio in Clovis, New Mexico. LeAnn was an experienced trooper when she stepped up to accept her first CMA awards. She was the real deal. When she befriended Bryan White and the two toured together, country fans loved them both. And when she'd logged three years on the road, LeAnn came off the touring circuit to live with her mom in Los Angeles. By this time BLUE had sold five and a half million copies, EARLY YEARS, UNCHAINED MELODY had sold two million, YOU LIGHT UP MY LIFE had sold four million, and SITTIN' ON TOP OF THE WORLD had sold a little over a million.

LeAnn was pictured on the cover of the April 27, 1999 edition of *Country Weekly* magazine looking trim and fit after a brief time when the road life had gotten to her and she'd gained a few pounds. She appeared to be every bit the rich, young, successful businesswoman that she declared herself to be in the story printed inside the magazine, where she is also pictured lounging in her newly leased San Fernando Valley mansion with her dog Raven. Like Shania Twain had said when I'd first interviewed her, LeAnn credited her parents for her ability to cope with all that had landed on her plate: "Materialistically, I'm a million miles away from that little girl who sang *Blue*," she told *Country Weekly* writer Larry Holden, "because I've got everything that I've ever wanted. But the values my mom and dad taught me are *all* intact." She planned to release two albums in the coming year: a pop album and a traditional country album with an additional five contemporary country cuts. "I'm anxious to bring the legendary country songs we recorded to a young audience, because there are kids who haven't heard them," she told Holden. "And I hope the more contemporary country songs capture an older audience as well. I truly believe if you deliver quality music, it transcends all ages."

Lila McCann is a young country singer who bases her operations out of the Pacific Northwest where she balances her high school studies, cheerleading activities, *and* weekend appearances on George Strait's portable Chevy Truck Country Music Festival. Lila's records are hokey, pop-flavored country which seems to make her hugely popular with young fans. Lila was 15 when she hit first with *Down Came A Blackbird*, and the Tacoma singer rode the young country wave right to the top of the charts with *I Wanna Fall In Love*, followed by *Almost Over You*, her second number one. She was a star on the radio and CMT, but she was the real deal, too, even if there was little of the controversy about her that surrounded so many young country artists. Lila had been welcomed into the family of country music performers that included Tim McGraw and Faith Hill, singing to 60,000 fans a night along with Lee Ann Womack

LILA McCANN

and John Michael Montgomery on George Strait's tour. She was featured in her own CMT special, she was cover girl for an edition of *American Cheerleader*, and *Time* magazine had named her the most successful new artist for 1997.

Lila's sophomore album, SOMETHING IN THE AIR, was released in spring 1999. *With You*, the lead single, debuted at number 62 on the *Billboard* chart and headed toward the Top 10. On a cheerfulness chart from one to 10, it was a 13. But the track was one of Mark Spiro's best productions to date, featuring innovative arrangements, soaring fiddle, and a pedal steel that was melded to an uplifting and thoroughly relentless band track. It was the kind of pop smash that broke artists. The single was good news for Lila's fans, but when they got their copies of the CD, they were not disappointed to find *With You* followed by the swampy intro to Lila and Mark's own *I Reckon I Will*. Mark Spiro and Don Schlitz wrote *Go Girl* for Lila, and it may become a signature tune when it is released to radio.

Back at home in Tacoma, Lila was driving her first wheels, a GMC Jimmy, one of those Chevy Truck-related products, slightly-pre-owned, that she had purchased with her earnings. Vince Gill, Steve Wariner, and Bryan White had sung backups for her on Bryan and Steve's *You're Gone*. Along with LeAnn Rimes and Amanda and Tyler Wilkinson, Lila had arrived. She was proud of the music she was making, but there were things it took a bit of getting used to. "I love being on stage," she told interviewers. "I love meeting the fans, meeting people that buy your records. I'm still getting used to that. For someone to come up and ask for my autograph, I'm, like, 'Okay, cool.'"

Lila is surprised when people make an issue out of the young country movement. "I think that people might have been shell-shocked, at first. But now they're getting used to it. . . . After all, it's not the first time this happened. Of course, talking about it can be a little boring. But on the other hand, being this young, I wouldn't have much else to talk about, anyway."

But it *was* the first time that radio had kicked off the veterans to stock their record libraries with teenaged country. There had been child prodigies before, but the contemporary country era was unique, even if some of its young stars were not sufficiently aware of the history of the genre to know it.

Amanda Wilkinson may just be the most authentic young coun- **AMANDA WILKINSON** try female vocalist on the radio these days. She and her father, songwriter Steve Wilkinson, and her brother, Tyler, moved to Nashville from Ontario at just the right time. Before long they were signed to Giant Records. Amanda was featured on the group's debut single, *26 Cents*, and her vocal put the group on the map, big time. The third single from the Wilkinson's album, *Boy Oh Boy* is not nearly as country as *26 Cents*, but you can't help but like the cheerful presence that Amanda exudes on the video.

Jessica Andrews was heard on THE PRINCE OF EGYPT NASHVILLE CD, **JESSICA ANDREWS** singing Byron Gallimore's *I Will Be There For You*, before she had put out a record to radio as a solo artist. This soundtrack debut was a perk from her Dreamworks label and paved the way for the introduction of her own CD, HEART SHAPED WORLD. At 15, Jessica is another fresh breath of air for generation "Y" country fans, just the vocalist that Music Row songwriters like Kerry Chater, Cyril Rawson, Cathy Majeski, and Stephony Smith were hoping would come along to record their songs. Jessica's cover of Carlene Carter's *Unbreakable Heart*, a song written by Heartbreaker Benmont Tench, really works well for Jessica. But the lead single should be *James Dean In Tennessee*, a song that puts the trendy corporate marriage of Hollywood and Nashville into perspective. It didn't work for MTM records, a few years ago. But it might work for Dreamworks, especially when you consider the planned corporate marketing strategy designed for Jessica's onslaught of the coveted radio numbers and sales numbers. Jessica's pretty good. Whether she will be lost in the corporate shuffle or will break free from the pack to distinguish herself from the rest of the young hopefuls, remains to be seen. *Hungry Love*, a swampy ode to teenage angst, could be the real deal, too.

Mandy Barnett, the young singer who had sounded so much like **MANDY BARNETT** Patsy Cline that she'd eventually ended up being Patsy in the musical revue "Always . . . Patsy Cline," a tribute that ran at the Opryland complex for more than two years, had been out-distanced by LeAnn Rimes in 1996 when *Blue* literally blew Mandy out of the minds and memories of country fans. In April 1999, months before the scheduled release date of LeAnn's new release, Sire Records released I'VE GOT A RIGHT TO CRY, a stunning new album by Barnett. Production had begun with Owen Bradley at the helm. When Owen passed away in January 1998, he had completed only four tracks. Harold Bradley finished up the project. When Larry Delaney received his review copy of this album at *Country Music News*, he raved about it over the telephone and insisted on playing several tracks for me right then and there. Coming over the thin phone line connection, songs like Don Gibson's *Give Myself A Party* and Delaney's favorite, *Mistakes*, had an eerie effect. The bluesy title track evoked the times the Bradleys and Patsy Cline had made their hit record magic together. A few nights later, I heard Mandy Barnett sing at the Opry. If country music has a future that is not totally shorn of its roots, this singer could lead the way!

THE LYNNS   Loretta's daughters Peggy and Patsy Lynn didn't want to ride on their famous mom's reputation, so they began showcasing themselves as the Honkabillys at Tootsie's Orchid Lounge on South Broadway in Nashville. "We didn't tell anyone who our family was, really," Peggy said, during the duo's CD release party in Tootsie's, "because it wasn't an issue, it was about our music. I would wear Momma's old stage boots and dress, but it was my secret. Our momma had shared with Patsy and me the gift of music, but you have to work to make your own way in life."

If Warner Reprise A&R rep Lisa Bradley knew who the two young women were when she caught their act at Tootsie's, she didn't let on. Lisa brought along Doug Grau a few nights later and the two Warner reps sat down with the Lynns. "I told them the our aunt was on this label for many years," says Patsy. "Doug Grau just kind of looked at us and asked, 'Who's your aunt?' I said, 'Crystal Gayle. Loretta is our mother, we're Loretta's twin daughters!'"

"You could have knocked him over with a feather," says Peggy. "He was, like, 'You're Loretta Lynn's daughters?'"

Honkabilly aptly describes much of the music on Peggy and Patsy's debut THE LYNNS, but radio didn't hear hits. Peggy and Patsy were the real deal when they performed live, but honkabilly didn't test market well as something to be put on contemporary country radio, something *Billboard* magazine writer Larry Flick hinted at when he reviewed an advance copy of the single *One Of These Nights*. "The Lynns are gifted songwriters, and have lovely voices as the beautiful harmonies on this record demonstrate. However, as good as this single sounds, it just does not do justice to this act's incredible live personality." Randy Lewis writing in the *Los Angeles Times* was more enthusiastic when he wrote, "Family harmony has been a rarity in country music since the Judds called it quits, but Peggy and Patsy Lynn, Loretta's 33-year-old twin daughters, bring it back with spunk. Their debut has a Carlene Carter-like maverick spirit, moving from traditional country to heartland rock to Buddy Holly-ish rockabilly." I wondered if what both of these guys were saying was that The Lynns were too old to make it the young country market as new artists. I wondered if maybe they were too good, too rebellious, too . . . maverick.

H eather and Jennifer Linley were more what radio wanted in twin sisters and they were the first out of the chute, so they had a head-start on The Lynns. The first two singles from their 1997 debut, JUST BETWEEN YOU AND ME, hit into the Top 20, and, after seven years of waiting tables in Nashville and plugging their songs whenever they could, the Philadelphia-born sisters were finally a success at 27 years old. The Academy of Country Music voted them the Best New Group and *Country Weekly* magazine named them Favorite New Group at the Golden Pick Awards. Their debut single, *Please,* was nominated for a Grammy. When the 1998 CMA Awards nominations were announced, The Linleys and The Lynns were both nominated in the duo category that had been owned by Brooks & Dunn for six straight years. It was a tough category.

THE LINLEYS

Even tougher, these days, is dealing with the number-crunching that goes on, especially considering the expensive budgets some labels run up when recording and releasing a new artist, budgets that are said to run from $250,000 to half a million dollars. A SoundScan printout for April 5, 1999 revealed that Mindy McCready had sold a whopping 1,145,435 units of her first album, but merely 272,145 units of her second one. "Now, I understand what all the panic their camp is all about," said my researcher via e-mail. "In corporate language, this is a stiff." Lari White's sales for her second RCA album WISHES had hit into the 300,000 level, but her highly-touted Dreamworks release had sold a disappointing 43,479 units. And Jessica Andrews' corporately packaged debut, HEART SHAPED WORLD, had sold only 2,958 units in its first week in the stores. "Next week will be crucial for this release," my researcher told me. He said he'd keep me informed. I hadn't asked him for a whole lot of figures, some of the hopeful acts were not even hitting the Top 40 with their product. It was not likely that they were selling significant numbers to impress any of the executives. But it was a pity because some of them were making pretty good music. When my researcher did report in, Jessica Andrews had sold only 4,330 in her second week, whereas Lila McCann's new album was selling at the rate of 23,000 per week.

LORRIE MORGAN

Calling Lorrie Morgan a contemporary country artist is to recognize that her career spans several eras, even reaching back to her father's time. Her long time association with country music has given her the perspective to take stock of the industry at the end of the century. Like Deana Carter, Lorrie Morgan came from a country music family. Given the genuinely country name Loretta Lynn Morgan when she was born on June 27, 1959, the youngest daughter of the 'Perry Como of Country Music', crooner George Morgan, Lorrie made her first Opry appearance on the stage of the Ryman Auditorium at the age of 14, singing *Paper Roses* to an appreciative audience who gave her a standing ovation. She first sang and toured with her father, then married to George Jones' steel guitar player, Ron Gaddis, Lorrie toured with Jones in the late 1970s. Early Lorrie Morgan releases were *Two People In Love, Tell Me I'm Only Dreaming*, and a duet on *I'm Completely Satisfied* recorded with her father before his death in 1975.

By 1980, Lorrie was separated from her first husband, a single mom with a daughter to raise, and off the road. Country music was in her blood, however, and she began to sing at the Opry, becoming a member in 1984. In 1986 Lorrie met and married bluegrass singer Keith Whitley. The liaison produced another child, but ended tragically with Whitley's untimely death in 1989. Just how shocking this loss was for Lorrie is clearly set out in her tell-it-all biography, *Forever Yours, Faithfully*, a 1997 best-seller written with George Vecsey.

Signed to RCA in 1988, Lorrie hit the Top 40 in 1989 with *Trainwreck of Emotion*, a song fans related to her personal life. She next scored two Top 10 hits with the weeper *Dear Me* and *Out Of Your Shoes*. Five

Minutes was her first number one. Always a vocalist who charged her performance with emotion, Lorrie continued to put out hits, not the least of which was her moving duet with Keith Whitley, *'Til A Tear Becomes A Rose*. Her next three releases — *We Both Walk*, *A Picture Of Me (Without You)*, and *Except For Monday* — went Top 10. *Something In Red* had more impact with her fans than the number 14 position on the chart where it peaked would indicate. Moving to BNA Records in 1992, Lorrie hit the top of the chart with *What Part Of No*, a song that expressed the emerging women's viewpoint in country music.

> Sir, if you don't mind, I'd rather be alone
> From the moment I walked in tonight, you've been comin' on
> If I told you once, I told you twice, I'm just here to unwind
> I'm not interested in romance or what you have in mind
> What part of NO don't you understand? . . .

> (written by Wayne Perry/Gerald Smith)

Lorrie's 1996 duet *By My Side* with new hubby Jon Randall let her fans know that she had found peace of mind, once again.

One of the things Lorrie had most wanted to do, right from the time she signed with RCA, was to record an album of standards, the same kind of lush easygoing songs she had listened to as a child in her parents' home. She'd even gotten assurance from Joe Galante, before signing, that someday, she would get the opportunity to do so. In 1998, SECRET LOVE, an 11-song CD of lushly produced tracks like Ira and George Gershwin's *They Can't Take That Away From Me* and Bart Howards' *Fly Me To The Moon* was issued by BNA. Produced by Richard Landis, the orchestral arrangements conducted by Tom Bruner were literally a bouquet of nostalgia into which Lorrie was able to cast truly heartfelt vocals. Dedicated to her father, George Morgan, the package was a brave move, but one that Lorrie knew her fans could appreciate, even if it might not get the airplay on Top 40 country radio.

Lorrie Morgan is outspoken when it comes to defending country music against the current trend to number crunch and against FM formats that are faceless and seamless. She is not a fan of the current consultant-driven situation, at all. "It has been directed to us for the past couple of years now," she says, "what to record, what's radio-playable. 'Oh it'll never get played on radio.' That's not the point of country music. The point is reachin' the fans. The fans will decide what they want to hear on the radio, if they let them. It's more country music business than country music. I hate for somebody to tell me what I can and cannot record because I think it's always been about the heart. When they start telling us not to record something because radio won't play it, well, I'm sorry, I don't think that's what the fans want to hear. Like I say, ultimately, the fans are the ones who buy the records."

Lorrie would like to see a return to the days of AM radio-type programming when the DJs had personalities. "It's almost like the disc jockeys can't play what they want to play," she declares. "I don't know who these consultants are — someone has never come up to me and said, 'Hi, I'm a consultant,' because, if they did, I'd say, 'Let's you and me go out and have a drink and talk.'" The missing ingredient, today, Lorrie maintains, is emotion. "I'm not really dogging disc jockeys, I'm dogging whoever it is that is calling the shots of what they are allowed to play. Because, back in the olden days when artists used to love to go in and visit with Ralph Emery on the AM radio and they'd play all kinds of music, and Ralph would play something that maybe was the first time it was ever played and because of the response, by word of mouth or whatever, maybe that would end up being a big record . . . but it doesn't work that way any more."

When I suggested that the contemporary dilemma is one we've all gotten in, together, and that perhaps its up to the singers, fans, radio people, *and* labels to get us out of the situation, Lorrie had some revealing things to say. "We've tried that. We've had these panel discussions. And you go in and talk to the label and they say their hands are tied and so and so's hands are tied. It's one big vicious circle."

I wondered, who was it that was tying everybody's hands? But Lorrie wanted to talk about the change that needed to be made, not to point fingers at anyone. "You know, every seven years, things change. I really believe we're getting ready to see one great big change in country music. I think it's going to go back to where radio stations are more like the old AM stations where it wasn't so formatted. I honestly believe that in order to keep this business alive, that's what's gonna have to happen."

I wondered if, maybe, kicking the more mature performers off the Top 40 format and the emphasis on youth wasn't one of the greatest problems country music had to face. Lorrie said, "You know, it's funny, in this business, the country business, they put so much emphasis on age, but in rock, the older the better, you know what I'm sayin'? Now, my gosh, let me play this 19-year-old record, it's so much different, now."

In April 1999, Lorrie Morgan's new BNA Records album MY HEART was in the record stores. The first single, *Maybe Not Tonight*, a duet she sang with her favorite singing partner, Sammy Kershaw, hit onto the country charts with a bullet. It was just the tip of an iceberg, as far as I could hear. After a brief holiday from the pressure of charting with contemporary cuts, Lorrie was back with a vengeance and riding tall in the saddle. She was featured in the *Girls' Night Out* Special on CMT, which seemed to be in some kind of rotation, like a jumbo-sized video.

One Saturday night when I was at the Opry, Lorrie hosted a broadcast segment. She was right at home on the Grand Ole Opry House stage. She had been there almost all her life. She was so well-suited to be introducing all of the great traditionally inclined artists. Lorrie Morgan loved country music and everyone in the audience knew it. I wondered if the Opry wasn't just about the most important bastion of country music tradition, a haven or safe place for the music where it couldn't be number crunched into unemotional statistics. "I think as long as we can keep the Opry alive and keep it goin'," Lorrie told me, "we'll always have that safe place for the great traditional music and music people. But I've gotten a little scared now, too, because they've closed Opryland . . . and now our audiences are less than what they should be for the *Grand Ole Opry*. It's kind of scary." Of course, the Opry had moved before. It had begun at WSM in Studio B and had stayed a good long time at the Ryman Auditorium. It could go back there where it would be more accessible. Out here, miles from town, on the defunct theme park grounds that were being strip-mined into a shopping mall, the Opry had been number-crunched away from Music Row by real estate speculators and hotel operators. It just might be dying.

When someone like Lorrie Morgan who has been born and raised in Nashville, someone who has followed in her famed father's footsteps, and kept the traditional spirit of Nashville country music alive in the 1990s, expressed concern, I knew that there really was a problem with country music. And I sensed that if there was likely any group of people who were going to do anything positive to rectify the situation, it would likely be country women who would be at the forefront of the healing process.

Afterword

☆ ☆ ☆

ANY MAN OF MINE

☆ ☆ ☆

This is what a woman wants . . .
Any man of mine better be proud of me

(Shania Twain)

As I was closing in on the final pages of this book, I naturally began to cast backward glances, looking for a figure or a theme in this history of country women artists to emerge which would neatly summarize all I had discovered. Oddly enough, I found one way of seeing the whole in the unexpected resistance I had met at the management and corporate levels while conducting my research and interviews in Nashville. The source of the resistance proved to be another writer, Laurence Leamer, author of *Three Chords And The Truth (Behind The Scenes With Those Who Make And Shape Country Music)*, a title he'd lifted from Harlan Howard. I learned very quickly not to mention the "L" word during my time spent in Nashville. People there felt betrayed by Leamer. They'd welcomed him into their world, onto their buses, into their dressing rooms, and into their lives and livelihood, but they'd been treated in the end like tabloid subjects by a cunning investigative reporter bent on writing the most controversial book ever written about Nashville.

In *Three Chords and the Truth*, little compassion is shown for experienced singers like Emmylou Harris or Mary Chapin Carpenter, and the somewhat puerile Mindy and Mandy bashing seems, well, a little unfair. It was one thing to point out that many of the young singers were being exploited, but another to reveal their innermost thoughts — *if* the speculations the author presents in the book were indeed *their* thoughts and not thoughts made up or heard third or fourth hand. Leamer seems preoccupied with seeking out ex-husbands, ex-lovers and ex-bandmates, digging up juicy gossip presented as fact. And he paints unfavorable portraits of almost every *woman* he discusses in this book.

Women fall victim in *Three Chords And The Truth* to a male journalist's zeal to write the ultimate exposé. Female singers are often treated like objects, their careers like commodities, and their lives as disposable fodder for the author's controversies. On the back cover of the book with stars beside their names we find: "Wynonna: the real story of her descent into a self-destructive lifestyle . . . LeAnn Rimes: how a masterful PR plan transformed an unknown into a teenage phenomenon . . . Shania Twain: the true story of her upbringing and rise to success told for the first time, so different from the image manufactured by the media . . . Reba McEntire: how she struggled to escape a life of poverty and a bad marriage to become the first woman superstar of today's country." Obviously, Leamer had never studied the actual lyrics that Harlan Howard had fashioned so fastidiously in his songs, checking to see how his lines would be perceived by women. Yet it was Harlan's words that were emblazoned on the cover of Leamer's book. Go figure.

Why hadn't Leamer gone after the rackers and distributors? I wondered. Why hadn't he gone after the hit men, as had been done in a book by that title? Why had he picked on so many women? I knew for a fact that he'd not realized how his exposé was being received by those he'd written about, even when they refused his telephone calls when he repeatedly called to get a quote from artists for his book promotion, endorsing what he had written and thanking him for doing so.

Reading *Three Chords and the Truth* you are encouraged to believe that every single facet of Shania Twain's career has been made up and that every note she sings on her albums is digitally pasted together by her husband — led to believe that she cannot sing at all. Fellow women artists have entirely different opinions about Shania Twain. "Shania has oodles of talent," says Janis Gill. "Mutt has refined her talent. There's nothing wrong with that. Vince helped *me* a lot. We should all have that. What a wonderful team they are, Mutt and Shania. I can't say enough about the quality of their records. There's a lot of attention to detail. Roy Cummins is the manager of my horse farms. He looks after all of my horses, and he works with Shania's horses on and off. I have only met her a few times, but I am aware of all of the trials and experiences she's been through." Besides, she is one heck of a songwriter.

Recent events seem to contradict Leamer's opinions about country women artists, but also suggest a source for his kind of chauvinism. On May 5, 1999 the Academy of Country Music staged their gala awards show on the West Coast. While Garth Brooks was named the Artist of the Decade and the Entertainer of the Year, Faith Hill won Female Vocalist, Single and Video for *This Kiss* and she and Tim McGraw won Vocal Event of the Year for *Just To Hear You Say You Love Me*. Jo Dee Messina was named the ACM's Best New artist and Dixie Chicks walked away with album, group and new group awards. In a special presentation, Shania Twain was awarded two "Diamond Record" awards for THE WOMAN IN ME and COME ON OVER. Both albums had sold more than ten million records.

The real progress made by women can be clearly seen when you compare the *Billboard* album chart, based on sales, with the *Billboard* airplay singles chart. Seven of the Top 10 albums on May 4th as reprinted in *Country Weekly* are by women: 1. Shania Twain, COME ON OVER. 2. Dixie Chicks, WIDE OPEN SPACES. 5. Lila McCann, SOMETHING IN THE AIR. 7. Faith Hill, FAITH. 8. Harris, Ronstadt, Parton, TRIO II. 9. Patty Loveless, CLASSICS. 10. Jo Dee Messina, I'M ALRIGHT. But when it comes to airplay, the Top 10 singles include only two cuts by women: Lee Ann Womack (*I'll Think Of A Reason Later*) and Dixie Chicks (*You Were Mine*). The women are the artists the fans endorse by purchasing albums, but the men are the acts propped up by partisan treatment from their male peers at radio and by the good ole boys on Music Row.

When it comes to awards, the top country awards have always been heavily weighted in favor of males. Since 1970, the ACM has only awarded Entertainer of the Year to a woman three times: Loretta in 1975, Dolly in 1978, and Barbara Mandrell in 1980. The CMA is not much better with Loretta in 1972, Dolly in 1978, Barbara Mandrell in 1981 and 1982, and Reba in 1986. Since that time, irregardless of the fact that, with the exception of Mr. Brooks, women have come to dominate album sales, the Garth era has been ... all Garth, George Strait, Vince Gill, Alan Jackson, and Brooks & Dunn. In the 34-year history of the CMA awards only Anne Murray in 1984 and Patty Loveless in 1995 have been named as winners of the album of the year award. Women may be "on top" when it comes to sales and winning Grammy awards, but they are still all-too-often in the missionary position when it comes to the business part of the country music industry and when it comes to winning the top Nashville-based CMA Awards.

Another book I read during the time I was putting this book together was James Dickerson's *Women On Top (The Quiet Revolution That's Rocking The American Music Industry)*. Dickerson's book is a polar opposite to Leamer's when it comes to viewing people, especially women, as human beings. Dickerson may be presenting stats and crunching numbers as he makes his argument that women have finally assumed a dominant position in music in the late 1990s; however, his research leads him to discover that when it comes to influential female executives working in the music industry, Nashville is actually a leader. I'm not merely talking about Jo Meader Walker, the longtime CMA director who has been recognized and honored by induction into the Country Music Hall of Fame. Dickerson finds that in Nashville both royalty collection agencies, ASCAP *and* BMI, are run by women. Frances Preston at BMI worked her way up to her tower office in New York through the ranks in Nashville and still retains an office there. Connie Bradley at ASCAP is the daughter-in-law of legendary producer Owen Bradley. Not content with these facts alone, Dickerson went out and interviewed both women. He discovered that they are surprisingly humanitarian in their outlook, neither one being a radical feminist, although a certain networking of sisterhood power-sharing just might be being exercised, here and there. These women were not isolated examples. Dickerson continued his research and came up with the news that of the two women executives heading up major labels in the United States, at that time, one of these was Sheila Shipley Biddy, the senior vice president and general manager of Decca in Nashville.

When he moved on to A&R execs, Dickerson discovered "Renee Bell at RCA Nashville, Kim Buie at Capitol Nashville, Margie Hunt at Sony Nashville, Susy Levy at Capitol Nashville, Nancy Brennan at SBK Records Nashville and Paige Levy at Warner Nashville." These women, Dickerson noted, "have had a significant impact by lowering the sleaze bar on that part of the industry, making it more difficult for sleazemasters to weasel their way into the companies." Dickerson praised Renee Bell highly for her skills at RCA in Nashville, often quoting the women execs who had come to respect her abilities. He pointed out that Sandy Neese, vice-president of media relations at Mercury, was part of a "good ole girl" network of female executives who had all pitched in to put Shania Twain's *The Woman In Me* over the top. Shania Twain credited Sandy Neese for picking the title of the album from several being considered. When James Dickerson moved on to women who had become successful and influential managers, he began with Lib Hatcher, writing, "Lib Hatcher is probably the first successful solo female manager. When she plucked Randy Travis from obscurity and transformed him from an insecure country singer into someone who had potential as a recording artist, she had no female role models to follow."

During his research for *Women On Top*, James Dickerson also discovered that it just might be that a woman and not a man had discovered Elvis. He asserts that Sam Phillips' partner, Marion Keisker, was far more than merely a secretary working at Sun Records, and that Phillips, at first, failed to see the potential in Presley, in fact, he was scarcely interested in the singer at all. Dickerson sites the example of a woman executive hopelessly in love with her boss who was willing to take a back seat when it came down to all the credit-taking. Whether this is fact or fancy on the author's part would take a whole book to discuss. But, according to Dickerson, during Elvis Presley's time in the U.S. Army, Elvis had not forgotten the role that Marion Keisker had played in his career. Keisker, who had left the music business for a career in the armed forces herself, was being accosted by someone backstage at a concert when Presley interceded by explaining, "Captain, you don't understand. You wouldn't be having this today if it wasn't for this lady!"

All of this is certainly a brave assertion on Dickerson's part. Sam Phillips is widely known as the person who fostered rockabilly. Few men in the music business want to hear anything that would detract from his legendary status. But Dickerson paints a picture of Marion Keisker as the person who not only picked Presley out of the usual lineup of people who hung around the studio office waiting to make their recordings, she also opposed selling him off to RCA. In the 1950s, no one would have believed that a woman could have such foresight, but Dickerson suggests she may have been the investor behind Sun Records. When men were in such a position, they gave themselves the illustrious title of Executive Producer.

Dickerson then spoke of Bonnie Garner who worked with Mark Rothblaum to manage Willie Nelson before moving on to manage Marty Stuart's career on her own. When Dickerson got to Pam Lewis, Garth Brooks' co-manager during the crucial years, he had made his point. In the 1990s, women were no longer merely pretty faces and voices stuck up there to front bands and sing songs written for them by men. Women were making decisions at every level in the music business, especially in Nashville. This represented an enormous shift in power from past years, changing the working conditions on a daily basis.

When Joe Galante, Chairman of the RCA Label Group Nashville, came back to Music Row after a brief absence in the 1990s, he cleaned house. *Country Song Roundup* writer Elianne Halbersberg asked Joe how difficult it had been to do so. "Change is always difficult," said Galante. "When I came back, I saw a town that had almost doubled in size. . . . Because this is a radio-dominated format, I couldn't make RCA's roster any bigger, so we created BNA to get Mindy, Kenny, Lorrie, Lonestar and John Anderson on the air." When Halbersberg asked, "Who was your greatest risk?" Joe had no hesitation, naming the time he signed K.T. Oslin even while his colleagues objected to her being 43 years old at that time. "To me, age was never an issue," Galante said. "People don't buy into age for the most part. They buy into personality."

And when Halbersberg asked if Galante would have signed Mindy McCready if she'd been 30 pounds heavier with the same talent as K.T. Oslin, Joe just said, "I don't know. K.T. came in as a singer-songwriter, so physical appearance was not as important. Personally, I think she was very sexy. . . . Mindy was not signed because she's got a great figure, but because of her personality and vision of what she wanted. I look for something that separates the artist, a philosophy people believe in. It's not about 36-24-36." All Music Row signings are not being made with such foresight and compassion. There were, no doubt, executives of both sexes who wanted the 'next' Beatles or 'next' Shania but who lacked sufficient vision themselves to discover someone entirely original. Those narrow-sighted execs were the cloners . . . the people who really did want K.T. Oslin in Mindy McCready's body.

When I viewed Lorrie Morgan, Mindy McCready, Martina McBride, and Sara Evans singing *Stop! In The Name Of Love*, doing the old

Supreme's moves, broad smiles on their faces as they sweated it out under the lights for their CMT Special *Girls' Night Out*, I had to agree with Joe Galante. Each one of these RCA/BNA artists did have their own personality. And it had been Mindy's idea for the four of them to band together, hadn't it? Sara was obviously nearly ready to give birth, a situation that in the past would have kept her away from television cameras, but in 1999, women were intent on celebrating life and music — so were their fans.

My conclusion was that the contemporary dilemma in country lay not at the feet of any of the singers. The contemporary dilemma takes place in the arena of human existence. It is a dilemma that all human beings face today, a problem found in day-to-day confrontations between corporations and individuals. When corporations buy up the 'Ma and Pa' radio stations, they erase individuality. When corporations hire consultants to advise them on demographics and trends, then manufacture product designed to sell rather than to entertain or heal, the singer and the song are left out of the equation entirely. When I asked Ralph Murphy just how the current situation in country music had come about, he replied, "You know, everyone says that in country music everything begins with a song, but they're always forgetting that. Now that sales are dropping off and things are getting weirder and weirder, the focus is back on the song again, where it's supposed to be." And these songs have begun to change under the influence of a new generation of women singer songwriters, away from alcohol-driven hurtin' songs toward positive, uplifting lyrics. Despite the battles with the corporate mentality trying to control country music, the girls have found reason to have fun.

Sara Evans was already in the studio cutting her sophomore album — resigned to the fact that while critics had liked her debut THREE CHORDS AND THE TRUTH, it had stiffed at radio and bombed in the record stores — when Joe Galante offered her a piece of advice. "All the songs you love are the sad, tear-your-heart-out songs," he said. "Try to write a positive love song. I think it will really help your career." That song was *No Place That Far*, her first number one hit. Country music had originally addressed the downtrodden and underprivileged, soothing the rural population with honey-sweetened melancholy. Today, people want at least some of their country music to be upbeat, inspiring, telling positive stories of fulfilled love and marriages that work. Cheatin', drinkin', hurtin' and divorce are no longer the only stuff of country music.

Shania Twain, the most controversial female country singer of the contemporary era, continued her "Come on Over" tour in 1999, sweeping back across the vast Canadian landscape to sold out repeat performances. The dailies featured her in five-page spreads with centerfold posters when she arrived in their city. CMT Canada featured her on *Shania Sunday*, an eight-hour-long TV Special during which lucky fans who won phone-in contests were to get to meet with her backstage, to be flown to regional centers to see her perform. The tour was grander than any Anne Murray or Michelle Wright tour, at least as huge as Garth's Canadian tours. Canadian writers pointed out that despite the criticism Twain had received in the American media concerning the dress she'd worn at the Grammies, the triumphant result of that appearance had been that she'd stolen the thunder from most of the other performers and created the ultimate buzz. People weren't talking about Madonna's Geisha Girl costume or performance, they were talking about Shania. Her album sales soared again and COME ON OVER was at the top of the *Billboard* country album chart, again, a year and a half after its release. Resistance just seemed to melt away in her path.

Vancouver *Province* writer John P. McLaughlin interviewed Marc Bouwer, the designer who clothed her. A by-line declared that "Shania Twain's videos and Marc Bouwer's fashion sense have altered the look of country music forever." McLaughlin's story led off with the hook, "Mention the name Shania Twain and the first thing people think of is the way the woman looks. Not half bad, they say. The man who gets to dress Twain — the gig from paradise — is New York fashion designer Marc Bouwer. He's also designed for the likes of Faith Hill, Toni Braxton, Sigourney Weaver and Pamela Anderson."

When McLaughlin reviewed Shania's Vancouver show, his headline read, "It's Fun First with Shania." The *Province* printed numerous testimonies made by Shania fans who were from all walks of life and every age group from first-graders to grandmothers. Twelve-year old Bobbi Smith joined Shania onstage to sing *What Made You Say That*. In a period of time during which the business part of the music business often stifled the radio, Shania was just a girl who wanted to have fun.

Then in September 1999, the CMA opened their arms to Shania Twain, awarding her not only a special plaque for international achievement but also the highly coveted Entertainer of the Year Award. On this televised night from Nashville, the artist formerly known as Garth Brooks was nowhere to be seen, and it was Vince Gill who handed Twain her first award. Appropriately, it was Reba McEntire — the last woman to win the Entertainer of the Year Award (in 1986) — who tore open the envelope and called Shania to the stage to accept the acknowledgment. The decision to once again name a female recording artist as the CMA's top achiever had been along time in coming, and was deemed a popular decision by a standing ovation from the audience.

For her performance on the show, Shania was in the pink, so to speak: pink stetson, pink western boots, pink longrider coat beneath, which, as she moved about the stage, the audience was able to glimpse not only a pink halter top and matching culottes, but also that famous pink navel. No one seemed to object, and many were merely relieved that she had not worn that same dress she'd worn to the Grammy Awards. To me, it seemed that Shania's defiant declaration: "Man, I feel like a woman!" had rung out like a final battle cry in a decade in which country women had seized the day and warmed a whole lot of cold, cold hearts.

Carlene Carter had prophesied the coming of Shania early in the decade when she told Mark Bego, "I think country music needs a breath of good-naturedness and a girl who can go out there and have fun. Other girls want to do that, but they're afraid they'll seem improper. Why can't you dance and have fun and wear short skirts?" Carlene had done just that in her *I Fell In Love* video. She'd been in love with *her* producer, Howie Epstein, and Shania Twain was in love with her producer, Mutt Lange. This crossing of the stars produced happy, transcendent music. Many recording artists like Lorrie Morgan would like to see more music and less business in the music business. Singers like Janie Fricke have opted not to pursue a record deal at all but to market their music solely through their stage performances and their websites. More people than ever are listening to women in country music because they are celebrating their music, singing intelligent, sometimes playful and ironic lyrics, and having good-natured fun, sometimes at the expense of men who will find it in their hearts to laugh and dance along, if country women artists have their way.

References

★ ★ ★

Anonymous. "George Jones Recovering." *The Rolling Stone*, April 15, 1999, page 35.

Anonymous. Gannett News Service Story. "Anne Murray Does Live CD, Will Appear In PBS Special." *Bellingham Herald*, February 23, 1998.

Anonymous. "Kathy Mattea Bio." Posted at *www.country.com*.

Anonymous. "Lari White." *The Tennessean*, August 29, 1998.

Bernell, Kellie. "Interview with Deana Carter." *The Country Network*, June 30, 1996.

Bessman, Jim. "Tillis Marks 'Time' On Arista Set." *Billboard*, May 23, 1998.

Biggs, Richard. "Sticks & Stones: Ways Mindy McCready Can Stay In The News." Nashville's City Weekly *In Revue*, February 23, 1999.

Bego, Mark. *Country Gals (The Superstars of Today's Country Music)*. New York, NY: Windsor Publishing Corp., 1994.

Brown, Jim. "Patricia Conroy: Pacific Coast Lady On The Fast Track." *Country Music News*, July, 1992.

Campbell, Glen (with Tom Carter). *Rhinestone Cowboy*. New York, NY: St. Martin's Paperbacks, 1995.

Cash, June Carter. *Among My Klediments*. Grand Rapids. MI: Zondervan Publishing House, 1979.

Catalano, Grace. *LeAnn Rimes (Teen Country Queen)*. New York, NY: A Laurel-Leaf Book, Bantam Doubleday Dell Books, 1997.

Charney, Dennis. "Myrna Lorrie: More Than A Myth." *Country Music News*, May, 1990.

Collins, Ace. *Tanya*. New York, NY: Saint Martin's Paperbacks, 1995.

Coulson, Sandy. "Delayed Success A Godsend: Deana Carter." *The London Free Press*, April 4, 1997.

Crosson, David. "The Queen Still Reigns: An Interview with Dale Evans." *Country & Western Magazine*, February, 1999.

Delaney, Larry. "Anne Murray in Disney World." *Country Music News*, February, 1991.

Delaney, Larry. "Canadian Country Music Awards Get Fresh Look." *Country Music News*, September, 1987.

Delaney, Larry. "Country Music Television: An exclusive CMN Report." *Country Music News*, September, 1987.

Delaney, Larry. "CMT (Canada) Airs Top 100 Videos of All Time." *Country Music News*, June, 1999.

Delaney, Larry. "Delaney's Dozen." *Country Music News*, January, 1999.

Delaney, Larry. "Family Brown: These Days." *Country Music News*, July, 1989

Delaney, Larry. "Fortune Smiles on Cassandra Vasik." *Country Music News*, June, 1993.

Delaney, Larry. "Lisa Brokop: What's Not To Like." *Country Music News*, January, 1999.

Delaney, Larry. "Michelle Wright . . . Nobody's Girl." *Country Music News*, July, 1996.

Delaney, Larry. "Michelle Wright . . . On Track." *Country Music News*, June, 1990.

Delaney, Larry. "Prescott Brown . . . And There You Go." *Country Music News*, May, 1994

Delaney, Larry. "Reba Takes Canada By Storm/Michelle Wright: Right Stuff." *Country Music News*, November, 1988.

Delaney, Larry. "Record Review: Lisa Brokop . . . When You Get To Be Me." *Country Music News*, August, 1998.

Delaney, Larry. "Shania Twain." *Country Music News*, December, 1977.

Delaney, Larry. "Special Box-set Review: Wanda

Jackson." *Country Music News*, December, 1997.

Delaney, Larry. "Stephanie Beaumont, Love & Dreams & Things." *Country Music News*, November, 1996.

Delaney, Larry. "Tammy Wynette - Gone at 65." *Country Music News*, May, 1998.

Delaney, Larry. "Terri Clark: Nashville Dream." *Country Music News*, November, 1995.

Delaney, Larry. "The World Of Lucille Starr." *Country Music News*, January, 1988.

Dickerson, James. *Women On Top (The Quiet Revolution That's Rocking the American Music Industry)*. New York, NY: Billboard Books, Watson-Guptill Publications, 1998.

Earle, Charles. "Grammy Schmammy." Nashville's Country Weekly *In Revue*, March 2, 1999.

Earle, Charles. "In, Out & About: Real Country Radio." Nashville's City Weekly *In Revue*. Feb 23, 1999.

Earle, Charles. "New Release From Westerberg; Reissue From Lone Justice." Nashville's City Weekly *In Revue*. March 2, 1999.

Escott, Colin. *Liner Notes: Emmylou Harris*, PORTRAITS, Reprise Archives 4 CD Box Set.

Flans, Robyn. "Love's Alive And Well — And Radio Loves It." *Country Weekly*, April 13, 1999.

Flick, Larry. "Singles: The Lynns, *Nights Like These*." *Billboard*, November 8, 1997.

Flippo, Chet. "Heather Myles Hits Highway At Full Speed." *Billboard*, May 9, 1998.

Gliatto, Tom *et al.* "The New Pop Divas." Cover story in *People Weekly* magazine, January, 18, 1999.

Gleaves, Rebekah. "Rock & Roll Hoochie Coup: Low-power Radio Looks For Listeners." Nashville's City Weekly *In Revue*, February 23, 1999.

Grills, Barry. *Snowbird (The Story of Anne Murray)*. Kingston, ON: Quarry Press, 1996.

Halbersberg, Elianne. "Quote / Enquote with Evelyn Shriver." *Country Song Roundup*, January, 1999.

Halbersberg, Elianne. "Quote / Enquote with Joe Galante, Part II." *Country Song Roundup*, October, 1998.

Hall, Doug. *The Real Patsy Cline*. Kingston, ON: Quarry Music Books, 1998.

Hall, Tom T. *The Storyteller's Nashville*. New York: Doubleday, 1979.

Hefley, James C. *Country Music Comin' Home*. Hannibal, MO: Hannibal Books, 1992.

Hilburn, Robert. "Did Lang Come To Praise Or Parody?" *Los Angeles Times*, April 4, 1987.

Holden, Larry. "LeAnn Rimes: I'm Learning How To Be A Normal Person." *Country Weekly*, April 27, 1999.

Johnson, Anne Janette. "Loretta Lynn Biography." Reprinted by label publicist from an article in *Contemporary Musicians* magazine.

Jones, Margaret. *Patsy: The Life and Times of Patsy Cline*. New York: HarperPerennial, HarperCollins, 1995.

Jones, George (with Tom Carter). *I Lived To Tell It All*. New York, NY: Bantam Doubleday Dell, 1997.

Kennedy, Paul. "Patricia Conroy: New Horizons." *Country Music News*, Spring, 1997.

Krewen, Nick. "Mary Chapin Carpenter's Taking Time To Get It Right." *Country Weekly*, December 1, 1998.

Leamer, Laurence. *Three Chords And The Truth (Behind The Scenes with Those Who Make and Shape Country Music)*. New York: HarperPaperbacks, 1997.

Lewis, Randy. "Record review: The Lynns." *Los Angeles Times*, November, 1997.

Lynn, Loretta. *Coal Miner's Daughter*. New York, NY: Warner Books, 1977.

McCall, Michael. "Canadian singer shows hint of country's future." *Nashville Banner*, March 26, 1987.

McEntire, Reba (with Tom Carter). *REBA: My Story*. New York, NY: Bantam Doubleday Dell, 1994.

McLaughlin, John P. "A Woman On A Mission: Brokop Says She's Destined For Country Stardom." *The Province*, March 18, 1999.

McLaughlin, John P. "That Dress!" *The Province*, April 1, 1999.

McLaughlin, John P. "Singer Savaged: Conroy Mauled By Dog." *The Province*, April 10th, 1997.

McLaughlin, John P. "It's Fun First with Shania." *The Province*, April 4, 1999.

McLaughlin, John P. "Looking Back And Ahead." *The Province*, December 29, 1998.

Mair, George. *The Judds (The True Story of Naomi, Wynnona, and Ashley)*. Secausus, NJ: Birch Lane Press, Carol Publishing Group, 1998.

Mandia, Pat. "Donna Fargo Living Happily Ever After." *Country Weekly*, September 22, 1998.

Mason, Bruce. "Whistler Lines Up The Dots." *The Province*, July 21, 1989.

Matella, Helen. "Country-swing The Dots Specialty." *The Edmonton Journal*, January 26, 1989.

Matella, Helen. "Vivacious Dots well worth seeing." *The Edmonton Journal*, February 3, 1989.

Melhuish, Martin. *Oh What A Feeling: A Vital History of Canadian Music*. Kingston, ON: Quarry Press, 1996.

Millard, Bob. *The Judds: The Unauthorized Biography*. New York, NY: St. Martins Paperbacks, 1992.

Morgan, Lorrie (with George Vecsey). *Forever Yours, Faithfully (My Love Story)*. New York, NY: Ballantine, 1997.

Nash, Alanna. *Behind Closed Doors (Talking with the Legends of Country Music)*, New York, NY: Alfred A Knopf, 1988.

Nash, Alanna. "Record Review: Highways and Honky-tonks." *Stereo Review*, September, 1998.

Newcomer, Wendy. "Lee Ann Womack Can Think of Many Reasons for Happiness." *Country Weekly*, May 4, 1999.

North, Peter. "Dot's Good! Vancouver Band More than Gimmicks." *The Edmonton Journal*, February 3, 1989.

North, Peter. "Jackson Cranks Up Country Fans." *The Edmonton Journal*, May 2, 1998.

Novak, Ralph. "Record Review: Stepping Stone." *People Weekly*, September 14, 1998.

Oermann, Robert K. "Sweet Inspiration: Singer Kim Richey Releases Second Collection Of Songs From The Heart." *The Tennessean*, March 8, 1997.

Oermann, Robert K. "Not Just Whistlin' Dixie." *The Tennessean*, February 7, 1998.

Parton, Dolly. *Dolly (My Life And Other Unfinished Business)*. New York, NY: HarperPaperbacks, 1994.

Pareles, Jon. "Cabaret: K.D. lang, Country." *New York Times*, May 10, 1987.

Paxman, Bob. "Mindy McCready: Learning as She Goes." *Country Song Roundup*, October, 1998.

Pond, Neil. "Chick Picks: When It Comes To Hot Licks, The Dixie Chicks Rule The Roost." *Country America*, September, 1998.

Pond, Neil. "Martina McBride: I'm Little But I'm Loud." *Country America*. February, 1998.

Rambeau, Catherine, S. "Country Videos Take High Tech To The Limits." *Country Weekly*, April 13, 1999.

Reid, LuAnn. "Lisa Brokop Cover Story." *Country Wave*, October, 1994.

Riese, Randall. *Nashville Babylon (The Uncensored Truth and Private Lives of Country Music's Stars)*. New York: Congdon & Weed, 1988.

Riley, Jeannie C. (with Jamie Buckingham). *From Harper Valley to the Mountain Top*. Lincoln, VA: Chosen Books Publishing Co., 1981.

Rohrer, Trish Deitch. "Twain's World." Cover story article in the February 1999 issue of *Cosmopolitan* magazine. One in a series of articles featuring winners of *Cosmopolitan* "Fun Fearless Female Awards."

Rowland, Tom. "Grand Alt. Opry." *The Tennessean*, February 24, 1999.

Savage, Candace. *Cowgirls*. Vancouver, BC: Greystone Books, 1996.

Schroeder, Dave. "Lucille Starr (Part One: The Early Years)." *The Rana Review*, Fall 1988.

Schroeder, Dave. "Lucille Starr (Part Two)." *The Rana Review*, Winter 1988.

Simmons, David. "For The Sake Of The Song: Cinderella Story, With Her Recording Career On Hold, Matraca Berg Hits New Heights." *New Country*, June, 1996.

Smith, Chris. "Trisha Yearwood." *US* magazine. February, 1998.

Starr, Victoria. *k.d. lang: All You Get Is Me*. New York, NY: Vintage Books, 1994.

Stevenson, Jane. "Dawn Does Mom Murray Proud." *Toronto Sun*, January, 1999.

Tosches, Nick, *Country: Living Legends and Dying Metaphors in America's Biggest Business*. Rev. Ed. New York, NY: Charles Scribner's Sons, 1985.

Tucker, Tanya (with Patsi Bale Cox). *Nickel Dreams (My Life)*. New York, NY: Hyperion, 1997.

Tweed, Shannon. "Dixie Rhythms." *Albany Democrat-Herald*, July 10, 1999.

Usinger, Mike. "The Road Less Travelled: Lucinda Williams." *The Georgia Straight*. February 11, 1999.

Van Valkenburg, Nancy. "Anne Murray Enters A New Phase Of Her Life." *Salt Lake City Examiner*, Oct. 1998.

Dellar, Fred, Alan Cackett, and Roy Thompson. *Harmony Illustrated Encyclopedia of Country Music*. New York: Harmony Books, 1986.

Wallin, Pamela. "Interview with Reba McEntire." *The Pamela Wallen Show* CBC-TV, 1998.

Weiss, Marc. "Lang Carries a Torch for Country." *Los Angeles Herald Examiner*, April 4, 1987.

Whitburn, Joel. *The Billboard Book of Top 40 Albums*. 3rd ed. New York, NY: Billboard Books, Watson-Guptill Publications, 1995.

Whitburn, Joel. *The Billboard Book of Top 40 Country Hits 1944 to the Present*. New York, NY: Billboard Books, 1996.

Williams, Hank Jr. (with Michael Bane). *Living Proof*. New York, NY: Charles Putnam's Sons, 1979.

Williams, Janette E. "Faith Hill: Secrets Of Her Success." *Country Song Roundup*, October, 1998.

Williams, Jett (with Pamela Thomas). *Ain't Nothin' As Sweet As My Baby*. New York, NY: Harcourt, Brace, Janovich Publishers, 1990.

Williams, Lycrecia (and Dale Vinicur). *Still In Love With You: The Story of Hank and Audrey Williams*. Nashville, TN: Rutledge Hill Press, 1989.

Wix, Kimmy. "Some New Attitude From Pam Tillis." *www.country.com*, June, 1998.

Wolliver Robbie. "Strawberry, Wine, Women and Song: Matraca Berg's Formula For Success." *Country Weekly*, January 28, 1997.

Wood, Gerry. "George Jones: A Radio Alien Is Granted Asylum." *Country Weekly*, November 24, 1998.

Woodworth, Marc (editor). *Solo (Women Singer-Songwriters ... In Their Own Words)*. New York, NY: Delta Trade Paperbacks, 1998.

Zimm. "Concert Review: K.D. Lang & The Reclines at the Roxy." *Variety Daily*, Wednesday, April 8, 1987.

ACKNOWLEDGMENTS

☆ ☆ ☆

The author would like to thank the following people for their help with the manuscript. Ken Ashdown at Mercury Records for the open-ended interview with Shania Twain. Dick Damron for his insights into the intricacies of many situations. Cathy Taylor, who made things a whole lot easier in Nashville, and Aimee Roberts, Bryan Taylor, Monty Hitchcock, and Susan Weber at Monty Hitchcock Management, Nashville, for the hospitality. Ralph Murphy at ASCAP for the friendship and the contacts in the songwriting community. Harlan Howard for the Predators hockey tickets. CCMA Publicity Director Richard Flohill for the press opportunities. Janice Pickwell and Bruce Woodward at Cyberstore Systems for the introduction to cyberspace. Diana Kelly and everyone at the Merritt Mountain Music Festival for all the help. Dee Lippingwell, Maggie Scherf, Don Wise, Laureen Muir, and Kevin Statham for the live action photos. Bob Hilderley and Susan Hannah at Quarry Press for the support and guidance. Tom Harrison for pointing me in the right direction. Fred Koch and Bob Colebrook for believing in my journalism from the start. And everyone in the country music family, from the musicians and recording artists to the agents, publicists, and managers who welcomed me aboard, and the many friends I have made over the years in the country community.

Special thanks to Larry Delaney at *Country Music News* for diligently reading the drafts and galley proofs and all the help with the research. For a complimentary copy of *Country Music News*, The Voice of Country Music in Canada, and a subscription form, telephone 1-613-745-6006 or fax 1-613-745-0576.

LYRICS

☆ ☆ ☆

Every effort has been made to provide complete and correct copyright publishing information for the lyrics quoted in the text.

Man, I Feel Like A Woman. By Shania Twain & Robert John (Mutt) Lange. Copyright 1997 Songs of Polygram International Inc./Loon Echo Music Inc.(BMI)/Out of Pocket Productions Ltd. Controlled by Zoma Enterprises Inc. (ASCAP) for the U.S.A. and Canada.

The Woman In Me (Needs The Man In You). By Shania Twain & Robert John (Mutt) Lange. Copyright 1995 Loon Echo Music (BMI); Out of Pocket Productions, all rights controlled by Zomba Enterprises, Inc. (ASCAP) for the U.S.A. and Canada.

No One Needs To Know. By Shania Twain & Robert John (Mutt Lange. Copyright 1995 Loon Echo Music (BMI); Out of Pocket Productions, all rights controlled by Zomba Enterprises, Inc. (ASCAP) for the U.S.A. and Canada.

When Boy Meets Girl By Tom Shapiro, Terri Clark & Chris Waters. Copyright 1995 Great Cumberland Music/Diamond Struck Music/Tom Shapiro Music; Sony Tree Publishing Company Inc. (BMI)

I Want To Be A Cowboy's Sweetheart. By Patsy Montana. Copyright 1936 MCA Music (ASCAP).

It Wasn't God Who Made Honky Tonk Angels. By J.D. Miller. Copyright 1952 Peer Southern (BMI).

Crazy. By Willie Nelson. Copyright 1961 Tree Publishing, Inc. (BMI).

I'm A Honky Tonk Girl. By Loretta Lynn. Copyright 1960 Sure-Fire Music (BMI).

Don't Come Home A-Drinkin' (With Lovin' On Your Mind). By Loretta Lynn/Peggy Sue Wells. Copyright 1966 Sure-Fire Music Company (BMI).

Harper Valley P.T.A. By Tom T. Hall. Copyright 1967 Newkeys Music (BMI).

Rose Garden. By Joe South. Copyright 1970 Lowery Music (BMI).

Ride, Ride, Ride. By Liz Anderson. Copyright 1967 Fred Rose Music (BMI).

Woman To Woman By Billy Sherrill. Copyright EMI Algee Music Corp. (BMI).

9 To 5. By Dolly Parton. Copyright 1980 Velvet Apple Music (BMI).

Born To Run. By Paul Kennerley. Copyright 1981 Irving Music, Inc. (BMI).

Fire Of The Newly Alive. By Rosanne Cash & John Leventhal. Copyright 1992 Chelcait Music (BMI)/Lev-A-Tunes (ASCAP).

If There Is A God On My Side. By Rosanne Cash. Copyright 1990 Chelcait Music (BMI).

Miss Chatelaine By K.D. Lang and Ben Mink. Copyright 1992 Bumstead Publishing/Zavion Music, SOCAN.

Piece Of My Heart. By Bert Berns/Jerry Ragovoy. Copyright 1967 UNICHAPPELL Music (BMI).

Woman's Work. By Sheree Jeacocke, Lou Pomanti & B.J. Cooke. Copyright 1989 Sheree Music Pub/Dreamin' in Public/Bonnie J. Cooke (SOCAN).

Take It Like A Man By Tony Haselden. Copyright 1991 Milhouse Music, (BMI).

Girls Will Be Girls. By Montana, Reeves & Allison. Copyright 1993 Sixteen Stars Music, Annie Green Eyes Music, Jim's Allisongs (BMI).

80's Ladies. By K.T. Oslin. Copyright 1987 Wooden Wonder Music (SESAC).

Mama Was A Workin' Man. By Rebecca Ann Hobbs, Don London & Mike Darwin. Copyright 1988 Beckaroo/Careers BMG Music Pub/Tracks of Don Music (BMI).

Mi Vida Loca. By Jess Leary & Pam Tillis. Copyright 1994 Dream Catcher Music (ASCAP)/Ben's Future Music (BMI).

How Can I Help You Say Goodbye. By Karen Taylor-Good & Burton Collins. Copyright 1993 Reynsong Publishing/Burton B. Collins Pub/W.B.M. Music Corp/K.T. Good Music (BMI).

I'm That Kind Of Girl. By Matraca Berg/Ronni Samoset. Copyright 1990 Patrick Joseph Music/Warner Tamerlane (BMI).

Independence Day. By Gretchen Peters. Copyright 1992 Cross Keys Publishing (ASCAP).

Girl's Night Out. By Brent Maher & Jeffrey Bullock. Copyright 1984 Wellbeck Music Crop/Blue Quill Music (ASCAP).

Cleopatra, Queen Of Denial. By Pam Tillis, Bob DiPiero & Jan Buckingham. Copyright 1991 Tree Publishing/Little Big Town/American Made Music/Duck House Music (BMI).

Highway Robbery. By Michael Garvin/Bucky Jones/Tom Shapiro. Copyright 1988 Cross Keys Publishing/Terrace Entertainment/Universal Polygram (BMI).

That Don't Impress Me Much. By Shania Twain & Robert John (Mutt) Lange. Copyright 1997 Songs of Polygram International, Inc./Loon Echo Music (BMI); Out of Pocket Productions, all rights controlled by Zomba Enterprises, Inc. (ASCAP) for the U.S.A. and Canada.

XXX's and 000's (An American Girl). By Matraca Berg & Alice Randall. Copyright 1994 August Wind/Longitude Music/Great Broad Music (BMI) and Mother Dixie Songs (ASCAP).

Hey Cinderella. By Suzy Bogguss, Matraca Berg & Gary Harrison. Copyright 1993 Famous Music Corp/Loyal Dutchess Music/Warner Tamerlane Pub/Patrick Joseph Music/Maria-Belle Music/August Wind Music/Longitude Music/Lazy Kato Music (BMI).

He Thinks He'll Keep Her. By Mary Chapin Carpenter & Don Schlitz. Copyright 1992 EMI April Music Inc/Getarealjob Music/Don Schlitz Music/Almo Music Corp (ASCAP).

Wild One. By Jamie Kyle, Pat Bunch & Will Rambeaux. Copyright 1993 WB Music Corp/Daniel the Dog Songs/Warner Tamerlane/Pat Bunch Pub/Reynsongs Pub (BMI).

Wide Open Spaces. By Susan Gibson. Copyright 1997 Pie-Eyed Music (BMI).

John Wayne Walking Away. By Jerry Boonstra, Doak Snead & Austin Cunningham. Copyright 1998 Starstruck Angel Music (BMI) & Songs Matter Inc/Famous Music Corporation (ASCAP).

An Innocent Man. By Kent Agee & Will Rambeaux. Copyright 1997 These Mortals Music (ASCAP) and Reynsong Publishing Corp/Bayou Boy Music (BMI).

Did I Shave My Legs For This? By Deana Carter/Rhonda Hart. Copyright 1996 Polygram Int. Pub/Door Number Two Music (ASCAP) and Miller Moo (BMI).

A Girl's Gotta Do What A Girl's Gotta Do. By Rick Bowles & Robert Byrne. Copyright 1996 Artbyrne Music/Diamond Storm Music/EMI Blackwood Music/Mike Curb Music/Sony/ATV Songs (BMI).

What Part Of No. By Wayne Perry/Gerald Smith. Copyright 1992 Zomba Entertainment (BMI).

Any Man Of Mine. By Shania Twain & Robert John (Mutt) Lange. Copyright 1995 Loon Echo Music (BMI); Out of Pocket Productions, all rights controlled by Zomba Enterprises, Inc. (ASCAP) for the U.S.A. and Canada.

PHOTOGRAPHS

☆ ☆ ☆

Photographs were supplied by individuals from their personal collections and by managers, labels, and publicists for many of the artists, including Mercury Nashville; Palmer Publicity Ink, Ltd.; Shoreline Records Inc; Stony Plain; Stubble Jumper Music Inc.; Intersound Country; Paradise Artists, Inc.; BMG Entertainment; MCA Records Nashville; Reprise Records; Asylum Records; RCA Records Label; Arista Nashville; Lyric Street Records; Capitol Records; apa Agency for the Performing Arts; Gehl Force Management; Monument Is Artistry; Frontpage Publicity; Warner Bros. Records; Dreamworks Records; BNA Records Label; M. Hitchcock Managment; Eminent Records; Iron Music; EMI Music Canada; Prestige Entertainment Inc; Force; Sunset Records. Special credit goes to the following photographers: Mark Tucker (Patty Loveless); Naomi Kaltman (Deana Carter); Bret Lopez (Lila McCann); Timothy White (Martina McBride); Andrew Eccles (Anne Murray, Sara Evans); Russ Harrington (Connie Smith, Terri Clark, Faith Hill); Matt Barnes (Dixie Chicks, Sherrie Austin, Patricia Conroy); Albert Sanchez (Lari White); Scott Bonner (The Lynns); Nancy Lee Andrews (Karen Taylor-Good); Frank Ockenfels (Kim Richey); Charla Beaulieu (Lisa Brokop); Laureen Muir (Rosanne Cash); Sandra Johnson (Mindy McCready); Mark Seliger (K.T. Oslin); Don Grashey Collection (Myrna Lorrie, Carroll Baker); Kevin Statham (K.D. Lang); Barry Gnyp (Farmer's Daughter); Don Wise (Michelle Wright); George Holz (Shania Twain); Dee Lippingwell (Dolly Parton) and Dee Lippingwell and the Merritt Mountain Festival (Carlene Carter, Kathy Mattea, Tanya Tucker).